11-13-75

CONTAINERIZATION

FIGURE 1 OCL cellular containership *Liverpool Bay*
(Courtesy of Overseas Containers Limited)

CONTAINERIZATION

J. R. WHITTAKER, AICS
Ferry Freighting (Croydon) Limited
United Kingdom

SECOND EDITION

with Preface *by*
GORDON S. C. WILLS
Professor of Marketing & Logistics Studies
Cranfield School of Management

HEMISPHERE PUBLISHING
CORPORATION

Washington   London

A HALSTED PRESS BOOK

JOHN WILEY & SONS

New York   London   Sydney   Toronto

First edition, 1972
Revised first edition, 1974
Second edition, 1975

Hemisphere Publishing Corporation
1025 Vermont Ave., N.W., Washington, D.C. 20005

Distributed solely by Halsted Press, a Division of John Wiley & Sons, Inc., New York.

Library of Congress Cataloging in Publication Data

Whittaker, J R
    Containerization.

    Bibliography: p.
    Includes index.
    1. Containerization. I. Title.
HE596.W46 1975   380.5'2   75-20247
ISBN 0-470-94115-4

Printed in the United States of America

Contents

Illustrations   vii

Preface   ix

Chapter 1   INTRODUCTION   1

Chapter 2   VESSELS AND EQUIPMENT   4
Consortia and Building Problems – Vessel Types –
Standardization - Barge Carrying Vessels

Chapter 3   PORTS AND TERMINALS   22
Established Port Structure - The Need to Invest - Grants,
Loans and Subsidies - The National Ports Council - Container
Handling Equipment - United Kingdom Developments -
Felixstowe - Tilbury - Southampton - The Clyde and Forth -
The Mersey - Inland Terminals

Chapter 4   THE THROUGH CONCEPT OF
            CONTAINERIZATION AND ECONOMIC
            GAINS   45
The Through Concept - Control by the Shipping Company -
CP Ships - Rate Cutting - Rising Costs

Chapter 5   THE ROLE OF THE RAILWAYS   65
The Beeching Report - Freightliners - British Rail Shipping -
Intercontainer - The French Railways - The German
Federal Railways - The Channel Tunnel - The Landbridge
System - Future Railway Development

Chapter 6 **INSURANCE AND THE NEED FOR A**
COMBINED TRANSPORT DOCUMENT 94
Established Procedures - Shipowners' Liability - Causes of
Damage - Other Factors Influencing the Insurance -
Combined Transport Documents - Faster Transmission of
Documents

Chapter 7 **EFFECT ON OTHER GROUPS** 116
Traditional Services - The Conventional Owner - Pallet
Ships - The Export Packer - Domestic Road Haulage - The
Freight Forwarder - European Container Movements -
European Roll-on Roll-off Movements - Dock Labor

Chapter 8 **DEVELOPMENT OVERSEAS** 158
Deep Sea Terminals and Feeder Ports - Less Developed
Countries - The Europe/Far East Container Service - The
Europe/Australia Container Service - The Problem of New
Zealand - The United States of America - Canada - Russia
and the Trans-Siberian Railway - India - South America and
the Caribbean - South Africa - East Africa - West Africa -
The Mediterranean - Italy and Sicily - Spain and Portugal -
France - West Germany - Belgium - Holland - Scandinavia

Chapter 9 **THE FUTURE** 301
The Rochdale Report - A Move Into Profitability -
Subsequent Growth - Nationalism - Computers and
Automatic Terminals - New Vessel Types

Appendix **FURTHER NOTES ON THE CONFERENCE**
SYSTEM 326
Evolution - The Need for Consultation and Publicity -
A New Rating Structure - Stability of Rates - A Change
of Outlook

Bibliography 336

Index 338

Illustrations

Figure 1 OCL cellular containership *Liverpool Bay* (Courtesy of Overseas Containers Limited)   Frontispiece

Figure 2 Sectional layout of fully containerized vessel (Courtesy of Seatrain (UK) Limited)   8

Figure 3 Container stowing in cellular holds (Courtest of Sea-Land Containerships Limited)   10

Figure 4 Wheeled and container traffic awaiting shipment by ACL roll-on roll off/container vessel (Courtesy of British Transport Docks Board)   11

Figure 5 Seabee barge carrier *Doctor Lykes* at Le Havre (Courtesy of Le Havre Port Authority)   20

Figure 6 Seatrain cellular containership *Asialiner* loading at the Clydeport container terminal at Greenock (Courtesy of Seatrain (UK) Limited)   38

Figure 7 CP Ships' container terminal at Wolfe's Cove, Quebec (Courtesy of Canadian Pacific)   53

Figure 8 World seaborne trade—weight of cargo carried 1937–72 (Courtesy of Chamber of Shipping of the United Kingdom)   59

Figure 9 Containers conveyed per annum by Freightliners Limited (Courtesy of National Freight Corporation)   67

Figure 10 Freightliner rout map (Courtesy of National Freight Corporation)   70

Figure 11 The Hull container terminal at Queen Elizabeth Dock (Courtesy of British Transport Docks Board)   82

Figure 12 OCL cellular containership *Liverpool Bay* (Courtesy of Overseas Containers Limited)   114

Figure 13 Roll-on roll-off traffic at Princess Alexandra Dock, Southampton (Courtesy of British Transport Docks Board)   138

Figure 14 OCL cellular containership *Cardigan Bay* at Southampton (Courtesy of Overseas Containers Limited)   165

Figure 15 ACT cellular containership *ACT 2* loading at Rotterdam (Courtesy of Associated Container Transportation (Australia) Limited)   176

Figure 16 Packer Avenue Marine Terminal at Philadelphia (Courtesy of Delaware River Port Authority)   196

Figure 17 Manchester Liners' cellular all-under-deck stowage container-ship *Manchester Challenge* (Courtesy of Manchester Liners Limited)   213

Figure 18 CP Ships' cellular containership *CP Voyageur* at Wolfe's Cove, Quebec (Courtesy of Canadian Pacific)   218

Figure 19 Roll-on roll-off vessel engaged in the West African trade loading at Le Havre (Courtesy of Le Havre Port Authority)   248

Figure 20 Deep sea and feeder vessels at Quay de l'Europe, Le Havre (Courtesy of Le Havre Port Authority)   270

Figure 21 The Container Terminal Amsterdam (CTA) at Amsterdam (Courtesy of Combined Terminals Amsterdam B.V.)   290

Figure 22 Prepared roll-on roll-off units at Helsingborg's Skane Terminal (Courtesy of Port of Helsingborg)   292

Figure 23 Short sea vessels at the Skane Terminal Helsingborg (Courtesy of Port of Helsingborg)   298

Figure 24 Earnings of the United Kingdom shipping industry in overseas trade 1971–1973 (Courtesy of Chamber of Shipping of the United Kingdom)   304

Figure 25 Sea-Land cellular containership *Sea-Land Finance* in the North Atlantic (Courtesy of Sea-Land Containerships Limited)   322

TABLES

Table 1 Size and age of fully cellular containerships (Courtesy of Lloyd's Register of Shipping)   306

Table 2 Merchant tonnage by type and country of registration (Courtesy of Lloyd's Register of Shipping)   309

Table 3 Merchant tonnage by country of registration (Courtesy of Lloyd's Register of Shipping)   314

Preface

by **Gordon S. C. Wills**
Professor of Marketing & Logistics Studies,
Cranfield School of Management

J.R. Whittaker's first edition of *Containerization* was an instant success. In the space of some 50,000 words, he said enough in 1972 to command a widespread and receptive audience, and deservedly so.

In 1975, Hemisphere Publishing Corporation is publishing the second edition of the title which has been 90 per cent rewritten and doubled in length. Such a transformation was almost inevitable such has been the continuing pace of development of containerization. Its rapid domination of the major sea routes is increasingly complemented by feeder services and inland shipments. New developments in Eastern Europe and the Third World are increasingly significant. The impact on dock facilities and organizational patterns continues to evolve. In summary, 1975 is a considerable distance further forward in the revolutionary process of containerization.

J.R. Whittaker takes us through the field with skill and in an eminently readable style. I believe this second edition will be as readily acceptable as the first.

August 1975

Chapter 1
Introduction

The concept of containerization is based on the advantages to be gained from a through transport system. From beginnings in the USA it is now generally accepted in the developed countries of the world that a standardized method of transportation of cargo across the oceans can offer definite economic gains.

For many years, marine transportation of cargo had been a labor intensive industry whereas it ought to have been an industry relying far more on mechanical appliances to move essentially heavy and awkward packages. Shipping companies, however, had built up fleets of conventional 'break-bulk' vessels and the industry had to be absolutely certain that containerization had come to stay before undertaking large capital expenditure. Port authorities were likewise encumbered with traditional cranage and handling devices with a limited lifting capacity, and they too had to decide on whether to provide, at enormous capital expenditure, the facilities necessary to attract the then limited number of container operators, or to continue providing their long standing customers with conventional equipment. Development by the lines was initially slow in the British shipping industry, and the first container service linking the United Kingdom and the United States of America was provided by an American concern. It soon became apparent though that the "box" had come to stay, and the industry began a major programme of investment in vessels and equipment.

Vessels earn a return on their capital outlay only when plying between ports, and are a liability at other times. One of the advantages offered by a fully containerized transport system is the ability to load and unload cargo of various types and sizes encased in standard sized containers, thus avoiding the necessity of handling many small packages one at a time during loading and discharge. Vessels can therefore be turned round far more rapidly and savings will occur not only to the shipping company through less time being spent in port but also to all those parties involved in the handling and movement of the cargo between the dock and point of origin or consumption. Apart from the cargo owners, port authorities capable of handling containers and road haulage operators able to provide chassis and flat bed vehicles will benefit, as well as British Rail with their excellent freightliner system which connects the ports and terminals with the main industrial centers.

From the time when the sailing ship was replaced by the steamship in the mid-1800's, to the start of the Second World War, merchant shipping had gone through a period of slow development. During the war however much of the pre-war merchant tonnage was lost, which presented the owners with an opportunity to re-build. This re-building really got under way during the early 1950's and, with the stimulus of an expansion in world trade, had increased by approximately 110 per cent by 1964.

These new general cargo vessels were of the conventional 'break-bulk' type and each unit of cargo had to be individually handled during loading, stowage and discharge, or if suitable, could be made up into pallet or sling loads to facilitate moving. This was an expensive, time-consuming operation which required a large labor force and comparatively little machinery. Vessels were delayed in port sometimes for as long as three weeks while labor was organized to be available as and when shippers forwarded export cargo to the berth, and stevedores were called in to stow the cargo in the vessel's holds in accordance with a complicated stowage plan drawn up in the shipping company's office. As a large part of the shipping companies' costs were being incurred whilst in port and more time was being spent in port than at sea, it is hardly surprising that many companies were kept going not by the running of a regular service between two ports, but by their own investment in other, more remunerative industries. Obviously, this was a situation that could not continue and some kind of radical change had to befall the world of shipping. This radical change was in fact forthcoming, and like many other major breakthroughs, came across the North Atlantic from the United States of America.

The founder of an inland haulage firm trading in the USA under the name of McLean Trucking Company began an experiment in integrated transport and formed a company called McLean Industries Inc. His name was Malcolm McLean and he firmly believed that savings could be made on a door-to-door movement if handling was kept to a minimum. In order to reduce handling at the ports and during loading and discharge, he maintained that if a container was used which could be packed at the exporter's premises, hauled to the dock on a flat chassis, lifted from the chassis on to the vessel and handled in a similar way during discharge and carriage to the customer's works, the necessary reductions could be made and a cost saving would follow. During the formation of the new company, McLean purchased a shipping company together with its subsidiary and he was now the owner of thirty-seven vessels of approximately 9,000 gross tons each, of which six were converted by McLean to carry containers. The first trial container run was in April 1956 when the *SS Maxton* carried sixty containers from New York to Houston. Soon afterwards, a regular service was being offered down the US East Coast from New York to San Juan in Puerto Rico. Owing to the lack of port equipment capable of lifting and moving the containers, these early vessels had their own gantry cranes, but in 1965 the company, which by now had changed its name to Sea-Land Service Inc., began installing dockside cranes at the main ports of call. Sea-Land's policy has always been, wherever possible, to own all the equipment involved in a through transportation system, including the cranes, whereas most other container lines rely on equipment provided by the port authorities and others. In 1966 the first transatlantic container service to Europe utilizing the ports of Rotterdam, Bremen and Grangemouth began. Shortly afterwards a feeder service was introduced from Rotterdam to Felixstowe, and the viability of the container as an alternative means of transport was firmly established.

Chapter 2

Vessels and Equipment

Consortia and Building Problems

During all this development the British shipping industry had looked on with considerable interest but possibly had not fully realized the significance of the containership. They were reluctant to change traditional break-bulk methods until they saw the possibility of their cargo being switched to the new American lines which were by now rapidly developing following the lead of Sea-Land. The capital outlay necessary to commence a service though was prohibitive, and the only solution appeared to be for a group of shipping companies to come together and pool their resources thus forming a consortium. Prior to this happening, however, the Irish owned Bell Lines had been running cellular containerships between the Tees area and Rotterdam, following the building in 1963 of the 499 GRT *Bell Vanguard*. This vessel together with seven more that have to date followed all have a capacity of between 70 and 118 twenty foot units, a service speed of around 13 knots, and are on long-term charter to Bell. Four such vessels were in operation by January 1968 and in June of the same year the first vessel belonging to a British consortium was launched in Hamburg.

This consortium had been established much earlier in September 1965 under the name Overseas Containers Limited and was formed by the amalgamation of The Ocean Steamship Company, British and Commonwealth Shipping, Furness Withy, and the Peninsular and Oriental Steam Navigation Company. A second consortium serving the same trade and working in collaboration with

4

OCL was also formed by the amalgamation of Ben Line, Blue Star Line, Cunard-Brocklebank, Ellerman Lines and T. & J. Harrison and trades under the name of Associated Container Transportation Limited. The formation of OCL alone involved a capital outlay of over £50 million but the consortia confidently expect to carry over 80 per cent of the available general cargo between the U.K., and Australia and the Far East. They are also active in the Pacific, OCL running between Australia and Japan, and ACT in partnership with Australian National Line from Australia to New Zealand and the east coast of North America.

With regard to the raising of capital finance the shipowners had, apart from their access to direct government funds, the facilities provided by such groups as the Shipping Mortgage Finance Scheme. The whole question of government aid is currently under review, and instead of such funds being injected irresponsibly, as was often the case, it now appears that aid will be granted where it can be shown that the result will not be complacency on the part of the builder, but instead an increased awareness of the competitive nature of the industry. In spite of nearly £300M in aid being granted to the industry since 1966, productivity is still poor especially in relation to Japanese, German and Scandinavian yards. The relative ease with which aid used to be obtained ran parallel to its extent, whereby 80% of vessel building costs would be forwarded to the prospective shipowner by the yards themselves, the remaining 20% being forthcoming from the government. These days are now past, and the owners must rely principally on government backed bank loans, spread over as long a repayment period as possible because of the extended delay in vessels becoming profit earning units, while grants are paid by the government to the yards.

Assuming that some form of assistance is to be given to the industry, to be effective it must enable the industry to advance in real terms and not merely allow it to remain in the same relative position to overseas groups. However, some of the recommendations contained in the Booz-Allen report, commissioned by the government in the summer of 1972 to look into the long term prospects of the British shipbuilding industry, may well not be put into practice. The intention was for the report to form the basis of future government policy, in a similar way that the

Geddes report of 1965-66 did, but the crucial recommendation that aid to the industry should be increased will probably be rejected on the grounds that the industry is not in fact in dire straits and should therefore be treated in a similar manner to other groups. In the short term, which will be further aggravated by capital investment being channelled to our offshore oil-drilling industry, such a policy might appear to severely jeopardize the future viability of British shipbuilding, but in the longer term it should encourage the industry to stand on its own feet in preparation to meet the competitive nature of EEC shipbuilding policy. Another important point in the Booz-Allen report is that the shipbuilding industry is too labor intensive and should reduce manpower from the current 50,000 to 39,000 by 1982. This is in line with the need for more modernization, which will probably be financed in future by the major financial institutions in Europe, and which should lead to productivity becoming internationally competitive, and the need for government aid to decrease.

Apart from the moral argument of maintaining employment in traditionally shipbuilding areas, it is of paramount importance, assuming that Britain is to maintain her long standing shipbuilding industry, to ensure that the industry has a sound future be it through government aid or from inherent changes leading to greater productivity. In this way it should be possible to check the move toward registration under flags of convenience, and to avoid the necessity of shipowners for example forming subsidiaries in the USA to take advantage of the generous subsidies allowed under the American Merchant Shipping Act of 1970.

An alternative open to shipowners wishing to secure new or replacement tonnage, and one that has grown considerably during recent years, is to lease their requirements from specialist firms. The attractions of leasing are immediately apparent because of the extent to which the industry is capital intensive. Apart from the high cost of the containership itself, the shipping company or consortium will have to provide up to three sets of containers per vessel, at an approximate cost of £1,000 per 20 foot unit. For a group to run several vessels each with a capacity of 2,000 containers, the problems of acquiring capital equipment in the early years before profits became evident were formidable. Because it is now clear, though, that the industry, while not being a particularly high profit earner, is generally able to show a credit balance, banks and finance houses are willing to become involved through either backing the leasing companies or offering finance direct to the shipowners. As an indication of the growth of leasing companies, it can be stated that during 1967 £19M was spent by them during the purchase of vessels and equipment, while in 1971 this figure had increased to £121M. One of the larger concerns, Sea Containers Incorporated, who now own 22 cellular containerships, over 38,000 containers and a variety of port handling equipment, increased its revenue during 1972 by 73% on the previous year. As more and more shipping companies and port authorities see the advantages in leasing, and especially because it is now becoming necessary to replace some existing equipment, this growth is likely to continue. It has in fact been estimated that 65% of all container orders during the next five years will be placed by leasing concerns.

To the lessee the advantages can be summarized as (*a*) less capital commitment, (*b*) freedom to utilize financial resources elsewhere, (*c*) rental payments allowed against tax, (*d*) necessity of using over a long period equipment that may have become outdated eliminated, and (*e*) the lessor may be able to take advantage of grants available in other countries that would not be directly open to the lessee. Equipment leased over a long period may also be painted to the customer's own specification.

During the early development of containerization it was uncertain who was to own and be responsible for the upkeep of the containers themselves, but the then Board of Trade (now the Department of Trade and Industry) had already ruled that only shipowners would be eligible to receive investment grants for containers. If the cargo owners, forwarding agents, or road hauliers were to own their own containers they would therefore be faced with the prospect of either leasing or approaching the finance houses, but this was a daunting prospect for many of them considering the cost of credit. They therefore pointed to the Board of Trade ruling which implied that the container was considered to be a part of the vessel, and as such should be the responsibility of the shipowners. It has in fact transpired that generally on deep sea routes the container is owned by the shipping company.

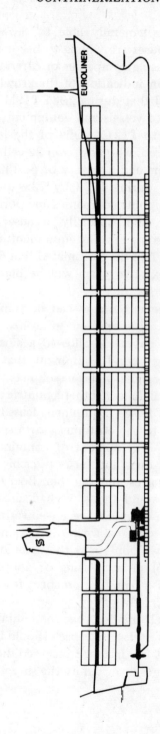

FIGURE 2 Sectional layout of fully containerized vessel (Courtesy of Seatrain (UK) Limited).

Vessel Types

Following this early development the green light was very much on and more and more owners were buying or leasing container vessels and the equipment necessary in a through movement of goods. During the transition period some lines began their container service by accepting containers for shipment on the deck of their conventional break-bulk vessels, and others began by converting their existing vessels to the cellular type of construction. Newly built vessels are now of three main types falling into one of the following categories, and generally a particular line or consortium tends to run one type only.

1. *The fully containerized vessel* with cellular type construction whereby loaded containers slide vertically downward filling every available cargo carrying space. The containers are held rigidly in position, one on top of the other, and may be stacked, in addition to six below deck on large vessels, up to four high above deck. By this means considerable extra cubic capacity is created, but problems with regard to stability because of the height of the deck cargo, and to lack of strength because of the wide hatchways follow. Poor stability can be overcome by a specially designed hull and through the siting of heavy fixed equipment within the vessel as low as possible, and weaknesses due to large open spaces at deck level can be compensated by strengthened hatchways. With regard to stability during loading and discharge, an automatic list-equalizing system whereby cross pumping of water ballast from one part of the vessel to another is possible, can be incorporated therefore avoiding jamming of containers in the cell guides. Vertical loading per complete stack of containers will be limited to approximately 130 tons which imposes an average weight per container of less than its actual capacity. Purpose built vessels will have a highly automated control system while at sea which can be operated by one officer only, and stabilizers will be fitted in addition to the usual ballast tanks situated in the double bottom and wings of the vessel. Among operators of this type of vessel are Sea-Land, United States Lines, Seatrain, Dart Containerline, Hapag-Lloyd, OCL and ACT.

2. *The partial container vessel* which offers roll-on roll-off

FIGURE 3 Container stowing in cellular holds (Courtesy of Sea-Land Containerships Limited).

facilities for cars, vehicles and heavy pieces of equipment, and some container carrying capacity. These vessels, apart from giving shippers a containerized service, are very attractive to the motor car manufacturers whose vehicles are simply driven into the car decks, and to shippers of cargo which, due to its size, is not suitable for containers. Extra long or bulky items as well as wheeled vehicles, which are being carried on an intermodal basis, are mounted on trailers and driven directly into the roll-on roll-off section of the vessel. Very large wheeled units such as heavy excavating equipment and even locomotives will have to be loaded on their own wheels, but whichever method is adopted the dangers encountered with lifting heavy pieces of equipment are eliminated. When container handling and roll-on roll-off loading or discharge are performed simultaneously very rapid turnround is possible and savings in port charges will follow. Containers are not normally loaded in the roll-on roll-off section of the vessel on deep sea routes, due to it being more economic to confine them to the cellular part, and to rely on handling by special cranes. This is in sharp contrast to short sea routes where pure roll-on roll-off vessels carry in addition to awkward loads, containers mounted on chassis and canvas-sided road trailers often hauled by their own tractor. A typical deep sea partial container vessel might have a capacity by weight of 75% container traffic and 25% roll-on roll-off, but there will often be a very marked wastage of cubic capacity in the roll-on roll-off section where construction of the decks must allow for larger traffic than may actually be carried on particular voyages. These vessels are obviously very flexible and other types may be purpose-built to carry in addition to containers, general cargo or primary products in bulk. The pioneer on the Atlantic of combined container and roll-on roll-off services was Atlantic Container Line, a consortium that brought together the resources of Cunard, French Line, Holland America, Swedish Transatlantic and Wallenius.

3. *The convertible container ship*, more common in the Pacific than in home waters, where the nature of the traffic demands a vessel capable of carrying containers and general cargo in one direction, and containers and bulk cargo in the other. For example, Matson Navigation Company ships containers and cars to Hawaii from the west coast of North America, and returns with contain-

ers and sugar and molasses in bulk. Similarly where marked differences in trade flows between two areas exist as would be the case between a developing country and Europe, the desirability of operating a vessel capable of exporting from Europe containerized general cargo and returning with bulk commodities is obvious. Problems with regard to container handling in the less developed country would exist but loading and discharge from the vessel could be accomplished through the use of ships gantries. Although not strictly containerships the *Pacific* and *Suecia* belonging to the Johnson Line of Sweden are convertible vessels carrying cars from the United Kingdom and Sweden to the Pacific west coast ports of North America and returning from Vancouver to Tilbury with forest products. Both commodities are carried on standard size platforms and stowed in cellular holds. Two 30-ton gantry cranes are carried. A similar operation to Johnson Line's is maintained by the Burnett Steamship Company which carries lumber from Canada's east coast to the United Kingdom and returns with European cars intended for discharge at Montreal.

During the period up to the end of 1971 building of pure fully cellular container vessels was dominant and 279 were in service worldwide at 1st January 1974. Increasing interest, however, is currently being shown in roll-on roll-off methods principally due to their flexibility in relation to cargo types and countries that can be served, and because of the negligible capital investment that need be committed to shore facilities. It is becoming less likely that cargo owners will have to use a container service, as other methods of unitized service are introduced or extended on particular routes, and it remains to be seen how the container vessel will fare in relation to roll-on, roll-off and to the LASH (lighter aboard ship) barge carrier, mention of which will be made presently.

The question of whether to utilize port authority container cranes or to provide vessels with their own equipment is not yet fully resolved. As already mentioned, the early services provided by Sea-Land depended on the use of ships' gantries, and this method is clearly a necessity when calling at ports without proper facilities. As the equipment is only productive though during the vessel's stay in port (a container vessel will be at sea for 80-90 per cent of its lifetime) and as it is very vulnerable to corrosion due to the impact of salt water, the system has disadvantages. These must be offset against the ability of calling at ports in less developed countries where container handling facilities may be nonexistent, and compared in turn with the advantages and disadvantages of the roll-on roll-off system with or without ships gantries. Over the long term it still remains to be seen whether world container traffic will grow at a faster rate than the provision by the ports of container cranes, but if this does prove to be the case owners will have to explore further the alternative ways of shipping and handling unitized cargo.

Standardization

In an integrated door-to-door system it is imperative that the container is capable of being handled by all the links in the chain, i.e., the vessel itself, the railway system, road haulage operators and the dockside facilities. To this end the International Standards Organization has recommended container sizes of 8 feet wide, 8 feet high and lengths in multiples of 10 feet with a maximum of 40 feet. Most of the lines have accepted the ISO sizes but some of the early operators, notably Sea-Land, had already decided on their own sizes (35 feet × 8 feet × 8 feet in the case of Sea-Land), investing immense amounts of capital in the process. Nonstandard containers are currently quite common in the Pacific trades where units often exceed 8 feet in height and there is a growing tendency within the USA for operators to invest in larger units up to 9′ 6″ high. There are two views on the most effective way of implementing standardization both of which are mainly discussed in the USA. Apart from the generally accepted principle of standardizing on the size of the container, some groups advocate that the carriers should provide flexible equipment capable of adjusting to varying sizes of container. This group points out, quite correctly, that the era of containerization has hardly started and that no one knows what the future holds in the way of further revolutionary changes. Some of these changes are already with us, and a transport system able to adapt will prove far more beneficial than one committed to carrying only a specified type of unit. It is also pointed out that

FIGURE 4 Wheeled and container traffic awaiting shipment by ACL roll-on roll-off/container vessel ' (Courtesy of British Transport Docks Board).

the user of an integrated transport system should benefit from the cost savings, and such a user would be far more able to benefit if he could utilize a container suitable to the carriage of his own traffic, which may well have peculiarities with regard to bulk and weight. As has already been stated the roll-on roll-off vessel has the ultimate in flexibility but will not be economical in all trades, while some container vessels have adjustable cells capable of accepting varying types of container. The advocates of standardized equipment maintain that the prices of such equipment are bound to fall when the manufacturers are able to enjoy economies of scale through the production of very long runs, and that many shippers and consignees could benefit if they mutually agreed to order and sell in quantities that completely fitted a stated size of container. In this way the exceedingly high minimum revenue to be earned by each container, imposed by some lines, would be reached and dead freight, i.e., that freight paid to a shipping company for space booked but not taken up, would not be incurred. This wastage of cubic capacity will also arise if the trend away from standardization to larger units continues, because of weight restrictions imposed by some countries when hauling containers by road or rail making it impossible to fill the container.

With regard to standardization of the vessels themselves the cargo operators have considerable advantage over the owners of passenger vessels, through being able to order 'off-the-peg' vessels, not therefore being committed to building up a fleet of vessels with their own peculiar characteristics, as demanded by the cruise-going public. This tendency is bound to expand when the future becomes clearer with regard to ship types, but further promotion of nonstandard containers can only lead to problems in ship design.

Barge Carrying Vessels

Mention should be made of a development taking place mainly in the United States of America, which could affect the containership of today to a similar extent that the containerships have affected and almost replaced the conventional general cargo vessels. In an attempt to achieve even quicker turnrounds than the containerships were capable of, and to reduce operating costs as well as handling costs in port through even greater economies of scale, it was decided to build barge and lighter carrying ships that could load and unload laden craft direct to an inland waterway. The concept was to be known as LASH (lighter aboard ship), and since the early vessels operated by the Central Gulf Steamship Corporation of America appeared in 1969 linking the USA and Europe, the system has spread to many other countries. This basic principle of using in effect "floating detachable cargo holds" and relying on ship's gantries or other on-board handling methods for loading and discharging laden barges also lends itself to operation in those trades where containerships are not able to serve due to lack of shore handling equipment. The original intention was in fact for the LASH vessels to be used in trade with less developed countries, where in addition to ports being unable to accept containerships, it was not practicable to operate on an intermodal basis due to the generally poor inland haulage system. Cargo would therefore have to "break bulk" by whichever way it was shipped, but if the LASH system were to be used the vessel would be turned round on arrival in a fraction of the time taken by a cargo vessel.

In the event, however, the system was used initially to link the USA and Europe through New Orleans and Rotterdam using the Rhine and Mississippi rivers as water "highways". Each LASH vessel carries between 73 and 83 lighters (cargo capacity equivalent of approximately 1750 20-foot containers), each measuring 61 feet 6 inches × 31 feet 2 inches × 13 feet, with an individual capacity of either 20,000 cubic feet or 372 tons. Deadweight tonnage ranges from about 30,000-40,000 per vessel, and conditions in America have been especially conducive to building, in view of a 44 per cent subsidy. In addition to Central Gulf Steamship Corporation, Pacific Far East Line, Delta Steamship Lines, Waterman Line, Prudential-Grace Lines, Combi Line (a consortium formed by Hapag-Lloyd and Holland America Line) and Moslash are running LASH-type vessels, and as well as overlapping the present containership routes between the Gulf and Europe, have extended their interests to the Mediterranean, Australia, and as was the original intention to South America.

The trans-Atlantic LASH service operates by cargo being loaded to barges and transported down to the mouth of the Mississippi River where they are loaded to the main vessel for shipment across the Atlantic for eventual discharge at the mouth of either the River Thames or Rhine. From here they are floated to their destinations in the English or German hinterlands. Expensive port facilities are not required, the carrying vessel merely mooring to a buoy in a river estuary while the barges are either lifted off by a ship's gantry or floated out of their fixtures. The LASH vessel may thus be worked in an estuary while other more conventional ships wait for a berth to be vacated prior to discharge and loading. Port congestion is avoided and the vessels can be turned round within 24 hours or less using as few as five men working a deck gantry crane, thus realizing cost reductions even greater than those enjoyed by the most efficient containerized vessel.

Four distinct types of barge carrying vessels were proposed, each differing in the methods used for loading and discharging laden craft. The portal crane type, where barges are lifted out of their cellular compartments by a gantry capable of vertical and horizontal movement is most widely used at present, but the system suffers from a lack of flexibility. Vessels with floodable compartments are slightly more flexible, and are of a single hull structure with only two layers of barges. By varying the draught of the carrying vessel, and in conjunction with a floating hydraulic lift, barges are floated out of and in to the vessel, a portal crane not being required. The third category of vessel, which will be discussed presently, is known as "Seabee" (Sea Barge Carrier), and is fitted with an elevating stern platform on to which a pair of barges are floated when the platform is in a submerged position. The platform is raised and the barges are stowed in the required position by a movable belt. A more recent proposition is based on the air cushion principle and is similar in operation to the hovercraft. The carrying vessel is allowed to settle deeply in the water while barges are floated directly in or out. When loaded an air cushion is created between the solid sidewalls of the vessel and curtains at the bow and stern, through which the barges pass, and the whole vessel rises out of the water. Flexibility and simplicity of operation are thus not compatible, and it appears at present that the former is best sacrificed in favor of the latter.

Some barge carrying vessels also carry a limited quantity of containers on deck, in addition to those carried in the barges themselves, but due to the economic advantages inherent in a complete barge system, whereby reliance is not placed on container cranes and the necessity of mooring alongside a container berth is avoided, it is probable that barge traffic only will be carried in the future. Such cargo as baled cotton and wool, hogsheads of tobacco, heavy vehicles and machinery, fertilizers and other bulk commodities where it is more convenient to move in 370-ton lots as against complete vessel loads will be ideally suited for stowing in barges. Efficiently operated, LASH is capable of handling four lighters per hour representing a total of 1,200 tons of cargo. This compares with a cargo handling speed by roll-on roll-off vessels of up to 400 tons per hour, by fully cellular containerships of approximately 250 tons per hour, and by break-bulk vessel of 100 tons per hour.

Although it is generally unwise for LASH operators to directly compete for cargo more suited to containers over the established container routes, there are trades where a dual-purpose specialized ship capable of carrying LASH barges and/or containers is desirable. For example, Delta Steamship Lines run vessels that can be used for any combination of barges/containers between the US Gulf and the east coast of South America. At present due to lack at the South American ports of adequate handling equipment LASH barges predominate on the route, but as port handling and inland haulage conditions improve, Delta will be able to alter their ratio of barges to containers in favor of the latter.

The LASH system can therefore be said to be at its most competitive when collection and delivery of laden barges is effected by inland waterway as far away as possible from the mother ship, as could be the case on the Mississippi and the Rhine rivers, and when barge consolidation results in cost savings during towing on the waterway. In a similar way to containerization the LASH vessel is not delayed while its barges, or detachable holds, are loaded or unloaded with cargo, and turnround will be further quickened in ports where congestion is common through the vessel not having to wait for a berth, but instead taking on and discharging laden barges often at an estuary mooring. To be set against these advantages, however, is the reality that both Prudential Grace and Combi Line are said to be losing money. Prudential Grace found it necessary, due to financial difficulties, to sell its vessels to a finance house and then to lease them back. Part of the blame undoubtedly rests with the American International Longshoremen's Association due to their insistence on over-manning and levying penalty payments on barges handled by non-Association labor, even though Association labor is not always available.

As already mentioned an alternative to the LASH barge system is the Seabee (sea barge carrier) system. The difference between the two is essentially one of scale and method of loading, the Seabee barges being able to accept up to 850 tons of cargo compared with the LASH barge capacity of up to 372 tons. Each Seabee barge measures 97 feet by 35 feet and two such units are loaded simultaneously using an elevating stern platform. The vessels are restricted to carrying 38 barges, and as in the LASH system are flexible in the types of cargo that may be carried. The basic principle of moving commodities in large loads, but at the same time not in bulk but in quantities capable of relative ease in handling, often become more attractive as the load increases to an upper limit. The Seabee system would therefore appear to have the same advantages as the LASH system plus an ability to effect even larger savings in costs because of greater economies of scale. Partly due to this, Seabee vessels are attracting cargo emanating from as far north as the Great Lakes, and are filling a very real need by supplying space to those cargo owners unable to enter the tramp market but nevertheless dealing in commodities in relatively large tonnage.

While discussing LASH and Seabee mention should also be made of a development taking place in Europe that hopefully will once again enable the extensive inland waterway system of the United Kingdom to be used in a similar way to the rivers and canals on the Continent. A Danish consortium, Rudkobing VI, has developed a system of handling and shipping barges now commonly known as barge-aboard-catamaran (BACAT). The vessels have twin hulls and the early ones will be able to accept 10-140 ton barges specially constructed for this type of vessel, and 3-400 ton barges of the LASH type. The BACAT barges will be stowed on deck using a similar stern lifting elevator to the Seabee vessels, while the three LASH barges will be stowed between the twin

FIGURE 5 Seabee barge carrier *Doctor Lykes* at Le Havre
(Courtesy of Le Havre Port Authority).

hulls. Building is being undertaken by a Danish yard and the system is being marketed in the United Kingdom by the British Waterways Board and on the Continent by Holland America Line, a group possessing considerable barge carrying experience through their participation in Combi Line. By using a part of the 350 miles of navigable waterways within the United Kingdom as a conveyance for the BACAT barges themselves, and the Humber estuary as a mooring point for loading and unloading laden barges to the mother ship, shippers of full loads will be given the opportunity of moving materials such as coal, oil, timber, ores and fertilizers between the inland industrial areas of England and the hinterland of the Continent via Rotterdam.

The advantages of LASH and Seabee will thus be extended to the BACAT system through less time being spent in port, lower handling charges by using only four lightermen, and a "door-to-door" service being offered to cargo owners who previously were shipping in quantities too large to benefit from containers, but too small to charter tonnage. A further advantage is the BACAT vessel's ability to act as a feeder, i.e., collect and deliver laden barges at ports other than the ocean-going vessel's mooring point, for the LASH vessels. As already mentioned the BACAT vessel is able to carry three LASH barges and it will therefore be possible for cargo owners in the northern part of England to utilize the trans-Atlantic LASH system by having their cargo transported in LASH barges by a BACAT ship to Rotterdam for loading to a LASH vessel bound for the US Gulf. The confidence possessed by the Danish consortium in BACAT is indicated by their placing an order in January 1974 for a similar vessel to the first but three times larger, and it is to be hoped that the United Kingdom Government will give the system its backing by allowing the canal system to be extensively opened up, and in the long term for the locks to be widened to accommodate at a later date barges of greater dimension than the present BACAT type.

Chapter 3

Ports and Terminals

Established Port Structure

Britain's ports had traditionally been built up to handle loose cargo for shipment by break-bulk vessels. Many were designed and built during the days of the clippers and were sprawled in an untidy mess around our estuaries and coastline, where land was at less of a premium than today, and where many vessels were in port at one time, usually for an extended period.

Many of these ports survived and grew with the increase in international trade and an array of conventional dockside cranes and fork lift trucks, both with limited lifting capacities, were built up. The outlook looked good, and many port authorities became complacent, not bothering to invest in new equipment, which could have helped to minimize the ever increasing frustrating delays experienced by shippers and consignees during deliveries and collections from the docks, and not realizing that increasing industrial development outside their confines was gradually making it impossible to expand if the need arose. This period of prosperity soon turned into one of gloom when it was realized that apart from the lack of space, the ports were encumbered with antiquated handling methods, lack of deep water which would be essential to the larger cargo vessels, and communications more suited to small lorries and conventional railway wagons. The ports were further hindered through being too labor intensive which resulted in continually rising costs, and through receiving very little government aid following the Second World War. The complacency of the past coupled with the recent speed of new developments has therefore led to the problems of today centering principally around labor relations, finance and the cloud of threatened nationalization.

Shipowners were the party most affected, as a vessel tied up in port is a liability, and is only earning revenue at sea. This was an important contributory factor taken into account during the examination of shipowners' economies and efficiency when containerization was being considered. The initial reaction of shippers and shipowners was to move their operation to less congested ports, and indeed many services that had been running out of London and Liverpool, the two major trouble spots, were based instead on such ports as Ipswich and Felixstowe. These moves were accelerated following the increased use of containers and the concentration of container traffic at fewer ports, and this in turn led to the need for warehousing to decline, as the new transportation methods encouraged delivery to, and collection from, the industrial manufacturing areas by full container load. It therefore became necessary to close some of the old established dock systems controlled by the Port of London Authority as well as many private wharves. An example of the latter is Hay's Wharf which extended on the south bank of the river from Tower Bridge to London Bridge. It should be pointed out however that Hay's Wharf had had more than its fair share of labor disputes which in part contributed to the closure. Another casualty was Free Trade Wharf which closed for 'economic reasons'. A spokesman for the wharf was reported to have stated "there have been heavy losses which can no longer be sustained and the company does not consider that future prospects for a wharf of this nature give any encouragement" (*Financial Times*, 15 October 1970). These closures have meant that a considerable area of land has become available for development in London, and the Government in association with local authorities and the present landowners are trying to reach a compromize whereby some of the land is sold at a fair market value to the local authorities for housing, schools, and open spaces, thus avoiding haphazard large-scale office development by speculators.

During all this running down, a handful of wharves in London possessing great confidence in the continuance of conventional shipping methods, have greatly benefited from providing a service which is still in demand by many merchants. For example, the Danish company P. Bork and the Norwegian Fred Olsen Lines both have great faith in the future of palletized cargo, and have virtually shunned the container as the ideal unit of transportation. Their London terminals situated at Aberdeen Wharf and Millwall Dock are practically standing alone and thriving while other wharves and docks nearby are ceasing operations. Such developments have taken place without the spending of millions of pounds on modernization and without widespread redundancies. Generally, however, with the need for extensive areas of land for container stacking and unrestricted inland transport flow, coupled with the necessity, especially by short sea operators, to cut down their sailing times, handling facilities for the new vessels have tended to proliferate along the less crowded estuaries of rivers and at the smaller coastal ports where land was readily available for expansion.

While an explanation of the labor problems that followed the introduction of containerization will follow in a later chapter, a word should be said about the two ways the ports are manned. Since 1947 the major ports in the United Kingdom have been registered with the National Dock Labour Board, a central body controlling the conditions of employment in the ports. A levy has to be paid to the Board and the men working in the member or "scheme" ports must be registered dock workers, as well as union members. A large part of the port's day to day running is therefore taken away from the port authority, and some flexibility of management is lost. There are other ports, however, that fall outside the jurisdiction of the National Dock Labour Board, and while their labor force is usually made up of union members, the conditions they work under are not controlled by the Board. These are the "non-scheme" ports, and it would appear that dockers working in such ports are open to any sort of malpractice that management care to inflict. But in point of fact it is the "non-scheme" ports that generally have the best labor relations and where productivity is highest. An obvious example is Felixstowe where efficiency in handling cargo and documents combined with good management/labor relations has led to consistently fast turnround of vessels and road vehicles. Port and ship running costs are reduced and shipowners are able to plan sailing schedules with confidence. Closer control by the port authority, some of the members of which are often major port users as well, would therefore not seem to be detrimental to efficiency, but the point has been raised, most unfairly, that the method of running some "non-scheme" ports such as Felixstowe is the cause of the stagnation of some "scheme" or National Dock Labour Board ports such as Bristol. The future of several of the Board ports is thus in jeopardy, and the unions have pointed out that if Government aid in the form of subsidies, which would presumably go to the ports least deserving it, were forthcoming the need for the less efficient ports to compete would diminish and job security would be assured. It is to be hoped that if a common EEC ports policy is drawn up very careful consideration will be given to the elimination of subsidies that could be met out of profits.

The Need to Invest

By the mid 1960's it was obvious that drastic changes would have to take place in the ports to accommodate the containerships, but not all had the foresight of for example Felixstowe, which was by now rapidly expanding, and many with little capital resources saw their share of international trade gradually dwindling. Some tried to attract the palletized ships, or extend their facilities for the handling of bulk cargoes such as iron ore, coal and timber, but the future of these ports, bearing in mind that fewer and fewer would be required in the container age, was very uncertain indeed. Generally only the larger authorities with strong financial backing, or those ports under the umbrella of the British Transport Docks Board have been able to adapt to container handling, but even some of these will probably encounter serious difficulties when it is more certain where the shipping companies intend basing their European operations. Competition amongst the ports, not only within the United Kingdom, but on a much broader European front as well, will therefore be intense, and the need for even greater investment than has taken place to date will be uppermost in the minds of port authority management.

To give an idea of the magnitude of the expenditure involved in modernizing Britain's ports it should be stated that over

£200 million was involved during the period 1965-1969 (*Digest of Port Statistics* published by the National Ports Council 1970) and that more recently over £40M has been spent per year, principally on container and roll-on roll-off facilities. Without this expenditure the container ships would have had a limited area in which to operate and in the early days exporters situated a long way from a container port would have tended to despatch cargo for shipment by break-bulk vessels from conventional ports.

The conventional ports were always the limiting factor regulating the size of general cargo vessels, and these vessels were able only to grow in size by 14 per cent during the period 1950-1966, while tanker sizes increased by 82 per cent and tramping vessels (including bulk carriers) by 52 per cent. The two latter types of vessel had the use of highly efficient shore installations for loading and discharge in bulk and were thus able to turn round in a fraction of the time taken by the general cargo vessels. The approximate time spent at sea and in port for a conventional break-bulk cargo vessel is 40 and 60 per cent, and about half the time in port is due to delays while waiting for labor and handling equipment, and while making hatches ready. As over one-third of the total annual cost of running break-bulk vessels was incurred while freight was being handled in port, it was clear that without far more modern ports the savings possible through the running of container vessels could not be realized. It was to this end therefore that justification of the above capital outlay was sought.

Although the capital investment was enormous, and indeed some of the early container berths are still not making profits through trying to pay off their capital debt, the handling costs of cargo per ton at a container berth are substantially lower than those at conventional berths. Admittedly charges have also to be kept low to attract users but the outcome, bearing in mind that typically only one-tenth of the labor force employed at a conventional berth is employed at a container berth, is higher productivity with a resultant stabilizing effect on one of the shipping companies' most variable items of cost. Through the National Ports Council, mention of which will be made presently, port authorities should to a large extent co-ordinate their expansion policies, without harming the competitive element of day-to-day running, to avoid unnecessary duplication of facilities. This co-ordination should be extended on a national scale to determine whether proposed new port complexes such as Falmouth and Maplin are really necessary, or whether existing facilities could be added to, and on a smaller scale to avoid duplication of services, such as stevedoring, within a port.

The question of subsidized ports on the Continent will be dealt with under another heading, but mention should be made of the effect on the United Kingdom ports of the proposed Channel Tunnel. If it is accepted that the principal reason for building such a tunnel is to increase political unity between the United Kingdom and her EEC partners, and that to allow the tunnel to operate on a competitive footing it will have to be subsidized, it follows that the short sea ports will be facing competition from a method of cross channel transport operating on an artificially low cost basis. This will create problems for the short sea ports such as the extent of future investment, and of whether investment should be utilized to attract a different type of vessel to those currently being catered for. For example, a port may see its future as a base for one of the barge carrying ships mentioned earlier, or as a feeder port to accept containers transhipped on the Continent, instead of developing facilities for roll-on roll-off vessels or deep sea containerships. Until it becomes clearer what Government intentions are regarding such projects as the Channel Tunnel, it will remain very difficult for some of the ports to plan ahead without ending with duplicated facilities and a serious over-capacity problem.

Grants, Loans and Subsidies

Generally though the need to invest is a definite one and as the ports, other than those controlled by the British Transport Docks Board, were not nationalized the controlling authorities were encouraged to drag themselves out of their quagmires through the implementation of a 20 per cent modernization grant issued by the Government for approved projects. In view of the subsequent development of many of the ports it was possible to withdraw the grants at a later date, but due to the collapse of the Mersey Docks and Harbour Board and the subsequent lack of confidence in the profit potential of the ports, finance was not forth-coming from the money markets in sufficient quantity and it was necessary for the Government to announce at the end of September 1971 that in certain cases loans would be provided to the ports for the renewal of capital debt. These loans will be long-term but the ports will be encouraged to continue to borrow on the market whenever possible, and to repay before the expiry date if possible. The National Ports Council, which acquired wider powers at the beginning of 1971, must now satisfy themselves that any port authority applying for a loan is financially sound, and the Council may impose conditions on the authority which must be fulfilled prior to the granting of the loan.

In the struggle to attract the container operators to the United Kingdom, it should be pointed out that some Continental ports benefit greatly from subsidies provided by central or local government, who regard the ports as vital to the existence of a healthy economy. Dredging costs are normally paid for in full on the Continent by the Government concerned, while local authorities will absorb individual port losses and depreciation allowances. French ports are particularly heavily subsidized, the Government granting 60 per cent of the cost of berths and 80 per cent of other essential infrastructure, as well as the 100 per cent dredging cost. This has resulted in the spectacular development of Dunkirk, Le Havre and Marseilles, and in October 1972 a further £42M was allocated to maintain future progress in France. These subsidies, which are granted in a modified form to the Continental ports of Hamburg, Antwerp and Rotterdam amongst others, are designed to draw a greater share of the world's large deep sea container vessels, which in future will tend to load and discharge all cargo for a large area of Europe at one major terminal only and rely on feeder vessels for collection and distribution at other European ports.

As already stated, and in contrast to their over-generous assistance, the ports in the United Kingdom are obliged to finance total expenditure without subsidies, and are only occasionally in a position to secure a Government loan. This policy was recently pointed to by the Port of London Authority to justify an increase in charges when it was stated that they "enjoy no subsidies, direct or indirect and, unlike them, we have to pay for all our dredging". The United Kingdom ports are therefore regarded as commercial undertakings and as such, profit-making bodies.

In view of the differing basis of port subsidization where it exists in Europe, it will be difficult to establish an EEC common ports policy, but the first need, and one that the British Ports Association firmly believes in, is for the Continental ports to scrap all subsidies and allow the United Kingdom authorities to compete more fairly. Although repercussions would be felt by fringe groups partly or wholly dependent on the Continental ports for their livelihood in cases where the elimination of subsidies was detrimental to the port, the way would be cleared for the establishment of a common ports policy which would stimulate competition, and in the long term have a beneficial effect on efficiency. If such a policy is not drawn up it should be made clear to the Continental port authorities that according to a National Ports Council survey it would be possible for United Kingdom ports to reduce their charges by over 50% if the Government were to adopt subsidies on a similar scale as found on the Continent.

The National Ports Council

Prior to the introduction of containerization into Britain's ports, the then Conservative Government set up a committee under Lord Rochdale in March 1961 "to consider to what extent the major docks and harbours of Great Britain are adequate to meet present and future national needs, whether the methods of working can be improved, and to make recommendations". The establishment of the committee was welcomed by those people who believed that the only way to improve the methods of working in the ports, was by co-ordination of the interested parties, and by the introduction of more scientific and more commercially minded management. Unfortunately the effect of some of the Committee's recommendation was not entirely beneficial, and whereas changes such as the fairer re-assessment of port charges on a basis more related to cost, as against what the traffic could bear, were welcomed, other results such as the breakdown in internal communications, especially prevalent in London following the management shake-up, were not so desirable. Before new policies were introduced in London a lengthy process of discussion and deliberation had to take place at a time when it was vital that decisions should be made promptly.

The main recommendation of the Committee, however, was the creation of a National Ports Authority, with wide powers, but this was later changed by the then Minister of Transport, Mr Ernest Marples, into a weaker body, the National Ports Council. The purpose of the Council was to advise the Government on ports planning which would include guidance on where to concentrate handling facilities. This lead to the ports was essential, as ship-owners were free to come and go, if expensive duplication of facilities was to be avoided, but the lead was not strong enough as at this time the National Ports Council was purely an advisory body to the Government. Inevitably Government decisions were partly influenced by outside sources and the ports continued to develop without sufficiently firm guidance.

With the coming to power of the Labour party in October 1964, and the second reading of the Ports Bill much later in December 1969, it looked as though the threat of nationalization was to become a reality and the ports would after all have a form of central organization. The objectives of nationalization contained in the Bill were (1) the creation of a powerful National Ports Authority to plan and co-ordinate future port development, (2) to establish lines of management responsibility, the National Ports Authority being responsible to Parliament for the running of all ports handling over five million tons of cargo per year, (3) to reduce the number of port employers, such as stevedoring firms, and therefore to cut duplication and waste of facilities, and (4) to improve labor relations particularly through worker participation in management. Nationalization would obviously have had drastic effects, detrimental to the more efficient ports, but through the pooling of assets and central control, the National Ports Authority may have been able to avoid the present strife to be found in ports such as Liverpool. Compensation to banks and insurance companies and other bodies holding stock, and to stevedoring and lighterage firms, would have to follow nationalization, and during this period of uncertainty future development schemes had to be shelved.

On the election of the Conservative party to power in June

1970, however, the Ports Bill died and the threat of nationalization vanished. Any idea of a powerful National Ports Authority was discarded and the National Ports Council continued to function as an advisory body to the Government. The Council, although still not forming policy, is now a highly respected body and is invariably supported by the Government. It advises the Government whether or not loans should be granted to particular ports, and is currently trying to avoid a situation of over-capacity that would surely follow the building of a port complex at Maplin, or the over-rapid expansion at fast developing ports such as Southampton. It was indeed the Council that finally convinced the Government that the proposed container terminal at Falmouth was not a realistic proposition, and it is the Council, together with the British Ports Association, that is urging free competition between ports throughout the EEC.

Container Handling Equipment

The prerequisite of any efficient container berth is the ability to turn vessels round in days or even hours as against weeks, through the installation of purpose-built handling equipment. Much of the capital invested by the port will therefore go toward providing fast working giant container cranes and a terminal system capable of handling the containers at the same speed as the cranes. It is no use running a crane unloading at a speed of a container a minute if it is not possible to move the containers off the quay on to road vehicles, into the railway system, or to a storage area at a similar speed. To this end the port authorities use two types of crane—the 'portainer' and the 'transtainer'.

The portainer is used for loading and discharge of container vessels where speed is of prime importance. It consists of a gantry supporting a horizontal boom which can be stowed when not in use in a vertical position. The gantry is usually mounted on a dockside rail, thus enabling movement along the ship's length. Containers will be unloaded to flat-bed vehicles, railway wagons, or to further specialized handling equipment on the quay. The cranes have lifting capacities of up to 50 tons, and some such as the Twin Lift Portainer built by Paceco-Vickers quicken ship turnround even more by being able to handle two unattached 20-foot containers simultaneously. The transtainer, an advanced method of handling containers on the dockside, consists of an overhead travelling crane mounted on a gantry spanning either the whole marshalling area or a limited area only. It is used for moving and stacking containers within the dock area, loading and unloading vehicles and rail wagons, and can also be used for loading and unloading ships where a limited throughput of containers is involved. Transtainers may be either rubber-tyred or rail-mounted, but the flexibility of the former, where all four wheels are steerable, has obvious advantages. Several of the portainers and transtainers being installed today are suitable for later conversion to automatic operation controlled by a computer as in the Modular Automated Container Handling system (MACH) developed by Paceco. Such a system has been developed in anticipation of automated terminals, units being added to as the terminal expands, and throughput will be even faster than it is today.

In addition to, or as an alternative to the transtainer, many port authorities use straddle carriers in conjunction with a portainer system. These carriers are driven over a container and lift them vertically upwards, for moving or stacking up to three units high. Although useful for lifting and lowering, they are very cumbersome when used as a conveyance and are difficult, because of the operator's restricted field of vision, to manoeuvre safely. Indeed they often seem out of place in a modern handling system, although if developed further the present carriers could be the forerunners of driverless automated carriers of the future.

A further way for a terminal to overcome the problem of keeping containers mobile on the quay is to use the "chassis system". Here a container will never be placed on the ground, but will be lowered to a chassis which will either be hauled directly to the point of destination, or will be parked at the terminal awaiting collection by a tractor. As it is desirable in a container system to obtain the maximum possible usage out of all the equipment, the importer will be encouraged, through heavy quay rent and demurrage charges, to take delivery of the container without delay. Stacking containers on the quay will not be necessary and the problems associated with extracting containers at the bottom of a stack will not occur. Although the chassis system is very flexible, a larger back up area will be required to accommodate the containers and their chassis, but it is being increasingly agreed that flexibility and the absence of straddle carriers is to be desired.

United Kingdom Developments

In spite of the early difficulties during initial provision of or conversion to container handling methods, the United Kingdom now has 46 ports with specialized unit load services, 29 of these having lift-on lift-off gantries. From a throughput of 16.6M tons of unitized traffic in 1970 and 19M tons in 1971, the United Kingdom ports handled 22M tons in 1972 and had an £8.5M surplus on total capital employed of almost £600M, ranging from Dover with 12% down to Liverpool with 2% returns. Nineteen of the ports are nationalized and are controlled by the relatively efficient British Transport Docks Board set up in 1963. The Board manages to maintain quite good labor relations and an operating surplus of £8.4M was made during 1972.

The stimulus to the industry has come from the need for a more efficient international transport system, and from competition amongst the ports for the container and roll-on roll-off operators, but now that the ports are either equipped or are formulating definite plans based on anticipated demand, and as relatively fewer ports will be required in the future, efficiency will become increasingly important in attracting the container and roll-on roll-off ships. Apart from the smaller ports specializing in short-sea container and roll-on roll-off traffic, it is becoming less important to the shipping companies where a port is situated, due to inland haulage charges on international traffic usually being assessed not on the distance of the inland haul, but on the location of the collection or delivery point in a grid system. Ports in the southern part of the United Kingdom will therefore be competing directly with those in the north, and it is of little use building a prestige terminal if the management running it or the labor force employed are unable or unwilling to allow the berths to be used to achieve their maximum possible productivity. Those authorities too slow to adapt or too quick in providing specialist facilities will find themselves in serious financial difficulties.

Unit load berths are operated in two main ways. The berth may either be under the direct control of the port management and be open to any shipping lines if spare capacity exists, or a single shipping line or consortium may be the only user under a tenancy agreement with the port authority. The tenant may take over the berth equipped, or more usually provide his own sheds, handling devices and labor, as in the case of Fred Olsen at Millwall Dock, London, and of Sealand at Grangemouth. While the port authority will admittedly lose direct control over a single user berth, the throughput will often be more than double that achieved at a common user berth. An example of extending the tenancy principle to embrace what is in effect a port within a port is the Victoria Deep Water Terminal, a private company, controlling an area of 17 acres within the old dock precincts of London. Situated far up river at Greenwich, the terminal would appear to contradict one of the strongest arguments in favor of Maplin: that future container berths should be sited as near to the Continental ports as possible. Admittedly the terminal is very well connected to motorways and other main roads, but the service given to users of the terminal which handled 28,000 containers during 1973, is a major factor contributing to its success. Short sea vessels, Seabee barges and groupage traffic are currently being catered for, and an example of the terminal's ability to quickly change to accommodate developments, is the fact that it could be the United Kingdom's first automated container terminal following adaptation of its existing container cranes. The terminal has a potential annual throughput of 53,000 containers and is investigating the feasibility of also handling roll-on roll-off vessels.

Felixstowe

One of the earliest ports to provide container handling equipment in an effort to secure for itself a place in the container revolution was the east coast port of Felixstowe. Felixstowe was strategically placed to act as a terminal handling feeder vessels servicing the early trans-Atlantic containerships, which were then docking at Rotterdam, and soon grew into a major terminal in its own right offering facilities to short sea container and roll-on roll-off vessels, and deep sea containerships, as well as the feeders.

A great deal of capital was required by the port of Felixstowe in adapting and extending its facilities to attract on a long-term basis the container and roll-on roll-off operator, and the then private Felixstowe Dock and Railway Company decided to invite the public to participate in the purchase of shares. The issue was a great success, and the subsequent expansion allowed the handling of 106,000 containers during 1972 representing M1.9 tons of cargo. Profits for the financial year ending September 1971 of £539,000 were 55 per cent up on the previous year's figure and rose by a further 50 per cent in 1972.

Three Paceco-Vickers portainer cranes are currently operating following a rapid growth pattern helped by the absence of any already existing outdated equipment and work methods, and high productivity, primarily due to the excellent management/labor relations, allows very fast vessel turnround. The latest development at the port was the opening in November 1973 of a £1M inland clearance depot financed by a consortium of ten companies including the Dock Company itself. The port has consistently kept abreast of growth in containerization and has often given a lead to other ports, but now that deep sea container vessels are becoming larger, and due to the limitation of water depth in the approach channels to the port, it may be necessary to increasingly rely on feeder and short sea services from the deep water Continental ports. The Dock Company's argument that ship sizes will not dramatically increase because the larger the vessel the longer its stay in port, and vice versa, is not very realistic, and becomes less so as the voyage time and sailing distance increase.

The future of the port though, whether in the field of providing facilities to all forms of vessels carrying unitized cargo, or whether in a more specialized role, is confidently assured through not only the current largely self-financed £10M expansion programme, but also through the willingness of other groups to invest a further £15M in ancillary projects such as warehousing and freight forwarding operations. The port's own plans will raise throughput to over 5M tons of unitized traffic per year, and in the longer term reclamation of a further 60 acres of land will allow additional general cargo and roll-on roll-off berths to be built.

Following development on this scale, directly attributed to the ploughing back of profits, it is to be hoped that the port's achievements are not to be overshadowed by the implementation by the present Government of policies for the nationalization of those ports with a throughput exceeding 5M tons of cargo per year.

Tilbury

A container berth needs sufficient space for the handling and stacking of the containers, and during the planning of facilities to be provided in London it was decided to construct a terminal at Tilbury where land was available for development, thus avoiding the expensive operation of demolishing existing structures prior to adaptation. It was also decided to go ahead and provide the facilities, at an estimated cost of £20M (which turned into an actual investment of £30M), before a definite demand for them existed. The Port of London Authority believed that shipowners would limit their ports of call in Europe, and so began their development with a view to attracting the owners, and making Tilbury one of the most up-to-date container handling berths in existence. Tilbury possesses nearly two miles of deepwater quay (up to 44 feet deep at some berths) forming thirteen new berths, six of which are for container traffic, two for roll-on roll-off traffic, three for packaged timber and wood pulp, and the remaining two for conventional break-bulk cargo. The complex today is the largest of its type in the United Kingdom and the second largest in Europe, and handled over 250,000 containers in 1972.

Following initial labor disputes at Tilbury, when the dockers refused to operate the terminal for two years, as a lever to obtain the best possible terms for port workers in general, the Port of London Authority began to be a profit-making body in 1971 with an operating surplus of £169,000, following several years of deficit, and increased this profit in 1972 to over £1.25M. These profits, however, are largely being used to finance the initial investment and it remains to be seen whether the terminal will actually make money. Three shift working allows the operation of Tilbury's eight portainers and the back-up system over a 24-hour day, and throughput at individual berths often exceeds 1,000 containers during this period. Efficiency of this order obviously acts as a boost to the morale of the PLA, but the Authority in its management of Tilbury faces a similar dilemma to that of Felixstowe—an inability to accept the largest of the containerships afloat today. In spite of this, the advent of containerization has proved to be of enormous benefit to the PLA, and cargo that was previously draining away to the more efficient ports has returned with vigor.

Southampton

Another forerunner in the provision of container berths is the British Transport Docks Board port of Southampton, where £3.5M was initially spent in the building of a 1,000 foot deepwater quay with two portainers, a roll-on roll-off linkspan, and twenty acres of paved working area. The facility began operations in October 1968 and is currently handling approximately 2M tons of container and roll-on roll-off traffic per year.

As in the case of Tilbury it was decided to build the terminal before any lines had definitely indicated their intention of basing their UK operation at Southampton, and also as in the case of Tilbury the project has been so successful that further development involving an outlay of about £18M is well under way. This involves the construction at the Western Dock of three container berths bringing the total to five berths and six portainer cranes. The container terminal is being worked under a three-shift, twenty-two hour day system, and the port's favorable geographical position making it the first major European complex for vessels entering the English Channel, is an argument in favor of further large-scale development. It would be possible to construct six more 1,000-foot container berths at the Western Docks, and as the potential container traffic passing over Maplin would only warrant the equivalent of two such berths at Southampton at the relatively negligible cost of £10M, it is to be hoped that the advice given to the Government by the National Ports Council will be heeded.

Development already completed at Southampton has meant that the port is a serious contender for much of the European

FIGURE 6 Seatrain cellular containership *Asialiner* loading at the Clydeport container terminal at Greenock (Courtesy of Seatrain (UK) Limited).

deep sea container traffic, and future expansion could make the port one of the principal container complexes of Europe.

The Clyde and Forth

The Clyde Port Authority formed in 1966 to control the river berths and docks stretching from Glasgow to Greenock, decided to construct a container terminal at Greenock and building began in 1967. The facility, known as the Clydeport container terminal, is situated at the lower end of the Clyde channel which allows easy access to the seaward approaches at all states of the tide. The 850-foot quay with a depth of at least 42 feet involved a capital outlay of £2.5 million and use is made of the adjacent Freightliner railhead. Clydeport was built primarily to provide facilities for Atlantic traffic, and it is principally this trade that contributed to a 40 per cent increase in throughput during 1972 to 500,000 tons. Three container cranes in conjunction with ten straddle carriers are in operation at the terminal and labor relations are generally very good. The port is controlled by a number of board members, many of whom are also port users, and at the same time as the authority is extending its control over its internal working by, for example, taking over stevedoring firms and a road haulier, the Government is also trying to obtain a degree of jurisdiction through appointing some board members themselves.

The six public trust ports on the Forth are controlled by the Forth Ports Authority and container facilities have been provided at two of the ports, Grangemouth and Leith. Grangemouth was a pioneer in the provision of such facilities, being the first United Kingdom port to have a container gantry crane. This crane was installed in 1966 for exclusive use by Sealand who were then using Grangemouth as a direct port of call for their early Atlantic containerships, and who were running the terminal on the chassis system, mention of which has already been made. The port now has two container cranes and a roll-on roll-off berth, and runs an incentive bonus scheme for its labor force whereby a throughput target is set, and a bonus is earned if the target is exceeded. Leith was provided with a container crane in 1968 and also has a roll-on roll-off berth, but is not as dependent on unitized traffic for its future as is Grangemouth. The port is well diversified, and in addition to catering for the Seabee barge carriers belonging to Lykes Lines, and break-bulk vessels operating to and from the Continent, is attracting groups providing services to the North Sea oil industry.

In a similar way to the Clyde Port Authority, the Forth Ports Authority is currently under the strain of paying off considerable capital debt, but following a deficit during 1970 and 1971 of a total of £790,000 the Authority made a profit during 1972 of £500,000. Another similarity with the Clyde is in the Government's insistence that some impartial board members are appointed who are not connected with any of the port users, such as shipping companies and stevedoring firms. If this move promotes greater efficiency it is to be welcomed, but note should be taken of another public trust port—Ipswich—where the board is composed of port users and local councillors, and where productivity is very high indeed. It should be remembered that what is good for the port is also good for the shipping companies either currently utilizing the port or considering doing so.

The Mersey

The dock system at Liverpool was built up from beginnings in the early 18th century, and consists today of several enclosed docks along the Mersey controlled by the Mersey Docks and Harbour Company, set up in 1971 following the collapse of the old Mersey Docks and Harbour Board which in its turn had been controlling port affairs since its establishment in 1858. One of these enclosed docks was the Gladstone Dock which had adjacent to it a dry dock. It was decided to convert this dry dock, as an interim measure pending completion of a far more ambitious plan at Seaforth, into a container terminal at a cost of £1 million. But everything was not running smoothly within the port, and it was announced in the summer of 1970 that the port was running a deficit of between £3 and 4 million. A persistent shortage of labor and an appalling strike record were blamed for shippers and shipowners switching cargo and vessels to other ports, which took much of the former revenue of Liverpool away, and which largely contributed to the collapse of the Mersey Docks and Harbour Board with debts of almost £100 million. To save the Board from going into liquidation the Mersey Docks and Harbour Company was incorporated by a special Act of Parliament in 1971, but a modest profit in the same year of £1.3 million was soon followed in 1972 by a loss of £1.76 million. The port employers had endeavored to recruit more labor, but due to union resistance this had to be abandoned, and closure of the more uneconomic docks followed together with the inevitable redundancies. About 2,500 men were expected to lose their jobs, but under the Jones/Aldington scheme which permitted severance payments of up to £4,000 per man, 2,800 dockers representing one third of the total labor force left the port during the period up to February 1973. The port's troubles were very far from over, however, and due to persistently slow and unreliable turnround of vessels, and in spite of the Dock Company's efforts to raise productivity through introducing modern methods of cargo handling, it became necessary, in accordance with the union's now changed policy, to recruit a further 500 men during the middle of 1973 on the supplementary register. A major management reorganization took place at the same time but the expected loss for 1973 increased to approximately £5.2 million. The accumulation of troubles on the Mersey has since led to the drastic step of reducing the port's capital debt of approximately £100 million by cutting the value of shareholders' investments by 70 per cent, and in view of the Government's earlier statement that it would not continually pump money into uneconomic enterprizes, many small and large investors could be very adversely affected.

When the Government announced that it would not prop up unsound organizations the port was deeply involved in the construction of a new £50 million container and bulk-handling dock complex at Seaforth, just north of the old Gladstone Dock, upon which the future of Merseyside appeared to be dependent. It was obvious that the Dock Company would be unable to raise capital on the open market, and the Government's policy would preclude financial assistance from public funds. It was subsequently announced by the Government, however, that grants would be made to the port in connection with contracts for Seaforth for the completion of ten deep water berths. The complex includes three container terminals as well as bulk handling equipment for grain, packaged timber berths, and general cargo facilities. It is too early to say whether these developments will place Liverpool on a firmer financial footing, but it is to be hoped that the labor problems which are already strongly in evidence at Seaforth, and which include the outright refusal to work some of the berths, are not indicative of a further period of unrest which could surely have only one outcome—complete lack of confidence of port users and the eventual downfall of Merseyside as a provider of cargo handling facilities.

Apart from the problems already mentioned which have led to slow vessel turnround and congestion surcharges reflected in freight rates, the port as a whole has a very inward looking mentality maintaining that it should not, on account of its own peculiar difficulties, have to face up to competition from other United Kingdom and Continental ports. But it is just such competition, if accepted by both management and labor, that could act as the stimulus to pull the port out of its persistent gloom. Worker participation could bridge the void between management and labor, and if handled skilfully could lead to increased productivity, a return to the port of many of the departed shipping lines, a check to the falling throughput of containerized cargo, and a reversal of the trend at break-bulk berths where, in addition to cargo handling charges having risen during the past 30 years from £0.35 per ton to £7.00 per ton, throughput per hour has fallen from 18 tons per gang hour to 11 tons per gang hour.

Inland Terminals

An important development arising out of containerization is the provision of inland terminals whose function is to perform some of the work that used to be carried out in the ports, and which greatly contributed to the inefficiency of a conventional cargo berth. This work involves the gathering of smaller consignments from shippers unable to utilize a full container, and packing them into containers prior to despatch to the container berth at the port. The terminals must therefore offer a comprehensive loading and discharge service for containers, and indeed often extend their facilities to accommodate in addition road trailers and railway wagons, and may also act as warehousekeepers.

Apart from the need to move such work away from the container berths, whose real function is merely to allow the fastest possible turnround of vessels, it is also desirable to carry out the work as near as possible to areas of production or consumption so that economies of scale through making up larger loads can be enjoyed over the greater part of the inland road or rail haul, therefore keeping costs as low as is practicable. The terminals are usually financed by a number of shipping companies, freight forwarders, or other groups connected with transport, shipping or warehousing, and should be looked upon as an extension to the port.

An early attempt at providing one such terminal in London was the establishment of Chobham Farm in April 1970, which was financed by Overseas Containers Ltd., Cunard, T. Wallis, Brown Jenkinson, British Rail, and Freight Terminals Ltd. A setback for the terminal came in June 1972 following unrest among registered dockers working in London, who saw their monopolistic position as the sole source of labor being threatened by the introduction of more normal labor into Chobham Farm for cargo handling. The terminal was picketed by the registered dockers and it became necessary to allow them to work there. The labor force soon grew to double its previous strength, but poor productivity followed, together with financial difficulties, and the closure of the terminal appeared imminent. After a small profit being returned in 1971 a loss of £100,000 was suffered during 1972, and British Rail and Freight Terminals Limited withdrew from the venture at the end of May 1973. The future was by now looking very bleak indeed, but it was announced shortly after the withdrawals that Containerbase Federation, a concern possessing vast experience in the running of inland clearance terminals in the United Kingdom, would as from July 1973 be managing Chobham Farm. This move followed the announcement by the remaining shareholders that £300,000 worth of working capital had been injected to avoid liquidation. Containerbase Federation has since changed its name to Containerbases Limited, and is now a holding company 76 per cent owned by OCL and 24 per cent by ACT.

An earlier example of an inland terminal, but this time

designed for the handling of freight in rail wagons, is the London International Freight Terminal (LIFT) at Stratford in east London. Whereas Chobham Farm is being run primarily to handle containers being shipped by deep sea container vessels, LIFT is made up of a number of freight forwarders handling rail wagons, and to a growing extent road trailers. Due to the speed and reliability in fact of moving UK/Continental traffic by road, the terminal's function as a rail depot is declining in favor of road traffic. But due to the high and inflexible method of assessing charges at LIFT some of this road traffic is being moved to one or other of the increasing number of smaller private terminals being operated by one or by several freight forwarders, where charges can be up to half those found at LIFT, and where service is often better.

Perhaps in future, or at least until European rail movements for general cargo come back into favor, rail freight terminals will be constructed only in cases where a definite demand exists. One such instance is for the handling of the Transfesa wagons, to be discussed later, which convey horticultural produce from Spain, and for which a private rail freight terminal is being constructed at a cost of £5 million at Paddock Wood on the proposed route of the rail link from the Channel Tunnel.

Chapter 4

The Through Concept
of Containerization and
Economic Gains

The Through Concept

The most desirable way to move goods from one country to
another is to use equipment constructed to be handled by all
parties in the transport chain. It is in the provision of such equipment that the advantages of the container become apparent. The
shipper is able to pack his cargo into the container at his own
premises, have it hauled by road or rail to a suitable port where it
is loaded to a containership, transported to the foreign port, unloaded to an internal transport system, and delivered to his customer without each individual package of the consignment being
handled at each intermediate stage. It is this intermodal concept
allowing a through movement which reduces considerably the
need for manpower, changes the system into a capital intensive
one, quickens cargo movements, reduces risk of damage and pilferage, and allows increased productivity in the ports. It should
therefore be possible to achieve savings over costs incurred during
conventional cargo handling, which involved the use of several
smaller operators, each of which could well delay the consignment
on its journey out of or into the United Kingdom. For example, a
typical shipment would pass through the hands of the original
merchant, a forwarding agent, a packaging firm, a road haulier
and/or the railway system, the port authority, dock workers,

customs officers, ships' stevedores, the shipping company, and a similar chain on arrival of the vessel in the overseas port, before final delivery to the consignee could be effected. Each operator would assess his own costs and charge accordingly, and each stage would require documentation covering that part of the journey only. Using a fully containerized system where a through movement is made possible, most of these intermediaries are eliminated, and it is possible to radically review documentation. Ideally the container should not be opened en route, and where effective locking systems have been used reduced pilferage has often been dramatic. It has been estimated that 20 per cent of all whisky shipped through New York was disappearing before containers were utilized, and while it is often difficult to explain shortages involving container cargo, and that usually the full container load will disappear if a theft does occur, insurance underwriters generally agree that over-all losses have fallen.

Advantages then should accrue to a number of bodies, but principally to the shipping company, and in some cases to the owner of goods. The extent of any beneficial effect to the owner of goods will depend on how easily he is able to adapt to fit in with the requirements of a containerized system. If he is able to accommodate full container loads (FCL) into or out of his factory or warehouse he will benefit to a greater extent than a shipper or importer dealing in less than container loads (LCL). The FCL exporter will have an empty container delivered to his factory or warehouse by the shipping company, will attend to his own loading, and will then have the full container hauled direct to the container berth again by the shipping company. Cargo will therefore be conveyed direct between the point of origin and the vessel, will not be subject to handling costs other than the inland haul and the lift on to the vessel, and the exporter will usually enjoy the benefit of a cheaper freight rate. The LCL exporter, however, will be dealing in consignments of insufficient weight or volume to fill the capacity of a container, and unless he agrees to pay a high minimum charge for the exclusive use of a container, he will be obliged, often due to the lack of alternative conventional shipping services, to deliver his consignment into one of the inland clearance terminals or containerbases. Here the shipping company will pack the goods with other LCL traffic, and will convey the loaded container by road or rail to the container berth. Due to the necessity of grouping such cargo prior to shipment, the LCL exporter will be charged a higher freight rate than that levied on FCL traffic, his cargo may have to wait while consolidation of a load is completed, and the possibility of damage during transit is present if other cargo in the container breaks loose. In spite of these apparent drawbacks, it is arguable whether the small shipper will be in a worse position than he was during the days of conventional break-bulk shipping.

A factor restricting the utilization of true through movements of intermodal equipment, and one especially prevalent in the United States of America, is the attitude taken by some bodies controlling the interests of firms engaged in the transport and handling of containers. These organizations were established during the days of conventional break-bulk shipping when groups such as road hauliers, railway companies, freight forwarders, port authorities, and shipping companies formed their own individual policies, in conformity with the controlling body where one existed. Consultation with other bodies controlling ancillary services was rare, and the result was the growth of a number of parochial institutions guarding their own working practices often to the detriment of closely connected and dependent services. Under conditions such as these it becomes very difficult for a container operator to act in a capacity other than that of transporting goods from one port to another, and to directly control the inland haul as well as the sea journey will be impossible. He will find it difficult to quote a through rate and will be open to sometimes harmful effects following policy changes undertaken by one or more of the other controlling bodies.

In an effort to overcome these difficulties one of the larger groups in the USA, the Federal Maritime Commission (FMC), entrusted by Congress with the proper discharge of statutory and regulatory responsibilities over the USA's waterborne trade, is trying to bring together all interests with a view to co-ordinating policies and establishing through rates. The FMC must authorize proposed rate changes put forward by the shipping companies, and is the controlling body responsible for ensuring that the companies do not exceed their rights through for example competing for cargo in a way that may unfairly harm other shipping companies or port authorities. The FMC has no jurisdiction over the affairs of freight forwarders, who have their own controlling body, the Interstate Commerce Commission (ICC), and if the ICC is unable or unwilling to approve an inland rate which is intended to form an integral part of a combined sea/land rate, the whole principle of a through charge becomes superfluous. Progress is therefore being held up due to the perpetuation of bodies that have no place in their present form in a modern transport system, and it is to be hoped that this misguided protection of self interests will end with the passing of new legislation in the USA. Intermodal shipments should be governed by conditions laid down by one controlling agency which would make it possible for operators to quote a through freight rate, issue a single bill of lading, accept single carrier liability, and permit recourse to one body only in such matters as arbitration.

Although the USA is generally recognized as the innovator of containerization, she is suffering more than other countries during attempts at co-ordinating the various groups engaged in cargo movement. Apart from the differences of opinion that exist between such bodies as the FMC and ICC, further difficulties are often to be found among the country's longshoremen. It was mentioned during the passage on barge carrying vessels that the International Longshoremen's Association is distorting the true cost of labor by over-manning, and imposing penalty payments on barges handled by non-Association labor. This attitude of ensuring that work previously carried out in the ports by members of the ILA remains there, is further exemplified by the insistence of the ILA that association labor should handle cargo passing through the port of New York whether containerized or not. This has resulted in the breaking down and repacking of all LCL containers originating from, or for delivery to, points within a 50-mile radius of the port, and another impediment is placed before the shipping companies in their efforts at offering a through service. It is understandable why some lines carrying cargo to or from the USA try to divert such cargo away from its traditional entry or exit port to other USA ports, and in some cases to Canadian ports.

Control by the Shipping Company

It will be plain by now that whatever the intentions of a prospective conveyor of intermodal equipment might be, these intentions will be affected to various degrees by other interests often making it impossible to develop them in the desired manner. The extent of any limitation will vary between countries, and the United Kingdom is better placed to accept changes of this type than is the USA. The trend will definitely be toward fuller control by the shipping company of all the links in a transport chain, and this is often achieved by the acquisition of interests in, or by the purchase of already existing firms running one of the subsidiary services. Diversification will also involve the taking over of companies engaged in fields not connected with the movement of containers in order to offer a comprehensive service to the firm's existing clients extending to for example air freight and insurance, and the entering of fields only loosely connected or not connected at all with shipping and transport.

The dangers of diversifying into areas unconnected with a company's present interests are obvious, but dangers can also be in evidence during diversification into a closely connected area. A full knowledge and understanding of the new field must be acquired, and this will usually be obtained in cases where a take-over or merger is proposed. But in cases where a company wishes to enter into the management of a new venture without acquiring the expertise, and also possibly the goodwill of an existing enterprise, the result can be catastrophic. For example, American Export Industries decided to expand its interests into port management through the development of a vast port complex at New York, but had to sell the containership terminal it had built to New York City, and scrap the remaining over-ambitious plans.

As it has already been established, however, that the shipping company should own the containers it is to the shipping company that one must look to provide the co-ordination required in a door-to-door movement. The need for co-ordination might result in such diversification as is illustrated by the purchase by Manchester Liners of two road haulage companies in the Glasgow area, and the acquisition by P & O of several firms engaged in the subsidiary activities of road haulage and freight forwarding. On a wider front Ocean Transport & Trading Limited is involved in tankers and bulk carriers, break-bulk services, industrial and domestic fuel distribution, wharfage and lighterage, and air and surface freight forwarding in addition to its container interests through the 49% holding in OCL. Furness Withy in addition to its involvement in OCL has entered the oil rig business and maintains a merchant banking interest, and P & O has committed over £30M to gas and oil exploration and owns property to a value of over £120 million. Diversification on this scale has usually followed the recruitment into shipping companies of top management who do not have a shipping background, as in the case of Furness Withy whose part-time chairman is Lord Beeching, and whose board also includes four merchant bankers and a past director of the Bovis construction company. Diversification and rationalization can therefore be complementary and the process is continuing today through, for example, the proposed purchase of Bovis by P & O and the Capitalfin Vlasov consortium bid for Shipping Industrial Holdings.

To return though to the difficulties often encountered by shipping companies running container services when trying to maintain control over its containers during the inland, as well as the sea leg of a journey, one can once again look at the USA. Some of the American railway companies had agreements with the container lines for the free carriage of one empty container to be positioned for pick up of cargo, for each revenue earning full one conveyed. This agreement terminated when the railway companies found the scheme uneconomic, due they say to the lack of co-operation of the shipping companies in programming the positioning of empty containers that had just delivered cargo sufficiently near to the point of collection of a new consignment. This type of dispute is typical of those mentioned earlier where controlling bodies representing groups of cargo carriers are unable to agree, but disputes can also arise within one of the groups only. Objections were recently raised by the container lines serving the US Gulf ports when a through rate to the hinterland area of the Gulf was proposed by lines operating out of the US west coast ports. The argument was put forward by the Gulf lines that the area was already well served, and if the through rate were agreed traffic would be unnecessarily drawn away from the area. In settling such disputes the FMC must decide whether a through service of the type proposed is really needed, but any decision against its implementation would be contrary to the Commission's basic commitment to the furtherance of through movements.

Control by the shipping company, then, will not always be possible in cases where other parties have a vested interest in an already established system, but control can be complete if the shipping company is able to directly influence the running of the subsidiary activity. This is illustrated by the use of "feeder" vessels which collect and deliver containers over a wide range of ports, while the deep sea container vessel restricts her calls to one or two ports in each country or continent. The principle of the ocean going vessel calling at as few ports as possible was recommended in the McKinsey Report (*Containerization: the key to low cost transport*, a report by McKinsey & Co. Inc., for the British Transport Docks Board 1967), but it is now sometimes argued that it is cheaper for the vessel to call at a number of ports and not to be burdened with the cost of operating feeders. Although this may be true from a pure cost point of view, it becomes less desirable as other factors are taken into account. Feeders can be of immense benefit to the cargo owner in cases where they short-circuit the deep sea vessel's otherwise necessary schedule, as would be the case where cargo shipped from the USA to the UK is transhipped at Le Havre by a feeder calling at a UK port, while the deep sea vessel continues her journey to her second and final port of call on the Continent before returning to the USA. This is in contrast to the alternative of the deep sea vessel discharging, for example, cargo for France at Le Havre, cargo for Belgium at Zeebrugge, cargo for Holland at Rotterdam and cargo for Germany at Hamburg, before finally docking in the United Kingdom. Whether or not the shipowner decides to operate feeder vessels will depend on the extra cost involved set against benefits accruing from possibly more cargo carried, and the greater number of voyages undertaken by the deep sea vessel due to faster turnrounds.

Perhaps the ideal way to operate feeder vessels is how Sea-Land is able to function through the company running their own terminals. Cargo handling costs at these terminals will be less than charges at common user berths, and due to fixed costs not varying with cargo throughputs, it will become more economical per ton of cargo handled as throughput increases. Sea-Land's constant flow of feeder shipped containers between the company's deep sea terminal at Rotterdam and Felixstowe, Preston, Grangemouth, Le Havre, Gothenburg and Aarhus, gives a very flexible service and a greater utilization of containers.

In cases where the shipping company has not developed its own fleet of feeder vessels, independent short sea lines running cellular vessels will undertake feeding on behalf of the deep sea company. An example is the Comar Container Line, who normally operate between Felixstowe and Rotterdam, but who are quite prepared to switch to other UK and Continental ports as and when demand changes. Feeders are maintained on a similar basis by independent lines in North America, but the distinction between feeding as it was originally intended, and diverting cargo from one area to another is very narrow. Vessels running between ports already well served by deep sea containerships such as Halifax and the US east coast ports, could be said to be diverting traffic, but vessels completing a natural extension from a deep sea container terminal to an area poorly, or not at all served by deep sea vessels should be classed as true feeders. This distinction does not of course apply when a line which would normally offer a service to a particular port opts to serve this port on a feeder basis.

CP Ships

An excellent example of a transportation company offering a through service is CP Ships, the container operations side of Canadian Pacific. Canadian Pacific started operations nearly 100 years ago as a railway company, but has now diversified and grown into the world's largest privately owned transportation group having interests in air freight, road transport, freight forwarding, container terminal operation and telecommunications, in addition to containership management. CP Ships run five cellular vessels on the North Atlantic between Canada, and the United Kingdom and Continent, and quite rightly look on the vessels as being just another vehicle, in the same way as their road and rail

FIGURE 7 CP Ships' container terminal at Wolfe's Cove, Quebec (Courtesy of Canadian Pacific).

transport facilities. Each phase of the freight movement is under their own control, and according to the firm's chairman, W.J. Stenason, "We arrive as close as we can get—short of a pipeline to every customer—to that straight line which is the shortest distance between two points". Inland terminals have been set up throughout the United Kingdom and on the Continent, and one document and one charge covers the container during its journey via Tilbury or Rotterdam, to their own terminal at Wolfe's Cove, Quebec. On arrival at Quebec their own cranes unload the containers for delivery by their own road or rail network in Canada and the USA to as far afield as Vancouver on the west coast. To achieve this full integration Canadian Pacific even built their own spur road to link the terminal at Wolfe's Cove to the main highways, and during the planning stage extended its own railway system right on to the dockside.

In addition to traffic generated by themselves, the rail subsidiary of Canadian Pacific also hauls, as a common carrier, containers belonging to other shipping companies, and this overlapping in part contributed to the recent rationalization of the trans-Atlantic container services of CP Ships and Manchester Liners.

Rate Cutting

During the early years of containerization shipping companies offering services on what were then thought to be highly profitable routes became involved in what can only be described as unhealthy competition. Owners were putting too many specialized containerships into trades such as the North Atlantic and Pacific, and the resulting state of over-tonnaging led to heavy operating losses being suffered. Due to the conference system (a shipping conference is a group of lines, jointly maintained, which co-ordinates sailings to give a regular service, and whose members agree to charge freight at predetermined rates) market forces following rate adjustments up or down could not operate, and many lines had to look at the sector of charges that was outside conference jurisdiction, as a possible source of rate reduction. This led in 1968 to Container Marine Lines, a wholly owned subsidiary of American Export Isbrandtsen Lines, issuing a through tariff to apply between inland points in the United Kingdom and ports in the USA. Two Atlantic conferences objected to the tariff, which in effect allowed free haulage from within the United Kingdom to Felixstowe, the port of shipment, by subsidization of the inland haul by the sea freight. A through rate was therefore being offered by Container Marine Lines that was the same as rates being offered by the other lines on a port to port basis only, and in backing the cheaper rate the FMC ruled that conference members should compete with each other to promote a better service. Although this ruling by the FMC appeared to be a step in the right direction, it should have been borne in mind by them that where it has been agreed to operate under the conference system, it is of little use introducing a system completely contrary to the conference system without first of all dismantling the conference. Without a firm agreement by the lines to either be bound by the conference or to operate outside it, a situation will be created of apparent conference loyalty undermined though by the granting of unofficial rebates. Due to this undercutting Atlantic Container Line withdrew from three conferences in August 1970, pointing to the insufficient power exerted by the conferences in trying to stabilize rates.

This unsatisfactory state of affairs continued and led to every carrier on the North Atlantic losing money during 1971. Although it is denied in some quarters that a situation of over-tonnaging exists at present on the Atlantic, there can be little doubt that it did exist earlier, and while the blame must be placed firmly at the door of the shipowners and the conferences that they form themselves into, a way should be found to avoid similar situations elsewhere if it is considered desirable to have any form of stability at all. But stability will in some cases be further threatened, and over-tonnaging will occur when loyalty to the conference by its members is combined in the same trade by an influx of non-conference shipping lines, often subsidized by their home states, charging rates in some cases up to 40 per cent below the published conference rates. Where freight is normally charged on what the traffic can bear, the largest savings to be achieved by cargo owners will obviously go to the owners of high-value cargo, and it is this more lucrative traffic that will be lost to the non-conference lines. This is another, and perhaps an even more damaging form of unhealthy competition, and can only lead to diversion of vessels to other trades or to their complete withdrawal.

An attempt at preventing unrealistic cutting of freight rates could be undertaken by the FMC and other controlling bodies if they were to ban all rates that were not sufficiently high to cover a predetermined share of vessel operating costs. This ban would apply to all lines whether conference or not, but would be difficult to formulate and administer due to the disparity of costs between lines from different countries. Another way would be to introduce a revenue pooling system whereby all lines belonging to a particular conference, or better still operating in a particular trade, pool their freight receipts into a central fund, before being reimbursed with a predetermined sum dependent on their fair potential capacity. Although pooling arrangements have been put forward by seven container lines on the North Atlantic, and by six Japanese lines in the Pacific, in an effort to stabilize the trades, the US Justice Department is unconvinced that they would be successful. Apart from believing that over-tonnaging does not exist on the North Atlantic and that rates in some trades are not being forced down by non-conference lines, they have pointed out that a revenue pool would stifle any remaining competition and lead to higher rates. As the system stands at present it is immaterial to the trade if a few lines are losing money, but if that loss were sufficiently large enough to make the existing level of rates uneconomic, after being shared by the other lines, an immediate demand to raise rates would be made. The Justice Department also maintains that a revenue pool, with its guaranteed percentage of freight return for the member lines, would act as a disincentive to the provision of special container types such as liquid tanks and open tops.

However much truth there may be in the validity of these arguments, the problem of over-tonnaging and disparity of rates will remain until a way is found to obviate them. It may be that larger groups should be formed, or that lines should agree to rationalize their services with a view to offering the shipper a regular flow of tonnage, which in turn would be of benefit to the shipowner through him being able to operate his vessels on a constant capacity basis. An example of recent rationalization is the CP Ships/Manchester Liners' agreement mentioned earlier, and of merger the proposed Sea-Land/US Lines grouping and the joining of American Mail Line and American President Line.

In the case of the proposed Sea-Land/US Lines merger, R.J. Reynolds Industries, who already own Sea-Land, have been trying to purchase the Walter Kidde and Co. owned US Lines for five years. Reynolds and Kidde both agreed to the merger in 1970, and the FMC gave their backing after laying down a number of conditions. They stipulated that both shipping companies should continue to function as entirely different groups, that their method of operation should be constantly open to close scrutiny by the FMC, that Reynolds does not sell or dispose of US Lines without FMC approval but that Reynolds should relinquish its interest in the line if the FMC thought it necessary, and that Reynolds registers its fleet under the American flag and recruits American seamen. Despite the FMC's agreement in 1973, the proposed merger was blocked in March of the same year by the US Justice Department, who are unconvinced of the ability of Reynolds to manage the two lines as separate entities. They rightly point out that policies taken by one line are bound to be formulated only after considering the effect they might have on the other line, and in view of the generally hostile attitude of the other shipping companies trading on the North Atlantic the success of the merger in its proposed form is doubtful.

Rising Costs

It will by now be clear that during the early settling down period following the introduction of containerization the problems that became apparent were many and complex. Apart from the change in financing new tonnage which meant that the prospective shipowner could no longer rely on substantial loans and grants from respectively the builder and the government, but instead had to approach the financial institutions, costs in general were rising at an alarming rate. The price of bunkers was already rising rapidly even before the recent oil shortage, and the longer-term outlook is anything but favorable when all forms of energy supplies are becoming scarcer. The cost of bunkers rose by over 55 per cent during the summer months of 1970 adding over £20M to the annual fuel bill of the UK lines, and crews' wages, port charges and repair costs were also escalating. The cost of vessel operation was often exceeding the revenue earned, and the added burden of paying off the initial investment in ships, containers, and sometimes terminals meant a steady drain on owners' reserves. A further problem arose following parity changes in currencies, and where freight rates in, for example, the North Atlantic trade had been based on the pound sterling, it became necessary to change to the then stronger US dollar to avoid heavy currency losses. The subsequent relative fall of the dollar has meant that owners are again looking for a more stable currency.

The advent of containerization, coupled with a feeling within the shipping industry that it had historically been functioning more as a service industry, instead of one committed to earning a realistic profit, meant that a series of freight increases aimed at lifting the industry to a higher profit plateau was unavoidable. A rise in freight rates on the North Atlantic during 1973 of approximately 35 per cent was soon followed by bunker surcharges, a container service charge, and a far more unsympathetic approach to the imposition and collection of demurrage. The level of freight increases would indeed have been even greater had it not been for the price freeze prevailing in the USA at the time. With regard to the question of demurrage it should be pointed out that cargo owners found themselves in a position not in evidence prior to the introduction of containerization whereby faster vessel transits and turnround times made it necessary to move cargo out of the container terminal area as quickly as possible. Documentation, however, was often taking longer in its journey between the seller, the banks and the buyer, than it was taking for the vessel to cross the Atlantic, and importers in the United Kingdom sometimes found it impossible to clear cargo away before demurrage became due. The severity of these charges was on a scale completely unknown during the days of conventional break-bulk shipping, and while it is appreciated that a disincentive to cargo owners using the container terminals as a temporary warehouse must exist, it should also be borne in mind by the conference that two days' demurrage will often negate any cost advantage to the cargo owner following use of a container shipping line. Maybe it is because the conference is aware of this that when payment is

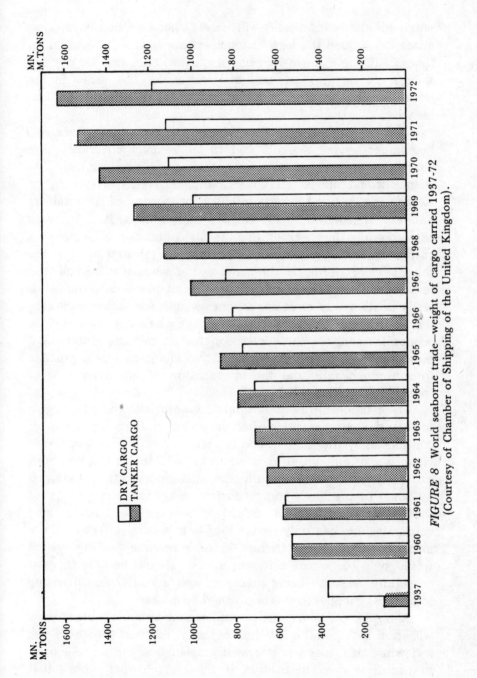

FIGURE 8 World seaborne trade—weight of cargo carried 1937-72 (Courtesy of Chamber of Shipping of the United Kingdom).

withheld the conference will rarely pursue their collection attempts through the legal channels. If payment were insisted on there could be a move by cargo owners to lines who do not sell their space on the basis that their vessels are the fastest in the trade, thereby obtaining a longer period for transmittal of documents.

Another burden now being borne by the cargo owner is a "container service charge", said to be a charge covering lifting containers on and off the vessel at the container terminal. This charge would appear to cover a similar service as stowing or stevedoring, but as the responsibility for stowing FCL containers has now transferred to the cargo owner, whereas it was always allowed for in the freight during the days of break-bulk shipping, a cost peculiar to the handling of containers (an extension of the ship) is being borne by the cargo owner when it is by right the responsibility of the ship. Maybe the "container service charge" is really another way of raising freight revenue, and if this is the case the lines should publicly state that their existing rates are not economic, and file an application for an increase. Intermodal movements should be accompanied by a charge as near as possible to a through rate, and the introduction of subsidiary charges (other than temporary) should be avoided.

The relationship between container lines, even those belonging to the same conference, is often prejudicial to the maintenance of confidence by the shipper, and can lead to heavy operating losses. When it was announced by Seatrain in 1973 that a loss had been suffered by their container division, the opportunity was grasped by some of the line's competitors to exaggerate the severity of the results. This type of in-fighting between the lines is time-consuming and can only have a long-term adverse effect on those involved. While the introduction of a revenue pooling system would help to obviate differences, lines should be able to exist peacefully without being made to, and a conference diverting some of its energies to this area would be desirable.

A regular container service implies that on some routes vessels will not be operating at full capacity for part of the time, and while this does not necessarily mean that the trade is over-tonnaged, it does mean that if the cargo owner desires that regularity of sailings be maintained, he will have to accept a level of freight charges relatively higher than those prevailing on routes where vessels are better employed. Consultation between the lines and the shippers would help to prevent the pricing of some lower value cargo out of the trade, and wider application of FCL and pallet allowances would encourage the shipper and importer to deal in container quantities, and would simplify the handling of LCL consignments. The merchant will thus benefit if he is able to offer cargo which easily lends itself to carriage by containers. For example, cartons can be loaded into a container without the need for special export packing, but a delicate piece of machinery may need the same crating that was being used when shipment was by break-bulk vessel. Loading times at the exporter's premises should be reduced, and if the traffic is of a regular nature, warehousing space will be available for other uses. The increased speed of container vessels will mean that less goods will be at sea at a particular time, which will put more money at the merchant's disposal for other uses. Containerization may also stimulate firms into exploring the export markets, if they can be convinced that foreign markets today should be looked upon as 'home' markets, only further away.

From the owners' point of view though it was clear during the early years of container shipping that costs had to be maintained, if they wished to establish themselves as a viable alternative to break-bulk methods of moving cargo. The intensity with which the lines were to utilize their vessels would not affect fixed costs, so a reduction in variable costs would be a major contribution to any savings. Quicker turnrounds would enable port charges to be maintained, and would help to alter the situation prevalent during break-bulk shipping whereby such charges often exceeded the cost of running vessels while at sea. (A conventional cargo vessel of about 12,000 tons was costing approximately £1,000 per day to run whether at sea or in dock, and was often in dock or awaiting a berth for the greater part of its life.) Although handling costs were reduced following the introduction of containerization, larger vessels had to be built to offset the loss of cubic capacity inherent in a containerized system. Due to the weight limit of each container, many units will not be filled to capacity by the time this limit is reached. As freight is usually charged on a per ton basis, except in cases where the cubic capacity per ton is very high (in excess of 40 cubic feet per ton, freight will normally be charged on a measurement basis), a subsequent loss of revenue realized is compared with that which could have been earned by a break-bulk vessel, which would be stowed to capacity if sufficient cargo were offered. It is interesting to note that Hapag-Lloyd recently lengthened its four Atlantic container vessels to allow the carriage of up to 1,100 20-foot containers, or their equivalent in other sizes, creating approximately 25 per cent extra capacity. An alternative though to charging freight on the quantity of cargo carried would be to levy a standard charge per container irrespective of weight or class of cargo carried, but this is unlikely to happen on conference routes due in part to the increased burden that would be placed on developing countries, who are engaged mainly in the exportation of raw materials and primary products, and who enjoy a cheaper rate due to the low value per ton of the cargo offered. Another alternative, which has now been imposed by a number of lines, is to levy a minimum revenue per container which must be reached prior to the operation of the tariff rate.

The realization of obtaining benefits from introducing systems aimed at reducing costs has been further hampered in the United Kingdom by the extreme shortage of labor at some ports following the Jones/Aldington severance scheme, which has led to long delays for vessels while loading and discharging. Further mechanical handling in the ports should be followed by the introduction of fully automated and programmed handling of containers, which will involve an extension of severance payments and the recruitment of a different type of employee with a more responsible outlook to operate terminals.

But in adding to the difficulties encountered by the British owner it should be stated that many overseas countries protect their own shipping industry by insisting that a given percentage of home-owned cargo is carried in their own vessels, and by giving other incentives such as tax rebates, depreciation allowances, and grants for new building programmes. The United States of America is particularly active in this field, and Russia looks on her merchant tonnage, which grew from 3.5 million tons in 1960 to 16 million tons in 1971, as a noncommercial operation.

It will not be difficult to understand that during the period 1962-1972 the returns obtained by many shipping companies through vessel operation were almost nonexistent due to out-of-date handling methods and poor management, and due to a general low level of trading and an over-valued pound. Conversion to a container system promised an eventual return to profitability, but in 1970 Cunard, P & O, Ocean Steam and Furness Withy all reported a falling back in profits. In order to prevent capital flows into the shipping sector being diverted to more remunerative industries, a satisfactory return had to be forthcoming, but initial losses were inevitable during the financing of the massive capital expenditure. These losses were aggravated though by largely un-controlled and intensive competition between the new container divisions, stimulated by a new breed of management, which reached their peak during the UK dock strike year of 1972.

The change that had to be forthcoming though did in fact materialize, and March 1973 saw the beginning of a general boom in the shipping market. World trade was expanding, sterling was stronger relative to other key currencies, freight rates had been raised to a more economic level, efficiency was improving, and as well as the investment of the previous five years in new tonnage being paid off, the specialized type of vessel involved was main-taining its value far better than, for example, break-bulk or tramp vessels. The container divisions of the major shipping companies are now generally a very major contributor to company profits, and P & O was able to increase its 1972 profit of £12M to £34M in 1973 partly through the company's participation in OCL. Similar-ly the profits of Ocean Transport and Trading increased from £10.4M to £19.1M during the same period, and both the other members of OCL, British and Commonwealth Shipping, and Furness Withy, returned increases on a similar scale.

While the much improved financial state of the container consortia is to be welcomed, it should not be forgotten that the change is in part due to the general increase in world trade, and any diminished rate of growth of this trade is bound to have an adverse effect on future profits. Much of OCL traffic is generated by countries having a high economic growth combined with political stability, but Ocean Transport and Trading, who have a 49 per cent interest in the venture, is increasingly diversifying into non-marine activities in order to cushion the cyclical effect on profits that ship management involves. British and Commonwealth

Shipping is currently relying on non-shipping activities such as insurance, investment, and North Sea supply work, to contribute over 45 per cent of its profits, and as already stated this trend is likely to continue throughout the shipping industry.

In an early report to the National Ports Council, Arthur D. Little Limited stated that "large containerships offering twice the container capacity (910 containers of 20 feet instead of 455 of 20 feet) need only carry 50 per cent more cargo to yield approximately equal costs per ton". In summary it will follow that economies of scale will be enjoyed if fewer, but larger vessels carry the same tonnage as previously, and extra benefits will also be in evidence due to building costs, fuel and crews' wages not increasing in proportion to the increased vessel size. Further economies will follow from the horizontal integration of shipping companies into consortia, and from the vertical integration of those firms providing ancillary services such as road haulage and packing. Conversion of a break-bulk service into a fully containerized one will prove to be more attractive where labor productivity is low, handling costs high, port turnround slow, and voyage time short. Merchants will be attracted to those lines offering a genuine service, in addition to the movement of goods from one port to another, and shipping companies will have to give more advice on matters such as packing, marketing, warehousing, documentation, distribution by road and rail, and even banking. The lines must realize that only customer satisfaction will promote increased business, and that this increase, coupled with a more even distribution of containership tonnage over world trade routes, will help to steady the continual rise in vessel operating costs.

Chapter 5

The Role of the Railways

The Beeching Report

The railway system prior to the closures recommended in the Beeching Report of 1963, had been built up over the years in such a way as to attract as much custom as possible from the travelling public and from the owners of merchandise. Cities, towns and villages were interconnected by a mass of lines, and services were run in the early years by privately owned railway companies competing with an underdeveloped road haulage industry. The railways were nationalized in 1948 but at the beginning of the 1950's were contending with rebuilding following war damage, and were facing increasingly fierce competition from the road haulage industry. Engines were still shunting wagons around in goods yards, and there was little emphasis on the more economic system of encouraging the regular movement of several wagon loads destined for the same place. Extensive plans for modernization were announced in 1955, but it was still not realized that the problem of relatively short hauls inherent in any small continent would be difficult to overcome. These short hauls meant that the need to contain time taken to group freight and to assemble trains was of greater importance in the United Kingdom than it was on the Continent or in the USA, where the hauls were much longer.

In 1961 the old British Transport Commission which had been established when the railways were nationalized was disbanded, and the British Railways Board was set up headed by the then Dr. Beeching. An encouraging note was struck by the British

65

Transport Act of 1962, which assumed that the railways could be financially self-supporting by 1968, but it was Beeching who made it clear that this would not in fact be the case, unless drastic steps were taken to run the system on a sound commercial footing. He advocated the termination of many passenger and freight services which were contributing particularly heavy losses, to quicken the introduction of diesel traction, and to investigate further the use of specialized freight services for raw materials such as coal and iron ore and for more general cargo traffic. It was for the last mentioned category of traffic that Beeching announced the new container carrying freightliner trains, which were to be purpose built, and were intended primarily for carriage within the United Kingdom, but with the possibility of later extension into overseas markets. These new trains followed Beeching's commitment to the principle of moving train loads as opposed to wagon loads, and ran parallel to his policy of combining extensive closures of uneconomic lines with modernization of the remaining track and services. In this way it was envisaged that the railways deficit would be cured, but the advantages of moving freight over the more flexible road system were underestimated. A case may exist for the subsidization of railway passenger services, but a similar case will be difficult to formulate purely on economic grounds where freight is involved. The generally quicker and cheaper alternative system of using road transport will continue to predominate, especially where full loads are involved, unless it becomes far more widely accepted by firms to establish their own private siding. Even then road transport will be more attractive unless these firms are able to deal in train loads, or until a system of moving over the railway network computer controlled single units with a capacity approximately equal to the present road vehicles, is established.

Freightliners

The freightliner system was inaugurated in the United Kingdom in November 1965, and during the following year 27,000 containers were rail freighted between London and Glasgow, Liverpool, Manchester and Aberdeen. Two years later a new

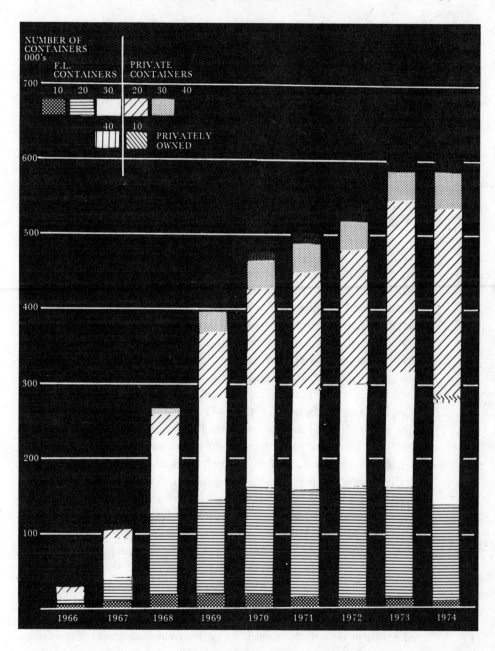

FIGURE 9 Containers conveyed per annum by Freightliners Limited
(Courtesy of National Freight Corporation).

company was formed following the passing of the Transport Act
of 1968, and management of the system was transferred from the
British Railways Board to Freightliners Limited. Ownership was
51 per cent with the National Freight Corporation and 49 per cent
with British Rail. British Rail was to provide the trains and
Freightliners Limited would supply the containers, operate the
terminals, and market the service.

The special-purpose trains are usually made up of fifteen permanently coupled low flat wagons capable of accepting ISO containers, and normally run overnight between terminals which may
be situated at the ports or at industrial centers. The terminals
are provided with a gantry crane which facilitates rapid transfer
between the rail wagons and road vehicles, or between the rail
wagons and a vessel either direct or via a back-up area. Haulage
may be undertaken by Freightliners itself, or an independent
haulier using the freightliner system or the trader will provide a
tractor to take delivery of a container at the terminal. Much of the
traffic will therefore be generated by the road haulage industry,
and Freightliners Limited will quote either terminal to terminal
rates or alternatively for those traders requiring a door-to-door
service, a through rate including the rail and road hauls.

Although the system was initially intended for domestic deliveries, it was designed on the ISO sizes of containers to enable
later absorption of traffic generated through maritime trade. This
maritime business now accounts for approximately 55 per cent
of total throughput, and ports such as Southampton, Tilbury and
Clydeport have been freightliner connected for several years. More
recently a 39-acre terminal was provided at Felixstowe following
long drawn out discussions with British Rail, the Dock Company
and the National Freight Corporation, together with other interested bodies. The terminal at Felixstowe, which was financed
eventually by the Dock Company, involved the spending of
£200,000, half of which went toward provision of the gantry. Discussions are now in progress with the Mersey Docks and Harbour
Company to assess the need for a terminal at Seaforth, an essential requirement if the port is to figure prominently in future deep
sea, as well as short sea container traffic. A boost to the maritime
side of Freightliners' operations occurred following the signing
of a multi-million pound contract with OCL and Ben Line

Containers, the British partners in the Far East container service, for the movement of containers between Southampton and inland freightliner terminals, and this traffic alone now accounts for 9 per cent of total business.

Although the freightliner system has been running successfully for eight years, and indeed is often the subject of study by railway authorities in other countries contemplating the setting up of a similar system, it is only just managing to become a profitable undertaking due to several reasons. Principal among these is the very large capital outlay necessary in building and equipping the terminals, but industrial disputes and the cyclical pattern of trading have also acted as a drain on resources. Operational problems such as a low average speed of train loads of only 35 m.p.h. being attained, while the maximum possible speed has been 75 m.p.h., have occurred. Similarly the 60-feet long wagons can carry two 30-foot containers, or three 20-foot containers, but when 40-foot containers are hauled the remaining 20 feet of space has often been unused. Handling of 40-foot containers at the majority of the terminals has also been difficult because the gantries installed have to be fitted with a larger spreader to facilitate lifting of the larger box.

Despite these apparent drawbacks the future of the freightliner system is assured, especially as successive governments are advocating the transfer of freight from the roads to rail, and throughput steadily rose to nearly 650,000 units during 1973. This figure, representing nearly 6M tons of cargo, is still considerably short of the 40M tons estimated by Beeching in 1963, but after allowing for Beeching's optimism, and a natural tendency for many United Kingdom merchants to avoid freighting by rail, the increase should be regarded as a considerable achievement for the National Freight Corporation, Freightliners Limited and British Rail.

British Rail Shipping

An extension to British Rail's inland freight developments came in 1968 with the introduction of British Rail containerships operating from Harwich to Zeebrugge and Rotterdam, and a

FIGURE 10 Freightliner route map (Courtesy of National Freight Corporation)

high-speed trans-European container service was thus offered to merchants. Harwich was chosen as the UK terminal due to its close proximity to the Benelux countries, which would allow the special-purpose containerships and shore installations to be utilized as fully as possible. If traffic was forthcoming in large regular flows British Rail, by using the already existing inland freightliner network, would be in a strong position on the North Sea and would be able to offer very competitive rates to industry.

Parkeston Quay was developed at Harwich as a container terminal and two purpose-built cellular containerships, the *Sea Freightliner 1* and *Sea Freightliner 2* were ordered to connect the terminal with Zeebrugge, while two modified vessels, the *Domburg* and *Colchester* were chartered to provide a service to Rotterdam. Although the Rotterdam service was discontinued in November 1973 following five years of operation, the efficiency and regularity of the services during the early years meant that shippers were finding it more economical and time-saving to forward cargo for the Continent to Harwich, from as far away as Glasgow and Liverpool instead of using one of the more traditional short sea routes out of Grangemouth or Hull, and a similar high standard of service was offered by the Belgian National Railways and the Dutch railways, within Belgium and Holland, and on to other European countries. This widespread support enabled the system to be used almost to capacity, and economies of scale were enjoyed which allowed a reduction in normal market short sea rates of up to one third. The initial containership operation, including new harbor works and the freightliner terminal at Harwich, involved an investment of £4 million, and it had a capacity to handle 122,000 containers per year. A development plan involving a further £0.5M to increase capacity by 50 per cent was completed in 1972, when the installation of a further two transtainers brought the handling facilities up to four transtainers and two portainers. The continuing success of British Rail's activities at Harwich, helped in no small way by the freightliner link, has since boosted the volume of tonnage passing through the port which in turn has led to congestion. Although some operators and freight forwarders are actively looking for alternative outlets to the Continent, the situation is likely to be eased following the completion of a £13M development scheme. This latest expansion at Harwich will include the provision for British Rail of a 1,250-foot extension to the container terminal at Parkeston Quay, which will improve the services to Dunkirk and Zeebrugge, and allow the introduction of new services if and when required.

Another development of British Rail's containership operation was the introduction of the sailings between Holyhead, and Belfast and Dublin. This link was due to commence in July 1971, but because of damage suffered by the Britannia Bridge over the Menai Straits following the fire of May 1970, the service was not fully operational until February 1972. Two cellular containerships, the *Brian Boroime* and *Rhodri Mawr*, each with a capacity of 184 20-foot units, maintain the link, and £7.5M was involved during the provision of the vessels and the three terminals. A network of freightliner routes connect Holyhead with London and the industrial centers, and these routes have been further boosted through the diversion to Holyhead of much of the Irish traffic formerly being handled at Liverpool.

The remaining route that British Rail have containerized is that between Portsmouth and the Channel Islands. This service formerly operated out of Southampton and Weymouth, but was consolidated at Portsmouth in October 1972 when the decision to containerize came into effect. It is maintained by the *Jersey Fisher* and *Guernsey Fisher*, each capable of accepting 80 20-foot units, and runs to St. Helier and St. Peter Port.

In addition to container services, British Rail are also active providing roll-on roll-off facilities. The French vessel *Transcontainer 1* connects Harwich to Dunkirk, while a joint service with the Zeeland Steamship Company provides two sailings per 24 hours between Harwich and the Hook of Holland. A third vessel of 7,500 tons is to be brought on to this service shortly. Other joint roll-on roll-off links are maintained through participation with French Rail between Dover and Boulogne, Dover and Calais, and Newhaven and Dieppe, while the Belgian Maritime Transport Authority is collaborating with British Rail in the running of the Dover to Ostend route. Services are also maintained from Folkestone to Boulogne, Calais and Ostend by the vessels *Hengist* and *Horsa* following an investment of £8M, and between Fishguard and Rosslare.

An often neglected alternative to both container and road

trailer methods of shipment, but one that is being actively encouraged by British Rail, is the ferry wagon. Ferry wagons were of course carrying freight between the United Kingdom and the Continent long before the introduction of containerization as we know it today, but the advent of the newer and possibly more fashionable systems caused the ferry wagon to fall out of favor. The present revival, however, has changed the pattern of dwindling tonnage to one of modest growth, and the 44,000 tons of ferry wagon freight passing through Harwich in 1973 represented a 6 per cent increase on the previous year. Problems though do exist, and perhaps the greatest is the in-balance of trade flows. Less than 500 ferry wagons are owned by British Rail, whereas the Continental railways own several thousand, and this has meant that historically Continental firms have tended to utilize the system more intensely than United Kingdom organizations. It is therefore often difficult for British Rail to fill wagons leaving the United Kingdom, but an improved service together with more co-operation with the railway authorities on the Continent is likely to mean a growth in outward tonnage and a more balanced trade flow.

At least until a decision is made on whether or not to construct a Channel tunnel, ferry wagons are likely to continue to be carried on vessels operating out of Harwich, to Zeebrugge and Dunkirk, and from Dover to Dunkirk. The service from Dover offers eight sailings per day using four vessels, which are also able to accept lorries and trailers, and will shortly be augmented by a fifth multi-purpose vessel, the *St. Eloi*. As mentioned above, Continental cargo owners make fuller use of ferry wagon services, and a further manifestation of this tendency is through the provision of far more private rail sidings at the premises of manufacturing concerns on the Continent. In cases where the United Kingdom buyer or seller also has a private siding, a through movement of goods will be possible of the type given by the road haulage operators for full loads, but still on a rather less flexible basis.

The majority of United Kingdom ferry wagon users though will deliver to or collect cargo from one of the freight rail terminals. In Stratford, East London the London International Freight Terminal (LIFT) was opened in June 1967, and replaced the facilities provided by the old Bishopsgate Goods Depot which was destroyed by fire. All the sheds except one are leased by freight forwarders from British Rail, and H.M. Customs and Excise provide clearance in and out at the terminal. Although the terminal was built primarily to handle ferry wagons, and is freightliner connected, the tendency recently has been for the resident freight forwarders to use it as a depot for road trailers, and indeed this type of traffic accounts for the majority of total throughput. British Rail are not unduly worried about this development as it does not restrict the freight forwarders to use of ferry wagons only, but instead allows them to offer a comprehensive service by road and/or rail without having to open, or even move to, a separate road haulage depot. As already stated, however, British Rail in conjunction with her Continental counterparts are trying to encourage more extensive use of the ferry wagon, and are introducing several multi-purpose vessels capable of shipping wagons as well as other unit load cargo. More terminal facilities are also being provided on a regional basis similar to LIFT, the latest being the Glasgow International Freight Terminal which was completed in March 1974. Others already exist at Manchester and Birmingham, and through the provision of customs control, some of the pressure is being taken off the customs offices at Dover and Harwich. In this way it is possible to load and customs clear wagons at, for example, Glasgow, rail them to Harwich for immediate shipment to Dunkirk or Zeebrugge, and then on forward them to destinations throughout the Continent.

Considerable expansion is due to take place in British Rail shipping services, especially on the Irish Sea where two new roll-on roll-off vessels are to be introduced by 1976, and while more emphasis will in the short term be placed on multi-purpose vessels capable of carrying combinations of containers/road trailers/ferry wagons, in the longer term the tendency may be to provide terminals and ships specializing in one type of traffic only. Thus it may transpire that one particular route is wholly containerized, while another may specialize in roll-on roll-off freight, and a third be confined to the shipment of ferry wagons only. This sort of long-term planning can only become a reality though when it is clearer what future policy is to be concerning the carriage of freight by road, and whether or not a Channel tunnel is to be constructed.

Intercontainer

A major factor contributing to the success of the British Rail containerships across the North Sea was the setting up in December 1967 of a co-operative company called Intercontainer. Intercontainer was formed through the participation of eleven European railway companies plus the Interfrigo concern, and consists today of twenty-three members plus the state railways of Eastern Europe. During the development of rail-borne container systems it was evident that problems were bound to arise in connection with the co-ordination of containers, or as they are called on the Continent, 'transcontainers', moving across frontiers from one railway network to another, and it was the intention of Intercontainer to obtain a degree of co-operation between its members, and to buy freight capacity in bulk for sale to individual members in smaller units.

Although owning a number of wagons, the company does not own any containers or terminals, but instead has the resources of the European railways to draw on backed up by 300 terminals for introducing to, or withdrawing containers from the system. The objective of the company therefore is not to run a service, but to point the way to the most efficient use of equipment throughout Europe, such as indicating routes where there are regular flows of traffic and co-ordinating the functions of the railway authorities and others in building up maximum capacity trains. Intercontainer will also accept traffic itself for making up into full loads, and with its contacts throughout Europe with forwarding agents and shippers, will be able to offer to the railways regular bulk traffic which should enjoy large rebates. A further impetus to the granting of these rebates is the general desire of the railways to encourage a transfer of long-distance road traffic to the rail system, and the actual tonnage conveyed has been further boosted by the deep-sea containership operators serving the European ports.

The administrative center of Intercontainer is in Basle where the fullest collaboration is maintained with shipping companies, container operators, and freight forwarders, as well as the railway authorities themselves. The company is represented in each country either by a recognized container operator, or by the railway authority in the country concerned, and needs the fullest co-operation from each member country to achieve full integration in rolling stock and commercial organization. For example, the company's early development in the routeing of traffic between Rotterdam and Milan was delayed due to organizational trouble at the freight depot at Milan, coupled with the extraordinary commercial practices of the Italian customs officials. A problem that has now been largely overcome was caused by the difficulty in the calculation of rates due to the complicated nature of the railway tariffs within countries, and the different methods of assessment from one country to another. Quotations often used to take several days to compile, while road hauliers were able to fix a price almost immediately, but Intercontainer have been instrumental in simplifying and wherever possible standardizing tariffs to conform to a common system.

The European rail terminals are linked by two rail networks, the Trans-Europ-Express-Marchandises (TEEM) used for single or small groups of containers moving on a localized basis, and the Trans-Europ-Container-Express (TECE) the international high-speed connection. TECE is currently carrying over 60 per cent of the British Rail container traffic generated by Freightliners Ltd. the United Kingdom Intercontainer agent, and the two networks combined increased their traffic from 85,000 20-foot equivalents in 1969, to 257,000 in 1971, and 440,000 in 1973. Using a rail-borne container movement the importance of finding an immediate back load is of less importance than it is to the road haulage operator, whose trailers can cost upwards of £100 per day when lying idle, because of the considerably smaller capital investment involved once the rail system has been established. The railways are therefore more able to accept cargo knowing that a back load may not immediately be forthcoming and are also able to compete more favorably with road the longer the distance involved. The longer the haul the less the significance becomes of delays at the terminal, and during the initial collection and final delivery of the container by road. If a short haul is involved these delays might often exceed the actual rail transit time by several days, and it is over these shorter distances that the road trailer is at its most competitive.

It is generally agreed that the railways are able to offer a method of transport for freight, and indeed for passengers, more sociably acceptable than that offered through carriage by road. Rail traction is cheaper, consumes less energy per ton of freight than road vehicles, and is pollution-free if electrification has been introduced. These are important factors to consider when planning future railway development, and they figured prominently during the preparation by the International Union of Railways of a planning document which discusses the possible improvement and speeding up of Europe's railway system. About £10,000M is likely to be spent over the next ten to twenty years in updating existing lines, building new ones, and increasing loading gauges to allow more widespread carriage of containers and other unit loads. Intercontainer will be able to play a major role in improving and expanding rail container services, and this coherent type of planning should be supported by the individual railway companies concerned. It is the intention of the planners to continue the development of rail links between eastern and western European countries, and this further encouragement of multilateral trade may one day play a not insignificant role in harmonizing relations between the European groups.

The French Railways

In a similar way to British Rail, but at a slower pace, French Railways (SNCF) have adapted their systems to make provision for a fast, reliable, and regular transcontainer service, and have developed the ports of Le Havre and Marseilles as depots for deep sea traffic, and Dunkerque for short sea traffic mainly to and from the United Kingdom. SNCF had little incentive to follow the type of railway development that was taking place toward the end of the 1960's in the United Kingdom, as the widespread use of private sidings which meant that 'door-to-door' movements could take place in wagons, made it unnecessary to set up a system of container terminals. More recently, however, SNCF has radically changed its outlook on containers, and through its subsidiary company, Compagnie Nouvelle de Cadres (CNC), which is also the agent for Intercontainer within France, it is actively selling the movement of both domestic and maritime freight by container. Container terminals similar to the Freightliner terminals in the United Kingdom are being constructed, and these will be used principally for consolidation and breaking down of container traffic where more than one origin or destination is involved, while door-to-door routing will still be encouraged for full loads, but by container in preference to the more usual wagons.

CNC's function is principally to market the carriage of maritime containers on behalf of the French railways, and confines its domestic container interests to the grouping of a number of individual containers which it offers for carriage to SNCF on a discount basis. CNC owns its own containers, while SNCF provides the rolling stock and offers services such as the "Container Express" which started in June 1969, and provides a fast overnight link between seven of the largest industrial centers in France. Eleven block trains run every night in each direction, and many incentives such as a rating structure which includes handling charges, and cheaper carriage of containers returning empty after a loaded journey, are offered. Apart from this highly specialized service, SNCF also run their 'Fret Express', trains which criss-cross the country to a fixed timetable, all of which can accept containers.

While SNCF and CNC are facing fierce competition from the road haulage industry, they are also closely collaborating with a company formed by road haulage interests known as Novatrans, to develop the use of "Kangaroo" services. Road trailers which may have crossed the channel from the UK on one of the roll-on roll-off ferries, are driven on to a low rail wagon for the long journey across France. On arrival in the southern part of the country the trailer is unloaded, hitched up to a traction unit, and driven by road to its destination. Following the success of Novatrans in France similar services are now operating through to Italy, and interests in the United Kingdom are to invest substantially in equipment to provide a Kangaroo service, largely in anticipation of the building of a Channel tunnel. It will therefore be apparent that the pattern of trailer freight in Europe could be radically changed if a tunnel were to be successfully built and if through transit times similar to those offered by the international road haulage companies could be achieved, the long hoped for large-scale transfer of road freight to the railways might well materialize.

The containerization policy of SNCF, while not interfering with the established use of rail wagons by, for example, the Spanish consortium of freight forwarders known as Transfesa, is not always conducive to the improvement of wagon routes. If SNCF is unable to adopt a slightly more flexible attitude, it might be that some of this traffic, which consists of perishables such as fruit and vegetables, will have to be transferred to the road system in order to avoid delays at the rail terminals. The Transfesa wagons are fitted with adjustable axles for use both on the wider gauge railways of Spain, and on the narrower gauge network of Continental Europe and the United Kingdom, and are currently being handled in the United Kingdom principally at the Hither Green rail depot. Due to congestion though at Hither Green, and again partly in anticipation of a Channel tunnel being built, the United Kingdom associate of Transfesa is contemplating the development of a £2 million private rail freight terminal on the proposed route of the Channel tunnel rail link with London at Paddock Wood. Another rail wagon operator that has been fairly successfully integrated with SNCF's container policy is the international railway-owned company for refrigerated traffic known as "Interfrigo". As mentioned earlier Interfrigo was one of the founder members of Intercontainer, and like Intercontainer has its administrative headquarters in Basle, and is represented by agents in 24 European countries.

The German Federal Railways

In contrast with some of the slower developing railway companies in Europe, such as in Italy, the German Federal railways (Deutsche Bundesbahn) have possibly gone too far in the provision of a rail network. Their policy has been to provide a service whereby a very large proportion of the available freight traffic could be moved by rail, often without relying on road haulage for initial collection and final delivery. To this end they have encouraged manufacturers to construct private sidings through the granting of Government low-interest loans, and their railway network of today which is far more extensive than that to be found in the United Kingdom, serves as an ideal distribution complex to satisfy the country's widely spread consumer markets.

The Deutsche Bundesbahn (DB) run an extremely efficient system and are very active in trying to persuade more cargo-owners to utilize the railways. If a town is not rail connected they will operate their own road vehicles for the collection and delivery of traffic between the town and the nearest goods rail-head, and indeed the DB is now one of the largest owners of road trucks in West Germany. They still face very fierce competition from the road haulage industry, but stringent regulations on the operation of road vehicles has kept this competition on a lower level than it otherwise would have been and has had the effect of transferring by legislative means some traffic to the railways. In spite of these measures the DB is operating with 20 per cent spare freight capacity at present, goods traffic increasing by only 4.8 per cent during 1973, but movements of kangaroo trucks are increasing more rapidly.

In formulating their container policy the DB carefully studied the freightliner trains running in the United Kingdom before committing themselves to any one type of system, and pointed to the limitation on the number of users of the UK system due to it only catering for the owners of full loads wishing to move their goods between the more important industrial areas which were equipped with freightliner terminals. They also indicated that the UK system suffered from a lack of flexibility because the trains were permanently coupled, and could not accept full wagon loads of the type to be found on the Continent. The DB now runs two rail container terminals at Hamburg, and if their trans-container trains can be operated economically over the more difficult short hauls, they will undoubtedly extend their loading capacities to cater both for the increasing volume of foreign as well as home trade. Partly to achieve this aim the authorities want to put into effect a twelve-year reorganization plan involving the construction of new lines, the improvement of existing ones, and the expansion of electrification. Freight trains would have priority over passenger services at night, and would at all times be run as far as possible as a separate entity. In this way the DB is hopeful of counteracting the revenue loss they suffered through the granting of preferential rail rates to the three new members of the EEC—the United Kingdom, Eire and Denmark—and is also hopeful of being able to finance the continuing spiral in the wage rates of railway staff. It might then be possible to convert a large deficit, if not to an operating surplus, at least to a paper surplus after allowing for EEC and national subsidies.

The Channel Tunnel

Perhaps the biggest boost to European rail movements of freight would follow the construction and successful operation of a rail tunnel beneath the English Channel connecting France and England. Apart from being a key link in the new types of rail system being planned on the Continent, a tunnel would allow British Rail to offer through container services not only on a domestic basis, but also to over twenty Continental destinations. The French, and to a lesser extent the German railways, would be in a similar position by being able to offer services through to the United Kingdom, and the resulting increase in revenues, particularly to the French, would help to put the authorities on to a far sounder footing.

A factor of considerable initial importance, but one that seems to be of lesser significance now that the potential monetary benefits have become more evident, is that of cost. The original estimate of approximately £366M rose during less than a year to about £900M, and if the project is completed this figure is certain to climb even further. The British and French governments will not be directly concerned with the raising of this capital, as it will be provided by a consortium of predominantly finance companies, but the Governments will provide guarantees of 90 per cent of the capital. Therefore in the event of the project being abandoned, or being unprofitable, the guarantees would come into force, and the companies would be responsible for 10 per cent of the financial commitment only. The companies involved, who are the sole shareholders in the United Kingdom parent concern, the

FIGURE 11 The Hull container terminal at Queen Elizabeth Dock (Courtesy of British Transport Docks Board).

British Channel Tunnel Company, are British Rail, Channel Tunnel Investments, Rio Tinto-Zinc, Morgan Grenfell, Robert Fleming, Hill Samuel, Kleinwort Benson, S.G. Warburg, Morgan Stanley, First Boston Corporation, and White Weld. A similar arrangement exists in France, and the companies' involvement extends only to the construction of the actual tunnel, the rail links being financed out of public funds.

Although becoming more expensive as time goes on, the expected profit margins from the venture are also likely to increase. During the first year of operation a total operating surplus of about £110M is forecast, which after allowing for debt service would leave net receipts of about £42M. It is estimated that in 1990 these figures will respectively be £332M and £242M, and in 2004 £1052M and £962M, which could well prove to be embarrassingly high. The receipts will initially be shared between the companies and the two Governments, but after fifty years the companies will have relinquished their interest through the redemption by the Governments of the capital outlay. The Governments by this time will have received about 85 per cent of the profits, and will take all subsequent revenue. The final decision on whether or not to begin construction will be taken early in 1975, following extensive tests and studies, and the thirty-two mile long twin rail tunnels would be scheduled for opening in 1980 if the go-ahead is given.

The main argument against a Channel tunnel is that it would draw far more heavy road vehicles into the vicinity of Folkestone, causing severe congestion especially during the summer months. The problem therefore is to introduce traffic into, and disperse traffic from the tunnel at terminals away from the tunnel entrance at Cheriton, and this could be achieved through the setting up of a number of inland transfer points on the route of the rail link with London where vehicles could join or leave a train. This would help to avoid heavy vehicles, some of which would be conveying cargo previously passing through the ports of Newhaven, Southampton, Dover and Hull, from converging on Cheriton, and the longer rail haul would not be detrimental to the economics of operating a road vehicle. In addition to keeping vehicles on their rail flats for part of the inland journey to help overcome road congestion, encouragement should be given to using the tunnel as a means of conveying freight by rail as opposed to by road. Freight from the United Kingdom would be generated by the Freightliner system from all over the country, and would be consigned direct via the container system of the Continental railways to buyers all over Europe. Following the successful completion of the modernization schemes of the Continental railways, a transit time similar to that given on a door-to-door basis by today's international road hauliers might be given, and a real swing in favor of carriage of freight by rail would be under way.

The rail link to London would run from Cheriton to a terminal at White City from where connections would allow through transits to and from the Midlands, the North and the West of England. Because it would not be possible to run the new types of Continental gauge high-speed trains over the existing track connecting Folkestone and London, the link would have to be a new one, and a conservative estimate of the cost is put at £120M. Admittedly this will have to be met out of public funds, but when it is remembered that a new rail link to one of the south coast ports will be needed whether a tunnel is built or not, and that generally railways are cheaper to construct than motorways, the spending becomes more justified. Social problems will arise such as property demolition and noise, but these are on such a small scale relative to motorway construction that the difficulties become almost negligible by comparison.

The differences in gauge between the Continental and United Kingdom railways are differences not in track width, but in loading. Rolling stock found on the Continent is higher and wider than that to be found in the United Kingdom, and is therefore unsuitable for operation on most of the existing British Rail track because of insufficient vertical clearance under tunnels and bridges, and insufficient horizontal clearance between fixed structures on curves. When running British Rail rolling stock over Continental tracks these physical problems of course would not arise, but legislation governing braking and other safety measures would have to be standardized throughout Europe before through trains could operate. Loading gauge difficulties would be easier to overcome in the Western region of British Rail's system, where the track was originally laid by Brunel to a seven-foot width (abandoned in 1892) to accommodate the more spacious type of carriages then in existence. These routes could therefore be used by larger loading guage equipment, but still running over the standard track width of 4 feet 8½ inches, without the necessity for extensive reconstruction.

The other main area of hostility to a Channel tunnel is formed by the ferry companies operating outside British Rail's shipping division. European Ferries has perhaps been the most hostile, but they are supported by the influential United Kingdom Chamber of Shipping in their argument that a smaller and more efficient fleet than has been estimated by the tunnel interests as being necessary to handle cross channel traffic in 1980, would in fact be required. European Ferries maintain that future ferries will be larger, and they are continuing to introduce new tonnage to their services. While correctly pointing out that shipping is more flexible than a fixed tunnel, and that if traffic flows change shipping can be diverted, they overlook the fact that because cross channel traffic is moving in any case over a comparatively restricted area, there is little room for diversion of cargo to alternative routes. A tunnel would therefore attract a large part of the traffic presently being handled by the ferries, but an initial price war, with the ferry companies widening even further the expected difference in the level of charges existing in 1980, would probably last for about five years. By the end of this period it has been suggested that the ferries would no longer be able to operate, and that they would have completely withdrawn from the route to concentrate instead on services out of the East Coast ports and Southampton. In contrast with European Ferries, the other major ferry operator, British Rail, would be cushioned from the effect of withdrawal of its shipping services by the additional revenue arising from increased freight movements made possible by a Channel tunnel, and indeed this revenue would more than compensate for the ship operation losses. Admittedly European Ferries must surely emerge from these arguments in a far from satisfactory condition, but this particular Government backed project is far less likely to become a monument to misguided state planning than some others currently being discussed, and the ferry companies would be better advised to accept the situation and concentrate now on the future development of alternative short-sea services.

While problems would arise following the construction and operation of a Channel tunnel, these should be put into perspective by examining the benefits as well. Passenger and freight transit times would be dramatically cut, and it would be possible for vegetables and other perishables grown in Southern Europe to be on sale in the United Kingdom markets more promptly than by using the sometimes erratic ferries. Environmental damage would be lessened if the majority of freight crossing the Channel were conveyed by rail container, but the risk of blockage and the subsequent state of chaos should not be ignored. The seasonal effect of motorized holiday traffic on a fixed structure such as a tunnel should also not be overlooked. Redundancies in the port and shipping services would be especially severe at Dover, and to a lesser extent at Folkestone, but some of these would be absorbed by the administrative and operational requirements of the tunnel.

The Landbridge System

Using an intermodal system the process of transhipping cargo from ship to rail and vice versa is simplified. This simplification has meant that where a large land mass existed, as illustrated by the USA and Russia, which formerly made circumnavigation necessary, it was now feasible to offload containers on one side of the continent and rail them to the other side where they would be loaded to a second vessel to complete the journey. Containers in effect would travel in almost a straight line between two points, the distance covered overland often equalling the distance covered by sea, and transit times would be considerably speeded up. This concept of combined land and sea transport has become to be known as "landbridge", and following initial development in the USA has spread to many parts of the world.

Factors that promote landbridge usage are many, but it is particularly of benefit to those owners of cargo who, while not requiring a transit time as quick as offered by the airlines, are nevertheless dealing in moderately highly priced goods where a faster transit, usually at a higher freight charge, is desirable. In these cases the cargo owner makes his own decision to utilize landbridge, but in other instances the shipping company may decide to establish a combined sea/rail system, usually in cases where it is found to be more economic, and does not put either his containership or a feeder vessel into the port of destination, completing the journey instead from an intermediary port by rail. Transfers of cargo to a landbridge route will also follow the establishment of rate differentials which make the all sea route relatively more expensive, where space shortages exist on containership routes, and where shipping services have been temporarily suspended.

Two of the early landbridge routes to be operated successfully were those connecting Europe with the Far East via either North America or Russia. Using the former route cargo would be shipped by container vessel from a European port to an east coast USA or Canadian port, where it would be loaded on to a rail wagon for the journey across America or Canada to a west coast port. Here it would again be loaded to a containership for the final leg of the journey to Japan. By this method the long sea voyage via the Panama canal would be cut out, and transit times would be considerably reduced. The North American route has not developed as fully though as the Russian route, which relies on the Trans-Siberian Railway for the overland link, and which has been able to boost its tonnage figures because of a shortage of capacity in containership services operating from Europe to the Far East and Australia. A full discussion of this Russian route will follow in Chapter 8.

The long voyage between the Far East and the North American Great Lakes via the Panama Canal has more recently been largely avoided through the introduction of a landbridge service. Cargo is being shipped by container vessel to Vancouver, where it is rail freighted to Windsor, Ontario, for on-forwarding to, for example, Detroit, by ferry. In this, and many other cases, a port or other maritime authority suffers through losing cargo to the landbridge route, and in this instance it is the St. Lawrence Seaway who must count the cost. Another example of landbridge having the effect of diverting traffic is to be found in the US Gulf to Europe trade, where cargo is being railed to Charleston for shipment, instead of being shipped directly out of the Gulf port of

New Orleans. The containership company concerned is guaranteeing a regular flow of containers to the railway company in return
for preferential rail rates, but due to these charges often being
well below normal domestic rates the Interstate Commerce Commission has been asked by some of the Gulf ports to investigate
with a view to fixing a more realistic charge.

In the United Kingdom there are possibilities of the railways
handling a considerable volume of entrepot trade, and if the port
of Liverpool manages to solve its financial problems containers
from the USA and Canada could be transhipped at the Seaforth
container terminal on to the freightliner network for carriage to
Harwich, where the units would be shipped to Zeebrugge to continue their journey on the Continent. Moving now to the Middle
East a landbridge connects Alexandria in Egypt by road to the
Red Sea port of Adabiya. Cargo is shipped from north European
and Mediterranean ports to Alexandria from where the road haul
to Adabiya takes only seven hours. From Adabiya links are
maintained by ship with Aqaba, Jeddah and Port Sudan, and the
service could even be extended to India and the Far East. Another
Middle East route has been developed by the Kadem Land Bridge
Company who have maintained a road link for several years
between Ashdod in Israel and Eilat on the Red Sea. Cargo has
been moving between Europe and East Africa since shortly after
the closure of the Suez Canal on this route, and Kadem, which is
owned by Israel's largest shipping company, Zim Navigation,
offered to ship 80,000 bales of Australian wool per year to importers in Greece and Turkey in half the time that was being taken
by sea. The wool would have been shipped from Australia to
Eilat where it was to be transferred to road vehicles for the
journey to Ashdod. From Ashdod it would then have been
shipped to ports in Greece or Turkey.

In a similar way as in Europe where the building of a Channel
tunnel, coupled with extensive railway modernization, is likely to
boost cargo moved over the rail networks, widespread development in the USA of the landbridge system could help to bail out
the largely bankrupt American railway companies. Co-operation
between the companies and the container lines has already prevented landbridge rates from being higher than they otherwise
would have been, and any steps by the ICC and the FMC toward

the raising of landbridge rail rates, as sought by the port authorities who complain of cargo losses, should be taken only after a consideration of the desirability of maintaining any sort of railway system at all. The feeling in nearly all the industrial countries of the world is that national rail services should be given a freer hand to compete with other forms of transport, and any movement toward building up traffic flows, even though they may initially be heavily state subsidized, should be encouraged, and should not have to face an immediate blockage as would follow intervention by the ICC and FMC. To what extent railway/shipping company co-operation should go, however, is debatable, and a landbridge operating as an extension to a shipping service, as in the Europe-Charleston-Gulf instance, or one operating as an alternative to a long and time-consuming sea voyage, as in the case of the North American and Russian routes, should be considered as legitimate alternatives to all sea carriage. But where, as is currently happening in the USA, a "mini" landbridge is operating purely to divert cargo to a port other than the one that would normally be used, a case may exist for closer examination of the economics involved. One such mini landbridge draws freight from the hinterland of the US eastern seaboard, which would normally be shipped out of a US eastern port, and rails it to such a port not for shipment by sea, but to join a railroad crossing the continent to a western seaboard port. From here it will join a containership bound for the Far East. The actual cost of maintaining this combined rail/sea route must be considerably more than that involved in the all sea link, but the rates charged are the same as those quoted by shipping companies using the sea route. It is in cases like these that some form of protection should be given to the ports most affected through cargo losses, and it has been proposed that the railway companies should publicize their rates in order that these rates may be challenged by the ports under legislation that states that such services should not be operated below cost. A further check to the rapid development of this particular mini-landbridge will follow the growing presence of Japanese lines connecting the eastern USA ports with the Far East, who are offering transit times via the Panama Canal approximately equal to those being obtained by the mini-landbridge operation.

Landbridge developments are desirable therefore where the overland haul, be it by rail or road, forms a natural extension to, or is a legitimate alternative to a sea voyage, and where an intermediary port is not purely being used to take advantage of the rail link that may serve the port. If cargo is not passing over the port authorities' quays, revenue is not being earned, and employment of dockers and other port workers will be subject to fluctuations directly attributable to the often short-term planning policy of some of the containership companies. Conversely, landbridge in whatever form it may take, will usually be beneficial to the cargo owner primarily through quicker transit times, and to the shipping company and the railways. Difficulties will arise though in issuing a through transit document until the FMC, who regulate the maritime part of the journey when US ports are involved, and the ICC who control the haul by road or rail in the US, are able to come together and formulate regulations applicable to both sectors.

Another instance of a group that was formerly largely unconnected with the handling and movement of maritime-generated container traffic is the airlines. Airbridge systems, which involve the shipment of cargo partly by sea and partly by air, are being developed to speed the through movement of goods and have evolved following co-operation between the containership companies and the airlines. While lightweight 20-foot aluminium containers suitable for conveying airfreight and strong enough to stand the rigors of a sea voyage are already in existence, and are being used on some routes, this type of movement normally involves the unpacking of cargo from more conventional containers at the transfer point between sea and air, and the re-packing into an igloo air container. It is anticipated, however, that it will shortly be possible to use 40-foot containers on a truly intermodal sea/air basis, which will be a further step forward toward integration of methods of cargo conveyance.

Future Railway Development

The purely economic viewpoints expressed in 1962 concerning railway development in the United Kingdom have largely been discarded by the present administration in favor of policy decisions based more on a total transport plan involving the roads and the environment. It was announced by the Government in November 1973 that £891M was to be invested in the rail system over a five-year period, principally to extend electrification and to improve existing track and signalling, and that some of the money needed would be channeled away from future road construction. It was realized that the railway system within the United Kingdom, in common with the majority of railways worldwide, is unlikely in the foreseeable future to run in economic competition with the road haulage industry, and that massive long-term subsidies would be required. It was also realized that however large the subsidies might be, only a small proportion of freight would be taken off the roads, bearing in mind that only 15 per cent of freight is currently carried by rail and a doubling of this figure would result in a comparatively small percentage fall in road traffic. The Government is therefore not looking toward a large-scale swing to the railways, but instead has in mind a lessening of damage to the environment as caused by the heavy road vehicle to say nothing of the motor car. Economic competitiveness is not now the principal criterion, and any large-scale cuts to the United Kingdom's current 11,500 miles of track are unlikely.

In spite of this change of outlook, British Rail will continue to try to improve its financial status, and while not shunning the smaller parcel and single wagon traffic, will nevertheless concentrate more on building up bulk cargo traffic. To this end it is likely that Government grants will be given toward the construction by industry of private sidings, and toward wider ownership of specialized wagons to convey commodities such as liquids and chemicals. Rail-borne bulk commodities, whether moving in train-loads or in computer-controlled single wagons directly between industrial sidings, are competitive with road transport methods, and further modernization of existing systems and track would allow British Rail in the first instance to boost the movement of train-loads, and secondly to develop a computerized system of control for single or small groups of wagons.

Where smaller loads are involved, and in the absence of computer-controlled wagons, there is little alternative at present in the United Kingdom to the majority of traffic being conveyed by road. This is due to the average freight haul only being about 40 miles, and in view of the time it would take for cargo to be loaded to a wagon and assembled into a train, the system would in no way be able to compete with the more flexible road haulage industry where units are smaller and transit times over short distances are much faster. This situation could however change if a Channel tunnel were to be built, because distances would become greater where through movements between the Continent and the United Kingdom took place. Imported goods previously arriving at a south coast port by road trailer following a ferry crossing by roll-on roll-off vessel, would instead be loaded to a rail container or ferry wagon on the Continent and conveyed direct either to their destination, or to a rail terminal for breaking down, and the time taken assembling a train would be of less significance. As mentioned earlier though, it is essential that the plans to build a large terminal at Cheriton near Folkestone for the transfer of road vehicles to and from the tunnel trains are disbanded if this switch from road to rail is to be achieved.

A topic of considerable controversy is whether, in order to encourage more cargo to be conveyed by rail, some form of restriction should be imposed on road vehicles carrying freight over distances exceeding 100 miles, as proposed in the Transport Act of 1968. Such restrictions on the freedom of choice should be used as a last resort and only then in cases where environmental damage is, or is likely to occur. Legislation should be replaced by encouragement, and any large-scale transfer of cargo from road to rail should be a natural occurrence, if severe capacity shortages are to be avoided. This encouragement is already illustrated by the investment programme that the Government has announced for the railways, and could be continued through a drastic cutback on spending on motorway construction. The real road needs in the United Kingdom are by-passes round towns to take traffic away from town centers, and freightways exclusively for commercial vehicles connecting key centers such as ports and rail terminals to nearby industrial centers. Increased capacity following the completion of new long-distance road trunk links soon becomes absorbed through a larger flow of all types of vehicle, and the continual building of such highways can only lead to the gap between road and rail freight widening still further, and to a devastating effect on our environment.

Chapter 6

Insurance and the Need For a Combined Transport Document

Established Procedures

During the planning and implementation stages of containerization it was not possible to produce a documentation system that would ideally be suited to the needs of the new transportation methods. Apart from the speed with which containerization was introduced, and the fierce competition among the lines and consortia, the situation was not helped by the various shipping and insurance acts which had been built up over the years in the light of practical problems that were met with in the carriage of break-bulk cargo by conventional vessels. The change to containerization was a radical one and it was not possible to immediately modify the existing shipping, insurance and banking procedures to accommodate the new methods. The insurance and banking fraternity were very conservative groups, and shipowners complained of a reluctance on the part of insurance underwriters to find out more about containerization and its possible benefits. Admittedly underwriters were not seeing the returns they would have wished for in the realm of cargo insurance, and the subject of containerization remained a controversial one.

Shipowners' Liability

A meeting of the International Law Association was held at The Hague in September 1921 with the object of securing agreement to a set of rules relating to bills of lading, indicating the rights and liabilities of shipowners and cargo owners. These rules became to be known as the Hague Rules, and have been widely used as the basis for formulating legislation within countries governing the carriage of cargo by sea. In the United Kingdom they are embodied in the Carriage of Goods by Sea Act, 1924.

The Hague Rules were formulated to establish the relationship existing between shipper and shipowner long before the introduction of container shipping, and consequently they are unable to accommodate some of the changed custom that has arisen following the sea carriage of containers. For example, the Rules state that "goods" does not include cargo shipped on deck, but a container vessel carries about 20 per cent of its cargo in containers on deck, partly to compensate for the loss of cubic capacity that will arise from using a vessel of cellular construction. It would appear then that the shipowner is in the advantageous position, should loss or damage occur to this section of cargo, of indicating that the Act of 1924 absolves him of any responsibility. Underwriters would then be unable, after settling a claim with the cargo owner to pursue the shipowner with a view to recovering all or part of the loss, and would therefore be faced with the responsibility of settling the entire claim. This was a daunting proposition bearing in mind the conditions to be found at sea, especially during the winter months on the North Atlantic. During one passage alone twenty-two containers were washed overboard from one of the early containerships, and obviously underwriters were far from happy with the situation. In order therefore to classify deck cargo, as far as shipowners' liability was concerned, in the same category as underdeck cargo, containership operators will generally exempt themselves from the Hague Rules, and accept the same level of liability for both types of cargo. This decision on the part of the shipowner has been strengthened in the courts, as illustrated by a case involving a shipment of encyclopaedias in a container, but by a conventional break-bulk vessel. The container was stowed on deck and damage occurred during the voyage. It was held that the ship was liable because that part of the Hague Rules appertaining to deck cargo did not apply, and the encyclopaedias were to be classified as goods, and were therefore the qualified responsibility of the ship.

Another clause to be found in the Hague Rules potentially of benefit to the shipowner was whether a container came within the definition of "package" or "unit". Article IV, Rule 5 of the Rules limited the liability of the shipowner, in the event of loss or damage, to £100 per package or unit, and if the container were so construed the underwriters' position would be precarious indeed. Early cases brought before the courts were given different judgements between countries, it being held in the USA that a container was to be thought of as one package, while in France it was indicated that where a cargo owner lodges a bill of lading covering one container, which also stated the number of packages within the container, the shipowner will be liable for each individual package up to the limit of his liability. The view of the USA courts was later amended when a case was heard involving the theft of a container carrying 99 cartons of leather from a terminal. The carrier tried to limit his liability to the container, which he maintained was a "package" or "unit", but the court held that his liability should extend to each individual carton within the container.

It is considered today that the rules drawn up at The Hague in 1921 are out of date not only when applied to the peculiar conditions of container carriage, but also to other forms of shipping. Article IV, Rule 5 had been consistently criticized by cargo owners and underwriters even before the introduction of containerization, due to the very low figure at which the shipowners' liability had been fixed. An amended Carriage of Goods by Sea Act was therefore passed in 1971 and shipowners' liability has been raised to 10,000 gold francs per package or 30 gold francs per kilo, whichever is greater. The 1971 Act, which is not yet in operation, will also contain a clause stating that if the number of packages in a container is indicated on the bill of lading, shipowners' limitation of liability will be based separately on each individual package, and not merely on the container as a whole, thus incorporating interpretations of the courts into statute.

Following the introduction of increased liability figures, it is now felt, and indeed supported by many shipowners, that the whole concept of liability limitation should be discarded, and that the owners should be wholly responsible for the goods in their care and liable for their full value in cases of loss or damage. This would of course remove the need for merchants to place their cargo risks in the insurance market, and underwriters would lose a corresponding amount of business. Shipowners would, however, insure for catastrophe losses, i.e. where the vessel, containers and all the cargo is lost, and they have stated that they would be able to stand the cost of routine loss and damage as found on individual voyages. This move on the part of the shipowner is partly to pave the way for the development of a combined transport document, to be discussed later, which would simplify claims procedure by establishing one combined transport operator as the party responsible for all segments of a through movement. Difficulties may become apparent though due to the entire cargo risk being carried by the shipowner, if it is found that the cost of meeting claims forces up freight rates. If this were to happen, and to avoid owners of good risk cargo subsidizing owners of bad risk cargo, it would be cheaper for the majority of shippers to continue arranging their own cargo insurance through their brokers with underwriters. The cargo owner would also be less inclined to ensure that this cargo was safely stowed in its container in the absence of any incentive, such as the possibility of a lower insurance premium as might arise through his own broker, and total cargo damage per voyage might well increase. Conversely the shipowner would be more careful ensuring that cargo was received in a sound and safe condition, if he were carrying the transit risk himself, and would reduce to a minimum any possibility of damage to the cargo while in his care.

Causes of Damage

Cargo for shipment by break-bulk vessel is forwarded to a quay where it will be loaded and stowed on board the vessel by a skilled gang of stevedores working from a detailed stowage plan previously prepared in the loading broker's or shipping company's

office from lists of cargo pre-booked by shippers. Cargo intended
for shipment by container vessel on the other hand, will either be
forwarded to a receiving terminal for stowage by the shipping
company into a container, or will be packed by the manufacturer
directly into an empty container previously delivered by the shipping company to the manufacturer's premises. If the shipping
company attends to stowage on behalf of the manufacturer the
quantity of cargo involved will be less than would fill the container (LCL), and where the manufacturer stows he will generally
be dealing in full container loads (FCL). It will follow that
responsibility for possibly the most important factor determining
whether or not cargo will suffer damage in transit, namely stowage, will for a large part of the cargo be transferred from the
shipping company to the shipper. In spite of the specialized nature
of a containership and the modern methods of handling at the
terminals, it is perhaps justifiably felt by some underwriters, principally due to the increased risk following poor stowage of containers by some shippers, that containerized cargo is more of a
risk than cargo shipped by break-bulk vessel. The opposite view
is expressed by the containership operators but the facts would
appear to indicate that while good stowage is important, it is the
type of cargo involved which determines how easy stowage will
be. For example, bales, bags and drums can be sold and shipped
in relative ease in quantities that will completely fill a container,
but more awkward shapes such as uncrated machinery and even
palletized loads will need extensive chocking and dunnage to
prevent movement inside the container.

It has to be admitted though that not nearly enough thought
is given to the packing of containers. Some shippers are not
entirely aware of the significance of stowage and over-economize
in their own factory packing thinking that the "box" is the solution to their packaging costs. While packing can be cut down in
some cases, over-economy can lead to damage through other cargo
breaking loose in the container, usually during heavy weather
at sea, and a very high packaging saving should sometimes be
avoided. Under the Carriage of Goods by Sea Act, 1924, the
carrier is not responsible for loss or damage to goods arising from
insufficient packing, but as he must also prove that damage was
attributable to poor packing, and as he will not usually examine

the contents of FCL containers prior to shipment, he will some-times find it difficult to establish that the proximate cause of the loss or damage was the type of packing employed. It should be mentioned, however, that cargo stowed in the hold of a break-bulk vessel is also liable to damage from other cargo, especially during heavy weather when some cargo is liable to shift or even break loose. It is indeed maintained by the containership com-panies that as containerized cargo is in a number of small units, the likelihood of this type of damage is lessened. Damage to containerized cargo will also arise from incorrect stowage, espe-cially when goods of different types are conveyed in the same container. Apart from weight being evenly distributed horizontal-ly, heavy items should be placed on the floor while lighter cargo is stowed above, and any empty spaces at the sides should be filled with wood or with a number of compressed air cushions which are now supplied for the purpose.

Containerization has therefore in effect added the burden of safe stowage to shippers dealing in FCL containers and has been accepted, more on a voluntary basis, by consolidators packing LCL containers. Admittedly the containership companies are able to issue advice on stowage, but where smaller shippers are in-volved, possibly moving FCL containers on an irregular basis and having their insurance premiums levied on their past record of claims, more practical help should be given. Good stowage is a fundamental requirement of safe carriage, and the small shipper should not be at a disadvantage because of a transfer from ship-ping company to shipper of responsibility for a skill traditionally carried out by the shipping company.

Apart from insurance claims arising from damage to cargo fol-lowing poor packing and stowage, losses will also be due to condi-tions peculiar to container carriage as well as to more conventional reasons. As containers are generally sealed during transit, pilfer-age of part of the contents will be less of a risk, but hijacking of the entire container and its cargo is common especially where high value and easily disposable goods are involved. If a damaged container is utilized it may not be waterproof and wet damage could result, while a completely sealed container may lead to condensation and sweat damage, especially when climatic varia-tions occur. Flashpoint cargo should not be carried in sealed containers because a build up of heat and the lack of ventilation could cause an explosion. This particular danger is not so apparent when hazardous cargo is shipped by break-bulk vessel, as it will be stowed on deck separately from other goods, or in a ventilated hold away from boilers. Tainting will either be due to utilization of a dirty container, or to stowage with other goods of an objectionable nature. Some commodities will be affected by temperature changes, an example being the carriage of a container filled with chocolates on the top layer of a containership bound for the Far East or Australia. Although the shipowner will not generally guarantee underdeck stowage because it is necessary for him, in order to load his ship safely, to distribute weight, he will guarantee such stowage where the cargo would obviously be damaged by heat, or indeed by cold, if shipped on deck.

Fire is a hazard at sea whatever type of vessel is involved. The containership, however, will again present its own special problems, the most important being the difficulty of access to underdeck spaces because of the close stowage of containers above and below deck. Fire fighting will be hampered, and jettison of containers will be difficult. An outbreak of fire in a conventional vessel could often be confined to one hold only, but a serious fire involving a containership will rapidly spread from one container to another and could soon become out of control.

In order to reduce damage to containerized cargo carried by purpose-built cellular vessels, a hull designed to produce low resistance to the water, and to keep heavy seas off the deck containers has been developed. Anti-rolling tanks are fitted to lessen the ship's motion, and a lower stress factor is placed on deck container stacks. But cargo in containers will still be subject to sometimes violent motion during transit by sea, road and rail, but damage directly attributable to these causes should not be greater by comparison to damage suffered by cargo shipped by break-bulk vessel. The one important exception is of course when containerized cargo has not been properly secured within the container, and the importance of proper stowage cannot be over-emphasized.

Before the advent of the cellular container vessel, containers were being shipped in the holds and on the decks of conventional ships. Satisfactory securing of containers was therefore difficult, and during this early period the record of claims presented to underwriters was very bad indeed. Premiums on cargo carried in containers by these vessels were thus raised relatively to cargo being handled by the cellular vessels, and cargo owners were quick to point out that any benefits of containerization were going to the shipowners and not to themselves.

It is indeed often said that cargo shipped by break-bulk vessel is more at risk than cargo shipped by containership. The risk to cargo while actually at sea, however, is not increased if shipment is by break-bulk vessel, but it will often materialize, due for example to outdated handling methods at foreign ports, that this cargo will suffer damage at some stage of its journey. This damage may be inflicted, due to the more exposed nature of the cargo, at the port of loading or discharge, while in store at a foreign port, or during transport to the buyer. What is more important then is the state of development of the country where discharge takes place, which will be reflected in the system of working in the ports, the internal transport facilities, and the state of the roads. These weaker links in the chain will remain until it is possible to introduce a proper through container system using intermodal equipment. Weak links will also exist though when small feeder vessels of a less stable nature than the deep-sea containerships are used, especially where a rough sea crossing is involved as will be found in the North Sea, and in addition to damage to cargo, it is not uncommon for several containers to be lost through washing overboard.

A final reason for possible loss or damage, but one of major significance, is due to the very high concentration of cargo at one time at one location. Large container vessels can carry more than 2,000 containers, and the total value of the ship, the containers, and the cargo can be in excess of £20M. A catastrophe loss would therefore follow from the constructive total loss of a large containership, and similarly containerized cargo at a terminal could be said to be at an unduly high risk because of the total value of goods and equipment concentrated in a relatively small area. The implications of catastrophe cover will be examined in the following section.

Other Factors Influencing the Insurance

There has been a tendency recently among some manufacturing and trading concerns to examine more closely what their real insurance needs are. Some have decided to carry part of the risks that their cargo is subjected to themselves, and to limit cover to consequential and FPA perils only. This decision may be influenced by the fact that fewer claims have followed from less damage to, and loss of containerized cargo. The value of claims may have fallen at a far faster rate than reductions to premiums, and this gap between claims and premium will be unacceptable. Generally it is the larger organization that is able to put into reserves a sufficient sum to cover losses, but the containership operator may also decide that he is able to finance himself day-to-day claims. Shippers will still retain insurance for consequential losses such as loss of further business following damage to, or destruction of cargo, and will insure their liabilities to the carrier as contained in the bill of lading indemnities. This latter category will include damage to the vessel or other cargo caused by poor packing of hazardous cargo, by misdescribed or misdeclared cargo, and by badly packed FCL container cargo causing damage to the container, the ship, terminal equipment or the haulier's vehicle. The shipowner will retain consequential and liability cover, and will also insure for catastrophe losses where the entire vessel and cargo is declared a constructive total loss.

The role of the underwriter is therefore slowly changing, and in future more emphasis will be placed on loss prevention. Risk carrying will decline while services such as surveys on equipment and terminals on behalf of the shipowner will increase, and more specific insurance for the shipper such as provision of cover as required by banks negotiating letters of credit, will be given. Underwriters will have less opportunity, through delaying payment of claims, of investing a large regular premium inflow, and due to generally poor returns from cargo insurance it may be that rates may have to rise. Another factor affecting the level of rates will be the narrower spread of risks that will occur following limitation of cover to more specific requirements. Catastrophe cover has traditionally attracted quite modest premiums, and has been partly subsidized by a comprehensive cargo cover allowing long-term spreading of the risks, and therefore an ability on the part of underwriters to meet the occasional really large claim without embarrassment. But if the demand for catastrophe cover is to remain, while cargo insurance declines, catastrophe cover premium rates will rise. It has already been stated that the combined value of a large containership together with the containers and cargo could exceed £20M and by the end of 1974 about 200 containerships on the main trading routes will have replaced 847 conventional vessels. Apart from the much higher individual value of the vessel, and the greater concentration of cargo per voyage, far more time will be spent at sea, and this intensity of usage will increase still further the risk factor and therefore the level of catastrophe premium.

Combined Transport Documents

If a through intermodal containerized system is to function effectively it is desirable that a single operator should organize and accept responsibility for all the different methods of transportation involved. Apart from the closer control thus obtained by the operator, be he a shipping company, consortium, freight forwarder, or other party, it would then be possible for a combined transport document to be issued tailor made to the requirements of the operator and the shipper, covering the through movement by any combinations of sea, rail and road.

The two fundamental problems that have arisen following the introduction of through container shipments are (1) difficulty of determining at which stage of transit damage occurred, and (2) differing levels of liability of the various carriers which have complicated settlement of insurance claims. Containers are sealed in the country of exportation either at the exporter's premises in the case of FCL units, or at an inland terminal or port of shipment where LCL units are involved. The seal is slotted on to the inside locking bar of one of the doors, and if the door is opened the seal is broken. It is checked at each stage of the journey and if the seal is found to be broken, the appropriate reserves can be taken out against the party responsible for the handling or movement of the container immediately prior to the breaking. It is therefore a comparatively simple matter to aportion blame for shortages, but where cargo is damaged complications will be apparent. Apart from a possible examination by the Customs authorities in the country of importation, the container will not normally be opened, and if damage to the cargo is apparent during final discharge of the container at the buyer's premises it will be impossible to determine at which stage of the journey the damage occurred. Other than damage directly attributable to bad packing, the cause may be due to a rough sea crossing, to careless handling at a terminal or whilst in the care of a road haulage contractor or railway company. Each party handling the container will certify having received the unit without positive reference to the contents, and the underwriter settling a claim with the cargo owner will find it difficult, if not impossible to apportion blame to the party actually responsible. If it were possible, however, to establish one party only as the carrier, with rights to limitation of liability, the underwriters' position would be eased as the carrier would accept responsibility for the container throughout its journey be it by sea, rail or road, and recourse by the underwriter to subcontractors would not be necessary.

The second fundamental obstacle to intermodal movement of containerized cargo is the varying levels of liability of the carriers. The Hague Rules allow the shipowner to limit his liability to £100 per package or unit, while road hauliers limit their liability to between £800-£1000 per ton and railway authorities operating under the International Agreement on Railway Transports, 1961 (CIM) rail convention usually have no limitation at all. A combined transport bill of lading or other document issued by a carrier responsible for a through movement would allow a single limitation of liability figure to be agreed, irrespective of where loss or damage occurred, and an underwriter settling a claim with a cargo owner would again find it much easier to come to an agreement with the one carrier when looking for part reimbursement of the claim. If the shipowner was one of the contracting parties he would therefore have to accept much wider liability to include not only carriage by sea, but also by rail and road. But if the shipowner is able to establish at which part of the journey the loss or damage occurred, he will be able to recover contractually from the subcontractor involved, if the loss or damage was occasioned during the inland part of the journey by rail or road.

These problems would be overcome if a through combined bill of lading or transport document could be issued by a single carrier, either backed by an insurance certificate also covering a through movement, or one which accepted full liability for the goods during all parts of the transit. If an insurance certificate were issued it would either be drawn up by a subsidiary company of the shipping company, incorporated for the purpose as happened in 1968 when P & O established a wholly owned subsidiary company called Leadenhall Insurance Co. Ltd. with a view to offering shippers "free" insurance, the premium being included in the freight rate, or it would be a certificate of a recognized insurance company or a Lloyds form. But if the transport document were one without any limitation to the carrier's responsibility the carrier would assume "strict liability" and would be responsible to the cargo owner for any loss or damage suffered by the cargo due to negligence during any part of the through movement. If strict liability were to become an accepted custom of shipowners, and they found it economical not to place the risk with the recognized insurance market, underwriters, as has already been mentioned, would have to look elsewhere for part of their income, and would become more involved in prevention of loss or damage and in reporting actual cases of loss or damage.

Containership companies and other carriers have so far only been partly successful in introducing combined transport documents. Several compromises have been adopted, and some others have been rejected, but until a uniform set of rules acceptable to the carrier and to the cargo owner, as well as to the insurance market and the banks, can be incorporated into a standard form these compromizes will remain unsatisfactory substitutes. Bills of lading covering container shipments have had to be adapted through incorporation of such clauses as "received for shipment", when cargo is accepted by the shipping company at an inland terminal, and "on deck shipment admitted" implying that should the container be stowed on deck the Hague Rules are still to apply and the cargo is to be classified as "goods".

An early attempt at introducing a combined transport bill of lading and certificate of insurance, or an "insured" bill of lading, was the ACT/OCL announcement that they intended to issue to shippers such a document which would cover the carriage and insurance from the time cargo was accepted by the consortium, until it was handed to the consignee in the country of importation. Difficulties were immediately apparent though in the proposed system. A banker negotiating a letter of credit will normally insist on a "clean" "shipped on board" bill of lading being rendered with the other shipping documents, and this could be supplied where the bill was issued only after the cargo had actually been shipped on board the vessel. Under the ACT/OCL proposal the bill would be a "received for shipment" one, which would be issued at the time of acceptance of the cargo by the consortia, and it was uncertain how the banks would react. ACT/OCL were still to be bound by the Hague Rules for the sea voyage, but their level of liability on the through movement would be considerably higher than the limitations in the Rules. These limitations of the carrier together with the insurance of the cargo, unlike the P & O venture mentioned earlier, would be covered by a Lloyds certificate and the placing of the entire risk with one body, would, in the opinion of the consortia, allow a reduction in insurance rates to be effected. In order to avoid the possibility of some cargo owners, probably with a good insurance record, continuing to place their cover with their existing brokers, and another group of cargo owners, probably with a bad record of claims, allowing the consortia to attend to their insurance, it was decided to make the insurance scheme compulsory. This would avoid all the bad risks being placed with the consortia's underwriters, and would be a further argument to reduce premiums. Before the scheme was put into effect, however, it was decided, particularly in view of the hostility of the British Shippers' Council, to determine what the reaction of the cargo owner would be and if it were found that the majority were against it, to look at the scheme more closely.

A questionnaire was accordingly forwarded in September 1968 to every identifiable shipper of cargo in the Australian trade, asking for their opinion of the scheme. Only about 10 per cent of those circularized bothered to reply, but those firms who did so were representative of the biggest shippers. It could be argued that those parties who had violent objections to the scheme would be more likely to voice their opinions, but on the other hand it would be unsatisfactory to assume that most of those who did not reply were in favor of the scheme. It was evident that the insurance rates offered through the consortia were attractive to the small and medium shippers, who numerically ran into thousands, but considerable opposition came from large or very large firms, both in the United Kingdom and Australia, who were able to negotiate more favorable rates through their existing brokers. This, together with the argument put forward by owners of low-risk cargo that they would be subsidizing the rates enjoyed by owners of high-risk cargo, led to the reluctant decision by ACT/OCL, on 21 October 1968, that they could not proceed with the scheme. The conventional type bill of lading was retained, suitably modified, and the sea carriage was again governed by the Hague Rules, while the inland transport by road or rail was under the jurisdiction of the appropriate acts and conventions, making it once again necessary to determine at which stage of the journey the loss occurred.

It will now be seen that if the problems of shipping by container on a through basis are solved by issuing a through combined transport document, another set of problems will immediately be created due mainly to the reluctance of the banks and insurance market to modify customs that have evolved over a considerable period of time. Partly in order to maintain a frequent and regular sailing schedule, shipping companies have come together to pool their container resources through the formation of consortia. Cargo for shipment by a consortium will be forwarded on a continuous basis to a container terminal or inland depot, not always for shipment by a specific vessel as used to be the case when forwarding cargo to a berth working a break-bulk vessel, but more usually with the intention of it being shipped by the next container vessel having spare capacity. Container cargo will therefore merely be "received" for shipment at the terminal or depot, and if it is desirable for a bill of lading or other transport document to be issued at the time of receiving, instead of later on at the time of actual shipment on board a vessel, the bill or other document will have to be a "received for shipment" one.

Banks though are often hesitant about advancing credit against a "received" bill and prefer a negotiable document specifying that the goods have actually been "shipped on board" a stated vessel. The need for such absolute documents of title however is becoming less, and large companies trading amongst themselves will usually only need a receipt for the goods issued by the carrier. Similarly goods are now usually sold to a specific buyer, instead of being sold while in transit, and there is less need for a negotiable bill of lading, i.e. one consigned to "order" and endorsed in blank by the shipper thereby allowing title to the goods to be obtained by any subsequent party at the discretion of a bank acting under instructions from the shipper. Combined transport documents will therefore often be acceptable to the shipper and the consignee when their function is restricted to being a receipt for the goods, and evidence of a contract of carriage only. But even in cases where a "received for shipment" document is acceptable to all the parties, it may be impossible to issue one without qualifying clauses. If the manufacturer packs his own FCL container at his premises, and the contents are not examined by the shipping company prior to shipment, the shipping company will be obliged to clause the bill of lading "said to contain according to shipper's load and count". In a similar way if a container is packed by a freight forwarder or consolidator with cargo originating from a number of different shippers, the shipping company will clause the bill "said to contain among other shipments goods described by the shipper thereof as follows". To obtain an unclaused "received for shipment" bill of lading it will therefore be necessary for the shipping company to pack the goods itself, as would be the case with LCL shipments forwarded to an inland terminal operated by the shipping company or consortium, or to have the goods tallied by the shipping company after receipt by them of an already packed container.

Partially successful through combined transport documents, as mentioned above, do already exist. Manchester Liners offer a through bill of lading and will insure for the same length of journey as covered by the bill. The insurance certificate is still a separate document though, and that part of the charge covering the insurance premium will be fixed without reference to an individual shipper's past record of claims. Objections similar to those raised in 1968 during the attempt by OCL/ACT to issue an insured bill of lading, will be forthcoming from several shippers, and it will often be preferred in such cases to arrange one's own insurance. Most other containership operators are prepared to issue through bills of lading, but these documents will still state that while the sea carriage is undertaken subject to the appropriate Carriage of Goods by Sea Act, the haul by rail or road will be subject to the separate conventions and agreements formulated to control inland movements. Freight forwarders operating through container and trailer services between the United Kingdom and inland Continental points will issue a "house" bill of lading. These "house" bills, which are not legally valid documents because they are not supported by any act or convention, evolved following co-operation between the Institute of Freight Forwarders and the International Federation of Forwarders Associations (FIATA). They are similar in appearance to a regular bill of lading, and when issued by recognized operators with sound financial backing are often accepted as security by the banks. The operator will still receive a conventional bill of lading from the shipping company running the cross channel ferry, but this bill will probably cover a number of consignments in the one container or trailer, and will be retained by the operator. Separate bills of lading merely for the sea crossing covering each individual consignment will not have to be issued, and neither will a certificate of shipment which lacks negotiability and is therefore less acceptable by the banks than a bill of lading. The freight forwarders' bill will cover the entire journey, and will contain provisions to allow carrier-type liabilities and responsibilities direct to the cargo owner. The introduction by ACL of their electronic freight documentation system, which involves the issue of a "Datafreight Receipt" instead of a bill of lading, primarily arose following a desire to speed up the transmittal of documents and as such will be discussed in the next section.

None of the documents mentioned above are able to satisfy all the requirements of a true combined transport document, but progress is being made in developing a form acceptable to all parties. This development must take account of the increasing tendency of operators arranging, and not necessarily performing the carriage, and they must be able to issue the appropriate documents covering a through movement whether by sea, rail or road, or by combinations of all three. The combined transport operator (CTO) of the future then will often be a consolidator or freight forwarder, owning no equipment of his own but able to co-ordinate through movements with the containership companies, railway companies and road haulage firms, or he will be a shipping company probably maintaining close relationships with railway and road haulage companies. As the combined transport operator will be the party undertaking the transport, he will also be subject to liabilities similar to those of today's carriers but to a level and range that has not yet been determined. (It has been suggested that CTOs will be liable for loss or damage to cargo up to a value of £1000 per ton.) But just as a shipping company undertaking a through movement against a combined transport document will have to widen his liability to include carriage by rail and road as well as by sea, the combined transport operator will also be liable to the cargo owner for loss or damage to the cargo while under his direct or indirect control.

It has already been mentioned that the Hague Rules governing carriage of goods by sea under bills of lading are not capable of being adapted to cover the intermodal movement of containers by sea, rail, and road systems under the proposed combined transport documents. An attempt at formulating a new set of rules tailor made to through intermodal movements is being made, and a proposed text is included in the Draft Convention on the International Combined Transport of Goods (T C M Convention). The Convention was convened in 1972, and although it still remains to be concluded, it is intended that cargo owners will eventually, under the terms of the Convention, have one contract only with a combined transport operator. The draft text will be incorporated into a combined transport document, and will establish the combined transport operator as the party undertaking and being responsible for the carriage. This new conception will clarify current disputes about whether the shipping company, other carriers, or the freight forwarder should be liable for the transport, and will determine the nature of the contract between the combined transport operator and the cargo owner. It is unfortunate that political and other problems have delayed finalization of the T C M Convention, and if further difficulties arise it could take as long as ten years to reach agreement. It is in fields such as these that international co-operation is needed, and it is hoped that this co-operation will be forthcoming. In addition to the draft text of the T C M Convention, the International Chamber of Commerce have also prepared a set of rules for a combined transport document, which ranges from definitions of terminology to liabilities of the operator.

The general principle of the combined transport document has been accepted by underwriters, but they are nevertheless concerned at the difficulties that will arise in apportioning blame, in cases of loss or damage, to the negligent party. The combined transport operator will limit his liability and claims on him will fall, while the underwriter will have to settle an increased number of claims without recourse. Furthermore, if the tendency for cargo owners to restrict their insurance to liability cover only continues, underwriters will lose a large share of premiums while the cargo owner will claim from the combined transport operator for more routine losses. But this tendency may be checked if a large number of cargo owners decides to continue to place their insurance direct with underwriters because they are able to negotiate a rate more favorable than the fixed rate as offered by the combined transport operator. Over-all claims will also be kept at a lower level where the cargo owner has a direct interest in reducing his record of claims and hence his premiums, through minimizing the risks to his cargo attributable to poor packing and stowage. Personal contact between the cargo owner and the underwriter or broker will also facilitate more rapid settlement of claims than could be achieved where the carrier, who may well carry on his business overseas, is the party with whom claims must be lodged and with whom possibly lengthy correspondence will ensue.

As the proposed form of combined transport documents will be issued at the time goods are received by the operator, and not at the time of shipment, the documents will have to be "received for shipment" ones. It has already been pointed out that banks are by tradition reluctant to negotiate "received" bills of lading because the carrying vessel and date of shipment will often not be known until a later date, but the banks are now becoming more flexible. (If a letter of credit allows shipment against "received" bills of lading, the negotiating bank will honor the draft.)

Under the proposed CTO Convention rules the combined transport operator will be the party undertaking the transport, accepting liability for the cargo, and issuing the combined transport document. This document will be used as a document of title, if one is required, and should therefore be acceptable by the banks even when issued by freight forwarders.

Faster Transmission of Documents

The more immediate concern of shippers and receivers of containerized cargo is the need for reorganization and simplification of documents currently in use. A standardized and aligned system of export documents was introduced by the then Board of Trade in 1965, following the establishment of a national committee of shipping, banking, exporting, and Government interests, and involved the cutting of a "master" document from which bills of lading, insurance certificates, certificates of origin, shipping notes, customs entries, and other documents could be prepared. The committee of 1965 was known as the Joint Liaison Committee on Documentation (JLCD), was made into an official board in 1970, and was renamed the Simplification of Trade Procedures Board (SITPRO).

SITPRO reported in May 1970 and called for standardization of documentation between merchants, shipping companies, port authorities, banks and insurers, etc., principally to pave the way for the introduction of computerized systems. The report indicated that export cargo was often held up prior to shipment while the documentation was being prepared, and that clearance in the buyer's country was likewise delayed while the documentation, which would often have to be negotiated by a bank, caught up with the goods. Merchants have always relied on the postal system to transmit documentation, which would involve despatching the cargo first of all, and then attending to documentation, knowing that airmail post would overtake the vessel and be available at the port of discharge prior to the vessel's arrival. But it was evident that delays as outlined in the SITPRO report would worsen with the faster transit times, especially on the North Atlantic, of the new containerships, and a quicker method of transmitting bills of lading, or an alternative to the bill of lading system would have to be found. The interests of SITPRO had thus widened, and it was the Committee who pointed out that delays in issuing bills of lading were often due to a lack of information accompanying goods delivered to the docks. The Port of London Authority therefore issued in April 1970 a new aligned shipping note containing similar information that the final bill of lading would show, and it was possible for the shipping companies to release bills sooner than had formerly been the case.

Release of bills of lading will also be quickened when they are prepared at an inland terminal or containerbase following receipt of the cargo. It would then not be necessary to wait for dock returns showing particulars of cargo actually loaded on board the vessel, but the bills would of course be "received for shipment" ones. Although banks will not usually advance credit against such a bill, officials of the Deutsche Bank stated in October 1970, following a meeting with one of the North Atlantic containership operators, that they were willing to accept for negotiation "received for shipment" bills of lading for cash against documents transactions.

An ability to obtain bills of lading quickly is to be welcomed, but it must also be possible to transmit the bill, or the information contained in it, without delay especially over the shorter deep sea routes. If the buyer is not in possession of the bill by the time the vessel arrives at the port of destination, release of the cargo may be delayed and heavy rent and demurrage charges will become due. This situation, which is potentially of considerable harm to the cargo owner, has been brought about following the desire of the containership companies to continually speed up transit times, in an effort to attract more cargo to their particular line. The benefits to the cargo owner of quicker sailing times, especially over trades such as the North Atlantic, are doubtful, and where delays during clearance of cargo have occurred due to circumstances outside the cargo owner's control he should not be presented with a bill from the shipping company for demurrage. The scale of this demurrage anyway, which will often exceed £100 per container, is wildly excessive, and steps should be taken

FIGURE 12 OCL cellular containership *Liverpool Bay* (Courtesy of Overseas Containers Limited).

to curb the misplaced power of some shipping conferences who are trying to enforce payment against the better judgement of some of the individual shipping lines.

An alternative to the bill of lading is the electronic freight documentation system, as introduced by Atlantic Container Line in May 1971. This was a real attempt by ACL to reverse the trend whereby new cargo systems were developing at a faster rate than new documentation systems, and involved the replacement of the traditional bill of lading by a non-negotiable receipt. The receipt was to be known as a Datafreight Receipt and is signed and returned to the shipper on receipt by ACL of the cargo. ACL then transfers the information in the receipt to the port of delivery by computer, where the receiver of the cargo is notified of its impending arrival. On presentation by the receiver to ACL of the notice of arrival, the goods are surrendered, and demurrage charges due to late arrival of documentation are avoided. While ACL retain the liabilities and exemptions contained in a bill of lading, they will still issue bills to those traders who must possess a negotiable document to satisfy, for example, letter of credit re-requirements.

The application of electronic data processing systems to container shipping is in its infancy. Apart from the necessity of the cargo owner being able to transmit documentation quickly, there is also a need for the shipowner to keep his paperwork moving at a faster rate than his vessels. Unless the terminal operator in the country of importation or transhipment is in full possession of disposal instructions, he will not know whether containers should be on forwarded by rail or road, or whether they are for local distribution. Terminals will soon become congested and containers will be delayed. These sort of difficulties could be overcome if a computer link up were established between the terminals in various countries and container movements would be fully controlled. Computers can also be used to collect and assemble information required prior to preparation of bills of lading and manifests, and this information will then be available for transmission to the port of destination promptly. Vessel loading will be fully computerized in the future and information of all types will be supplied to management for decision taking.

Chapter 7

Effect on Other Groups

Traditional Services

The complex business of moving cargo from one country to another has always depended on the activities of a multitude of specialized firms. The forwarding agent would gather all the necessary information about the consignment to be shipped, attend to much of the documentation, and instruct the exporter where and when to forward his goods to meet a suitable vessel. The export packer would crate the consignment in a suitable way to withstand handling and shipment. The road haulage operator would move shipments between the docks and the exporter's or importer's premises. These firms had been built up to attend to those parts of the movement of cargo that were outside the jurisdiction of the break-bulk shipowner. But during the development of containerization, it was clear that many of these firms would no longer be required to perform their traditional roles in the handling of goods if the newly formed consortia of shipping companies were to accept the responsibility for the through movement, and if they were to use their own intermodal equipment for the carriage of cargo between sellers' and buyers' premises. Considerable concern was shown by many groups and firms who were desirous of maintaining their long-established practices and opposition to the changes grew. This opposition was not necessarily against the new systems themselves, but was more often evident due to an inherent unwillingness to accept any radical change and, in the case of dock labor, because of the threat of redundancies and due to non-dock labor handling container cargo. The

116

decline in break-bulk shipping services would lead to the closure of many wharves, and the need for dock labor would become less. The formation of containership consortia and larger shipping groups, in conjunction with cuts in shipping services to many of the smaller ports, would mean less employment for ships' agency firms and loading brokers. To survive, those groups and firms adversely affected by the containership would either have to depart from the world of marine transportation, develop new skills in the peripheral areas of distribution, or operate their own container or trailer services.

The Conventional Owner

The break-bulk carrier operating conventional vessels is the party most likely to be directly affected by the growth in containerization but he is also the party more able to change his mode of operations. But break-bulk services will continue to be run, not only in those trades where containerships are currently operating, but also in trades unsuited to containerization. A lack of modern handling facilities in the ports and an underdeveloped rail or road system will generally preclude any large-scale build-up of containerized traffic and, in these trades, the break-bulk operator will either have a monopoly of the trade or face competition from the more flexible roll-on roll-off or LASH systems. Many ports are equipped with, and will continue to use, shore cranes with a limited lifting capacity and many other ports are so badly equipped that ships' derricks have to be used. Some ports, especially in the West African trade, are still worked using the "surf boat" method whereby, due to the lack of deepwater harbors, cargo is discharged overside to small barges and other assorted craft to be transported, with luck, to the shore. The break-bulk owner will also cater for the needs of shippers of traffic not suited to containers such as extra long or heavy units, and items with two dimensions in excess of the square internal measurements of a container.

A drawback in using break-bulk methods, when compared to a containerized service, is the reliability inevitably placed upon the labor intensive operation of physically loading and unloading the ship. Less labor is required to work a container port, and the employment of a higher paid and more highly skilled work force should lead to loading and unloading being carried out relatively free from the disruptive effects of constant labor disputes. It could be argued that a better service will therefore be offered to merchants who support the container operators, but the lines running break-bulk vessels point to the multitude of sailings out of different United Kingdom ports, some of which ports will have varying working conditions and agreements, as well as the competition that will result between the lines for the available cargo. This competitive nature will be less apparent where the lines group themselves into a consortium.

In contrast with the containership operators who, as already mentioned, have to restrict their ports of call, the break-bulk owner is able to call at many ports. This ability is especially valuable in those trades where many countries will be served, and where the movement of cargo between one country and another may be impossible due to geographical conditions, or difficult due to political relations. For example, vessels capable of this freer movement will operate from India through the Bay of Bengal down to the Malacca Straits and Singapore, on to the South China Sea, Hong Kong, the Philippines and along the Asiatic coast bordering the Pacific Ocean. Although part of this area is covered by the Far Eastern container service, which will be examined in Chapter 8, it will be a long time before most of the remainder of it will be in a position to finance the capital investment required to develop new port and terminal facilities.

The break-bulk operator then will either have a trade monopoly, usually involving a less developed country where handling facilities are poor, or will run a parallel service with containership, roll-on roll-off, or LASH lines. Cargo types will therefore often overlap among the different shipping methods but the resultant competitive nature of the trade will have a beneficial effect. Admittedly, the versatility of break-bulk vessels permits the shipping of many extremes of cargo, either below or on deck, from a few cartons of tinned food up to a London bus. The validity of this argument though is limited when it is realized that approximately 80% of general cargo is suited to carriage by container. Although there are trades where containerships are soon to be put into service, such as South Africa, other areas such as the

Persian Gulf have not even been considered as suitable for containerization. Break-bulk vessels will therefore continue, for variable periods of time, to serve a great number of trades and medium-term competition will be forthcoming, not so much from the containership as from the roll-on roll-off, LASH, pallet ship and groupage operators.

It cannot be denied though that where the containership has become the dominant mode of maritime transportation, several break-bulk carriers have had to completely withdraw or convert to a container system. Because of fewer opportunities for conventional shipping out of North American ports, both Pacific Far East Lines and United States Lines have had to begin converting some of their break-bulk vessels into tankers, and this process may continue now that the shipment of war goods to Vietnam has ceased. But if the process of containerization of a trade is taken to excess, as has happened in the Pacific, the resultant state of overtonnaging will adversely affect the containership operator, while the break-bulk shipowner, who is often dealing in cargoes unsuited to containerization anyway, will be less affected.

In spite of the withdrawal of a number of conventional services, the impact of the container on break-bulk shipping has been less than was at first thought. Break-bulk does not require massive investment in specialized ships and shore handling facilities, and neither does it require the containers themselves which may number up to three times the capacity of each container vessel. A container vessel is unable to ship cargo unsuited to stowage in a container, but a break-bulk vessel will often have one or more of her holds converted to accept containers. Where varying cargo types are being moved, or where limited shore handling facilities exist, but where at the same time a country is fast developing her port, rail and road systems, there will be ample scope for the semi-containership or part converted break-bulk vessel able to carry cargo conventionally and by container. Part of the West African trade is being shipped by such vessels, and Harrison Line are running vessels from Liverpool to the US Gulf capable of shipping container and break-bulk cargo.

Although many former conventional short sea operators who were running services between the United Kingdom and the Continent had to abandon their sailings, and run road trailer or container services instead utilizing the smaller number of roll-on roll-off ferries or cellular containership operators for the sea crossing, several other lines have managed to continue their services and are often thriving. Generally the shorter the sea crossing, the more competitive will the trailer and short sea containership operators be. It is of little use maintaining a labor intensive port handling system at either end of a very short sea crossing to transfer cargo between ship and shore when a similar transfer between manufacturer and road or rail haulier has already taken place, and a further transfer between road or rail and buyer is yet to come. The use of a road trailer or container, whether the cargo be a full load or groupage, will avoid individual handling of small pieces at the ports, and total transport costs should be less. But in trades where the sea crossing is relatively longer than the inland haul, the short sea operator will often find that his vessels are running to capacity. For example, General Steam Navigation is still running break-bulk services to France, Portugal and Italy out of Shoreham, and Hispania Maritime is operating similar vessels to Spain using a private wharf in London. Both lines are achieving fast vessel turnrounds at trouble-free ports, and it is largely this ability of maintaining good dock labor relations that has contributed to their success. Larger ports, with many restrictive practices, are often not flexible enough in supplying labor to a small short sea line, and their level of charges on both vessel and cargo is sometimes prohibitively high. Containership operators however are able to avoid some of the effects of high port charges by consolidating cargo into containers at inland terminals, and merely using the port to transfer the already packed containers between shore and ship.

The rapid development then of containerization over the last 10 years has sometimes meant that trades more suited to break-bulk methods are being served by containerships and indeed some other trades are supporting roll-on roll-off or LASH vessels when break-bulk ships or a combination of two or more different types would suit the trade better. While several cargo owners have shown a preference to use break-bulk vessels, and others are in fact reverting back where the alternative is available, some shipping companies are reviewing the situation and they will be more cautious in introducing new tonnage in the future. A decision to containerize a trade must be taken only after assessing the state of development of the countries involved, especially with regard to port facilities and rail and road links, and also after determining whether or not the terrain of the country will permit the inland transportation of individual units having a length of over 40 feet and a loading of up to 20 tons.

Pallet Ships

Palletization has been used for many years in the carriage of break-bulk cargo, and is also widely used for assembling cargo into unit loads of a manageable size prior to containerization. But the pallet is also used as the basis for a system of shipping in its own right, and distribution systems have become established among manufacturers and buyers involving palletization of cargo at a shipper's premises, for through delivery to the consignee's premises, utilizing in some trades purpose-built pallet vessels.

Specialized pallet ships may be custom-built at less than half the cost of a cellular container vessel, or an existing conventional break-bulk vessel may be converted at a moderate cost. These specialized ships are equipped with side doors large enough for a complete unit load (the cargo on its pallet) to pass through. The vessels, which predominate in the Scandinavian countries, are capable of rapid loading and discharge, as horizontal handling of cargo will be quicker and more efficient than vertical handling by crane. Fork lift trucks will transfer cargo between quay and vessel, and similar trucks will stow cargo in the vessel's holds. Damage to palletized cargo shipped by break-bulk vessel could at times be considerable, especially when access to holds was difficult and careless loading and/or discharge was in evidence. It was not unusual for palletized bag cargo to suffer a deep vertical tear, following violent contact with narrow hatchcovers and metal projections, which extended from top to bottom of the unitized load. But where pallet vessels are employed this type of damage will be practically eliminated due to the more positive aspect of loading and discharge through the side doors. The use of sturdy non-expendable pallets will also help cargo to travel more safely and if a market can be found for them after shipment in the country of destination, the extra cost over expendable pallets may be recouped. Cargo must be securely bound to the pallet by steel or polypropylene strapping, and in the case of bagged cargo the bags are often glued together using a dextrine solution to make the load even more stable. More recently the utilization of shrink wrapping has become popular as a means of securing goods to a pallet, and this method will also render the load waterproof, but will not afford protection from impact with other goods or objects.

As the main drawback in using break-bulk vessels for the shipment of palletized cargo is the narrowness of hatchcovers, conversion of vessels will either involve increasing the size of hatches, often considerably, or the incorporation of side doors giving access directly to the holds. While such conversions have in the past been quite commonplace, there is a tendency now to make provision for the carriage of other cargo types in addition to pallet loads. Fred Olsen, who strongly advocate the use of pallets, and who run several specialized pallet ships, are now introducing roll-on roll-off containership tonnage capable of shipping containers, trailers and private cars between the United Kingdom and Norway. P. Bork, who were also formerly purely pallet load operators, are also extending their loading capability to include the shipment of 10-foot containers, which are side loaded to their pallet vessels using fork lift trucks.

Whether a shipowner decides to carry purely palletized freight, or a combination of pallets and other types, the aim will be to reduce over-all operating cost, and indeed stevedoring costs for pallet loads will be considerably less than charges for stowing aboard a conventional break-bulk vessel in smaller pieces. Break-bulk costs for loading, stowing and discharge of predominantly nonpalletized loads will often account for half of an owner's operating cost. As well as lower stevedoring charges, other charges for handling cargo throughout a palletized system will be less. Although labor rates cannot be cut, labor costs can by the elimination of the necessity to handle each individual carton or bag each time it is moved from one part of the system to another, e.g., between the factory and the road vehicle or between the quay and the vessel. The extension of a palletized system into domestic distribution and warehousing will also allow considerable cost

savings and it is this type of through movement of palletized loads that the shipping companies and port authorities are trying to encourage. If cargo has to be palletized by the shipping company at a terminal or berth prior to shipment, a large part of the possible savings in handling charges will be lost. To obtain maximum benefit the pallet load should be assembled at the works of the manufacturer, and should remain as a unit load until received by the buyer abroad. The load will then be suitable for fully mechanized handling and labor costs will be reduced. It has in fact been estimated that if all suitable break-bulk cargo not capable of being containerized were made up into unit loads, several million pounds would be saved annually. It is the prospect of achieving cost reductions of this scale that may encourage industry to make more use of the pallet, whether the cargo is to be containerized or not, and a direct way of benefiting is to take advantage of incentives offered by the shipping companies and port authorities.

The saving in labor charges, coupled with a greater hourly throughput of cargo than could be achieved through handling and stowing small single pieces by crane and by hand, will allow the shipping companies to give incentives to owners of palletized cargo in the form of cheaper freight rates or the free transit of pallets. Containership companies for example will often give an allowance on the freight, whether the cargo is LCL or FCL, equivalent to the depth of the pallet base for measurement cargo, or to the weight of the pallet base for weight cargo. Similarly port authorities are now far more active in offering discounts against wharfage charges where through palletized cargo is offered, and these discounts will sometimes be quite considerable. The motivation behind such incentives is to allow the full mechanization of that sector of cargo capable of assembly into unit loads, but currently being delivered to the ports in smaller pieces, and a consequential streamlining of port systems.

Palletization may then be an alternative to containerization, or a method of facilitating the loading of container cargo. Merchants unable to fill a container and reluctant to ship LCL may well be inclined to adopt a system of palletization, and it may indeed be physically impossible for some shippers and receivers to accept a 20- or 40-foot container at their premises due to space limitations or because of problems of access for large vehicles. Port authorities handling palletized cargo will not have to instal specialized handling equipment, as use will be made of fork lift trucks and conventional cranes, both of which will be standardized port equipment throughout the world. When pallet loads are consigned on a through basis using a system developed around the pallet load, consolidation and de-consolidation will not occur, and charges associated with stowing and de-vanning LCL container cargo will not arise. It is in fact maintained by the Unit Load Council, whose findings have also been substantiated in a report issued by the Economist Intelligence Unit, that in some cases door-to-door shipment of palletized cargo will be cheaper than shipment by either break-bulk methods or by container methods. Over certain trade routes this may well be the case, but the more widely held view is that palletized cargo shipped by container will offer optimum savings. This latter view has probably been formulated though after an appreciation of the dominant position of containerized shipping in the main trading routes over palletized shipping systems. As container shipping has grown, break-bulk alternatives, especially on the short sea routes, have declined or become nonexistent, and the shipper of palletized cargo in insufficient quantities to fill a container or trailer is being forced into using the groupage operators, who in turn are utilizing the short sea cellular containerships or the roll-on roll-off ferries. As the groupage operators have adopted a sliding scale freight tariff, in contrast to the generally fixed rate per ton tariff irrespective of quantity, of the former short sea break-bulk operators, the shipper of smaller loads will find himself in a less favorable position with regard to costs than he was when he was able to ship break-bulk. Admittedly a large part of the groupage operator's cost will be accounted for by the inland part of the journey, but the disparity between the small and large groupage consignment, whether palletized or not, will also be apparent over port-to-port routes as illustrated by the London to Paris trade, which would traditionally have been carried by conventional vessels sailing directly out of London and discharging at a wharf at or near Paris.

As the pallet ships are generally looked upon as an alternative to containerization, they are not intended to directly compete with container systems but offer instead an alternative way for merchants to ship their wares. They will predominate away from the container routes and concentrate on those trades where cargo types travel perfectly satisfactorily by pallet, and where the facilities possessed by merchants are not ideally suited to container handling. The Scandinavian countries are one such area, and Norway in particular is enthusiastic over the system. A report from Norway indicates that in such trades as the South Africa to Australia run, where the quantity of cargo moving does not warrant the use of containerships, a unitized system based on the pallet would be as effective as, and cheaper than a containerized system. This opinion is borne out when handling speeds achieved working pallet ships are compared with speeds of container cargo handling. By using fork lift trucks in the holds of pallet ships, as well as on the quay, a handling speed of up to 300 tons per hour may be achieved while cellular containerships will seldom exceed 250 tons per hour.

It is possible that the jump from break-bulk shipping to container shipping has been too radical, and had it not been for the over-rapid growth of the container concept, a better compromise might have been the wider development of the more flexible pallet ship. There would then have been less necessity to introduce systems equally as expensive as the container system, such as the LASH barges, to provide a "new" method for cargo unsuitable for containerization. But the container system soon became firmly established, after some pushing from American shipping circles, and this influence is still having an effect today. Even in Scandinavia shipowners began to doubt the wisdom of further development of palletized systems, and several owners, fearing they would not be able to compete with the cellular vessels, invested quite heavily in containership and roll-on roll-off vessels at the expense of further pure pallet ships. Many other Scandinavian owners, influenced in part by American shipping policy, are converting their side loading pallet ships to semicontainer vessels. Unquestionably it would have been far more economical in the short term to develop world-wide shipping services based on the unit load principle, but whether the system would be able to cope in the longer term with the increasing amount of world trade is less certain. Whether the container or the pallet was to be the basis of future cargo shipping, it is better that a fairly universal standard, in the event represented by the container, was adopted, but it is unfortunate that this adoption has prevented the system of palletization from showing how it could have stood up to today's shipping and cargo handling requirements.

The Export Packer

The export packers are another group that will be affected by containerization. During the days of conventional shipping, most cargo other than bagged materials, palletized shipments, and loose pieces not requiring protection, required a strong wooden crate to ensure safe arrival at the importer's warehouse or factory, and specialized packing firms were established to undertake this work. Using a container on a through movement some of the risks to which cargo was formerly prone, especially those associated with rough handling at the docks, will be reduced, but the container should not be regarded as a method of transport whereby damage is eliminated. Container vessels will still have to cope with heavy weather, and will thus still pitch, yaw and heave whilst at sea. Road vehicles will continue to inflict violent pressures on cargo, even though in a container, due to braking, vibration and even dropping of the container itself. Some degree of protection will still be necessary, but to what extent will depend on the type of cargo. The ideal situation, as far as the cargo owner is concerned, is to have his consignments packed in cartons capable of being loaded in a container to fill completely its cubic capacity. This would prevent any movement of the cargo during shipment and would reduce to a minimum risks of damage during transit. Unfortunately, however, not all cargo owners are able to use cartons, and many shipments of a deadweight nature will reach the weight limit of the container before all the available space is used. In these cases, efficient chocking will help to prevent movement, but most shippers will take the precaution of providing some means of protection to avoid damage by other cargo breaking loose in the container. It may be thought wise to use a proper export crate, but this should be avoided where possible due to the greater weight factor which could well increase the likelihood of cargo shifting, and instead a better system for securing should be used together with the utilization of a skeleton crate made up merely of battens to prevent superficial damage. The export packer will therefore still be needed, but his function will in part change from solely building crates, to advising shippers and implementing these recommendations with regard to the most suitable protective measures required for each particular consignment. He will particularly be in demand at the inland terminals where groupage loads are assembled prior to shipment by container, and his specialized knowledge of all types of cargo, and the damage to which they are most prone, will be of the utmost use in packing different types of commodity into one container.

Domestic Road Haulage

It was to be expected that the domestic road haulage industry within Britain and other countries would have to change its method of operating following the growth in container traffic. The smaller firms based near the ports would find that much of their former break-bulk cargo had been transferred to carriage by container, and their dock delivery and collection services would have to be curtailed. Whereas the break-bulk shipping lines would accept cargo for shipment at a port, and discharge at a port, leaving the inland carriage to be arranged by the cargo owner, the containership operator will usually have an interest in the cargo during delivery to the vessel and during carriage to the buyer, in addition to the sea crossing.

The containership company's requirements regarding inland carriage will be satisfied in two main ways. If the company decides to operate the chassis system, where containers can be made mobile at any time through being mounted on a trailer at the terminal, the trailers will either be owned by the shipping company or leased to them by one of the leasing firms mentioned earlier. Independent hauliers will still be required though to haul the trailer to and from the terminal. Alternatively the shipping company will dispense with owning its own trailers and employ a road haulage company instead to supply the trailers and tractors and to undertake the haulage. The road haulage operator who is willing to build up and is able to intensively use a fleet of tract-ion units, or tractors and trailers, and to operate under contractual conditions, will be assured of a regular flow of containers, and will not have to pursue a limited amount of traffic on his own account. The shipping company will often dictate the type of trailer to be used by the haulier, specifying for example that the container be secured to the trailer using twistlocks and not chains. The haulier will therefore often find his range of operations severely restricted, and if the containership company decides to alter its ports of call, the haulier may be left without any custom at all. Added to this will be the necessity to offer very competitive rates to the shipping company, but generally a pattern of small but constant returns will be evident.

If the haulier wishes to spread his activities more widely he may utilize his depot, in association with a containership company or freight forwarder, as a terminal for handling LCL deep sea container traffic, or as a depot for the basing of a Continental road haulage operation. Cargo will be generated by the container-ship company or by the freight forwarder, and the haulier will again be acting as a subcontracted party to his principal, and will have very little say in the running and future development of the operation. As a safeguard the haulier may decide to run dual-purpose trailers with retractable twistlocks, and he will then be able to switch from container carriage to general haulage as conditions change. Other fields open to the haulier will involve the collection from and feeding to of containers generated by the Freightliner system and the United Kingdom haulage of con-tainers and trailers crossing the cross channel ferries on a non-driver accompanied basis.

The Freight Forwarder

With the introduction of containerization it was thought that those firms largely responsible for the co-ordination of the re-quirements of the cargo owner and the shipping company, former-ly known as forwarding agents, but now referred to as freight forwarders, would have little part to play in the new transporta-tion systems. The role of the forwarding agent had traditionally been to attend to the multitude of steps necessary in moving a consignment from the exporter's premises to the dock and subsequent shipment by a suitable vessel. Inland haulage and crating could be arranged by the agent, and he would attend to the preparation and lodging of bills of lading and customs entries, and attend to the varying documentation requirements of different countries. But the advent of through movements, not only in the deep sea trade, but also in the short sea routes to the Continent, brought the opportunity of arranging door-to-door transit of cargo sold on a free delivered basis. It was feared that much of this traffic would be handled by the organization actually running the service, and relationships for example between the container-ship lines and the cargo owner would strengthen, while relation-ships between the forwarding agents and the cargo owner would weaken. While there has definitely been a tendency for shippers to deal directly with the container lines, especially when FCL cargo is involved, there has also been a tendency for the forwarding agents, or freight forwarders as they prefer to be called, to use the container system to strengthen their own positions and to upgrade their activities. Many freight forwarders have become combined transport operators, consolidating cargo into full loads and arranging for its carriage worldwide, while others have special-ized in purely break-bulk shipping. The freight forwarder will therefore still perform the traditional role of the shipping and forwarding agent, but he will also have to develop "back-up" ser-vices for the container lines. He may consider building up his own fleet of road vehicles and enter the highly competitive world of European haulage, or he may decide to subcontract all the traffic he generates. The modern freight forwarder will also be obliged to either open his own warehouse, or to arrange storage on behalf of his client who may be situated in this country or abroad. These changes have inevitably involved a shaking out process, and those agents not possessing specialized knowledge, or unable through lack of finance or management skill to alter their func-tions, have had to cease trading or have become absorbed by larger groups.

The more important role now undertaken by the freight for-warders has meant that systems have had to be updated and new techniques adopted. Connection by telex is obligatory, and the larger agents are showing an awareness of the advantages of data processing. The computer will be used to process internal information, to handle documentation, and to transmit cargo and conveyance data between offices in different countries. New management techniques will often mean a re-organization of office methods, and the formation of larger groups will affect the traditional pattern of working and responsibilities still further. The service given by these radically altered agents may suffer following an obsession with introducing lines of responsibility, usually influenced by American practice, whereby the old system of an individual dealing with all the requirements of a number of firms, is substituted by departments within an agency specializing in one geographical area only. It is appreciated that where trailers have been put into service on United Kingdom/Continental routes, the loading of these trailers is facilitated when cargo information is channeled directly from the cargo owner to the appropriate department of the freight forwarder, but it is a pity that the system prevents an employee of the freight forwarder from obtaining complete knowledge of a firm's overseas trading activities, and of the products it deals in.

Either through owning his own equipment, or by subcontracting to haulage companies running Continental road services, the freight forwarder will usually advertize a part and full load service between the United Kingdom and the Continent. Good agents abroad will be necessary and branch offices in the United Kingdom will enable full coverage to be given to potential traders. Whereas a shipping and forwarding agent would normally arrange transportation of cargo through a shipping company, and the contract would be between the shipping company and the cargo owner, the freight forwarder will be acting as a combined transport operator and will enter into contractual obligations directly with the cargo owner. This situation will arrive irrespective of whether or not the freight forwarder is operating his own equipment. After a non-operating freight forwarder has obtained Continental trailer business and subcontracted it to a haulier, it has not been unknown for the haulier to approach the cargo owner direct and offer a more competitive rate, but a reputable operator who may have several agreements with other such firms for subcontracting, will be bound by a code of goodwill and will not knowingly encroach on another's territory.

Although many freight forwarders now advertize "sailings" to overseas destinations, it will invariably be found that they are in fact utilizing the services of containership lines, and are channelling cargo to the lines. In such instances the freight forwarder will charge the shipper the normal conference rate, and the shipping company will deduct an amount equal to the freight forwarder's commission when debiting freight to the forwarder. It is felt by several freight forwarders that their role of combined transport operators should be extended in cases where they have been instrumental in obtaining cargo for shipment, and that the containership companies should concentrate on ship management. It is maintained that the freight forwarders are in closer contact with shippers and importers, and that they have more time to attend to the varying requirements of the cargo owners and to advise them regarding the best method of shipment for particular consignments. The role of the shipping company and the freight forwarder will therefore overlap, but more co-operation between them would enable them to assist each other, especially where LCL traffic is involved. It is the freight forwarder who has the expertise to deal efficiently with LCL cargo, and he should be encouraged by the shipping company to develop such traffic, while the shipping company itself concentrates more on full container loads. Such a policy would help to reduce congestion at container terminals by spreading the consolidation and de-consolidation of containers over a wider area through increased usage of inland terminals. In addition to the handling of deep sea containers prior to shipment by the container vessels, inland terminals maintained by freight forwarders are also used for handling Continental road trailers and rail wagons. The terminals are usually established by a consortium of forwarders, and will ideally have Customs officers in attendance, and will also offer storage facilities wherever possible.

For a freight forwarder to function as an independent body, and to give proper advice to his client, he should avoid becoming directly involved in running vessels. Instead he should have access to all possible alternative shipping methods, and evaluate their suitability or otherwise for a particular movement of cargo. Unless he intends to specialize in acting as loading broker for a number of overseas shipping companies, he should also avoid the agency side of shipping, so that he is not unduly influenced by shipping companies. Where a more specialized service exists though, such as the operation of road vehicles to Eastern Europe and the running of the Trans-Siberian Railway through Russia, the freight forwarder will perform a valuable service by giving information to shippers and offering through rates to destinations formerly reached only in a roundabout way. The freight forwarder will, in such instances, be able to remain fairly impartial, and will not be affected by the policies as adopted by Transfesa, the Spanish consortium of freight forwarders operating rail wagons to the United Kingdom, who forbid their members to forward cargo by any means other than the rail wagon.

European Container Movements

The United Kingdom exports over 45 per cent of her foreign trade to Europe, obtains over 40 per cent of her imports from Europe, and expects to nearly double by 1980 her 1971 volume of trade. Much of this traffic used to be forwarded to a dock for shipment on a port-to-port basis by conventional vessel, and had to be on-carried in accordance with the buyer's instructions. But now most of this trade is packed either into a container or into a road trailer for through delivery to the buyer's works or to a depot close by. The container and road trailer are therefore competing with each other for the available cargo, and each has its advantages over the other.

The fully containerized system utilizing the short sea cellular-type vessels employs expensive and up-to-date port authority equipment of the type already described. The containers are packed at the exporter's premises, or at a container terminal, and make use of combinations of road, sea and rail means of transport during transit to the consignee. Much of this traffic will be obtained by freight forwarders and channeled to the short-sea cellular containership lines, although it is not unusual for the freight forwarder most active in supplying business to a particular line to be a subsidiary company of the line, or alternatively both the freight forwarder and the shipping company will be members of a larger group. The Freightliner system will also be responsible for a large proportion of traffic shipped by the container vessels.

Port authorities are usually more prepared to offer facilities for short-sea vessels in the form of roll-on roll-off berths, as distinct from container lift-on lift-off berths, due to the far smaller capital outlay necessary and because of the reluctance recently on behalf of the lines to add to their short-sea container tonnage. Because of the dependence inevitably placed upon ancillary facilities such as terminals, dock labor and railway systems, and because of the sometimes unreliable nature of some of these facilities, the short sea container system will suffer from a lack of flexibility. If one part of the system fails to function it will often be impossible to direct the vessel to another port, as it is possible to direct road trailers at very short notice to alternative ferries, and the system will come to a stop. Container vessels themselves are also inflexible in being unable to ship road trailers, while the roll-on roll-off ferries will convey containers on flats in addition to their more normal loading of road trailers. Containership facilities will tend to be provided by ports located away from the sea, and situated for example on rivers or estuaries, while roll-on roll-off ports will be located in relation to each other so as to cut the sea crossing to a minimum. London has therefore had to provide several short-sea container berths, while Dover has concentrated on offering facilities to the roll-on roll-off ferry companies.

Members of the European Economic Community have seen trade flows amongst themselves grow following establishment of the common external tariff which has had the effect of diverting sources of supply of some goods to within the market itself. It is important that the methods of transporting this larger share of traffic are to some extent regulated to avoid an unprecedented increase in the number of road vehicles operating between the EEC countries. To this end a common transport policy has been proposed, and restrictions on the running of road vehicles would have the effect of transferring a large part of EEC trade to the railway system. France and Germany at present have particularly heavy restrictions on road vehicles, and all the member countries are subsidizing their railway systems in order that competitive rail rates may be given. These policies will encourage further development of container systems, at the expense of road trailer systems, and the building of a channel tunnel would have a similar effect if it were utilized primarily for conveying containers on rail wagons as distinct from trailers. This boosting of container movements would in turn give a stimulus to the short-sea lift-on lift-off containership owners, and such operators indeed seem unconcerned at the adverse effects that a tunnel, if it were to be built, would have on their trade.

In spite of the optimism contained in forecasts for the future of short-sea container shipping, the picture has not always been favorable. Due to poor management and a feeling on the part of the container lines that cargo would be forthcoming in ever-increasing quantities, following the enlargement of the EEC, the service given by the containership companies used, at times, to be appalling. Coupled with this were attempts at re-paying the large amount of capital investment that were needed to finance the system, and many companies found that they were not even making an operating profit. The situation was not helped by the popularity of the roll-on roll-off ferries and comparisons such as the ability of full supporting documentation to accompany the driver of the road trailers which allowed prompt clearance of the vehicles on arrival in the country of importation, while documentation could not be as readily available for container movements, aggravated the situation further. Receivers of container loads often found that their handling facilities were not suitable for the unloading of containers, and several shippers were also unable to load containers. During the period 1970 to 1971 lift-on lift-off traffic passing through the United Kingdom ports fell by 1.4 per cent, while roll-on roll-off traffic rose by 12.9 per cent. Obviously such a situation could not be maintained and many container operators withdrew services or ceased trading after substantial losses had been incurred.

During 1973 however, when the swing from container to road trailer transport seemed to signal the end of most of our short-sea container shipments, to say nothing of break-bulk methods, a swing back to container shipping was apparent. Trailer rates had been forced up by heavy demand and shortage of equipment, and in some cases stood at double the rate for a comparative container movement. Cargo owners were again looking for alternative shipping methods, and the containership operators who had managed to survive the previous lean years found that traffic was returning to their services. This revival not only affected the container lines sailing between the south and east coast ports of the United Kingdom and the Continent, but also brought increased trade to those lines serving the United Kingdom to Spain and Mediterranean trades. Following EEC legislation, this trend is bound to continue, and the scope for future growth of short-sea container shipping is illustrated by one of the major North Atlantic containership companies deciding to put cellular tonnage into United Kingdom trade routes ranging between Scandinavia and Greece.

European Roll-on Roll-off Movements

Continental railway systems, largely financed by public money, have always been subject to a substantial measure of Government protection, and used to have almost a monopoly of freight traffic. The beginning of the decline in rail freight was heralded though in Italy in 1924 with the opening of the world's first motorway between Milan and Varese, and the long-distance carriage of goods by road vehicle became possible. Motorway systems soon spread throughout the Continental countries, and the need to manipulate the flow of goods became even greater if the railways were to remain as the principal conveyance of traffic. Each country had its own ideas on how best to organize its transport systems, and separate national policies gradually evolved, often having little in common with the policies of neighboring countries.

Following the Second World War and the proposals for the establishment of an integrated Europe, the opportunity presented itself to formulate a common policy between the European countries relating to trade, transport and agriculture. Transport was chosen as a field in which a common policy should exist because of its close relationship with trade. Freedom of movement of goods would have to be supported by freedom of movement of services, such as road haulage, and it was intended that through minimizing direct control on transport prices, freedom of choice would be offered to the potential transport user. Sadly though, the EEC common transport policy is leading to more restrictions on the flow of goods carried by road vehicle, as road permits have become a necessity before journeys can be undertaken and as taxation and regulations relating to drivers' hours and vehicle loading limits have been imposed. It should be admitted though that some of the conditions such as the limitation of drivers' hours to eight-hour periods, and the requirement that two drivers should accompany vehicles when the mileage is to exceed 280, are in the interests of safety and those countries objecting are doing so purely because the new regulations mean a change from their former method of operating. These new conditions are being introduced slowly, however, to give time for the former national policies to be phased out gradually, but the ultimate adoption of all the common transport policies is bound to distort the true relationship between road and rail systems. Running parallel with the harmonization of road transport there will be a constant pressure, originating from the common transport policies themselves, to move more traffic by rail, and it is felt in several quarters that the policies are largely a means for boosting rail freight.

It is accepted though that a large proportion of freight will continue to be carried by road, but it is considered by the EEC Commission that although free enterprize is to be encouraged, it should nevertheless be subject to controls over pricing. The common transport policy assumes that the road haulage industry in its present state is subject to constant variations in price, and as such the formation of larger groups operating within a narrow tariff band would stabilize the industry. An attempt has already been made to fix prices by a system of bracket tariffs, which are regulated bilaterally between each member state, but this type of compulsory rating, which is welcomed by the less efficient haulage operators, can be used too easily to benefit the railways. If the common transport policy is to function as originally intended, there should be a move away from bracket pricing as quickly as possible to allow the free movement of prices in accordance with traffic volumes and operators' efficiency.

Prior to the Community system of permits being introduced controlling the number of vehicles passing through member states of the EEC, traffic flowing between the United Kingdom and the Continent was wholly subject to the Transports Internationale

Routiers (TIR) system. The TIR system will continue to operate alongside the EEC permit system until the end of 1976 but by this time the changeover to the EEC system must be complete. Under the TIR system, carnets are issued to international road haulage operators by the International Road Transport Union in Geneva, which allow vehicles to cross frontiers of those countries running the TIR system without extensive Customs formalities. A vehicle will undergo customs examination only in the country where the journey starts and ends, and a formal bond undertaking will not be necessary to waive duty. The method has grown rapidly from the 1950's, and approximately 700,000 carnets were issued in 1970 compared with 3,243 in 1952. Due now to the gradual replacement of the system, the current annual total has fallen back to approximately 450,000 of which 46,700 were issued to British hauliers in 1972. TIR carnets will continue to be used though for trade with non-EEC countries.

European cargo movements can therefore be divided into container shipments as described in the last section, and road trailer shipments utilizing the roll-on roll-off ferries. The more flexible nature of trailers which are free to use a number of different routes and ferries lends itself to transits where speed is more important than cost, and when trailers are driver-accompanied throughout the journey, a transit time of three days will be offered for example between Italy and the United Kingdom. Less capital outlay will be required to establish a roll-on roll-off system and in the United Kingdom, as NPC/Government approval is not required for port schemes costing less than £1 million, roll-on roll-off berths have proliferated. The system also tends to develop in areas where cargo flows differ, and in Scandinavia where large amounts of lumber are exported which are not suitable for containerization, while inward traffic consists predominantly of goods suited to containers and pallets, the roll-on roll-off vessel is able to accommodate both cargo types.

Prior to the introduction of roll-on roll-off ferries, the Continental road haulage operators never envisaged a time when they would have actively to compete with United Kingdom haulage interests. They were slow to realize the significance of the ferries as a method of entry to their market, but very soon United Kingdom firms were making inroads into Europe and were offer-

FIGURE 13 Roll-on roll-off traffic at Princess Alexandra Dock, Southampton (Courtesy of British Transport Docks Board).

ing competitive prices for the carriage of goods. This move was further boosted by the problems found at the time by the short-sea cellular containership operators, such as severe congestion at Harwich and the state of unpreparedness of some of the rail terminals on the Continent. The TIR trailer system therefore rapidly developed as cargo owners in the United Kingdom began to appreciate the speed and reliability of a method where a constant check could be placed on their goods in contrast to being given vague or totally inaccurate information by some of the container operators. Continental interests, having been used to the lorry as the most efficient means of cargo transport to neighboring countries for several years, became extremely concerned at the prospect of much of this traffic being carried by "outsiders" and provision was made for the introduction of bilateral permits aimed at curbing the growth of United Kingdom road haulage concerns. The implications of bilateral permits will be discussed presently. This growth can be illustrated by the proportion of cargo being carried between France and the United Kingdom by British haulage firms which presently stands at about 80 per cent of the total. Although much of this traffic must surely be diverted to the channel tunnel if it is built, the confidence on the part of the ferry companies in the future of trailer traffic is illustrated by the continuing activity of European Ferries in ordering new roll-on roll-off vessels to add to their current fleet of 30 vessels operating on 12 short-sea routes.

All the European administrations control the number of international road vehicles passing through their countries by operating a quota system of granting permits. The issue of bilateral permits or co-operation permits as they are sometimes called, will be regulated between the two countries concerned. A British haulier, for example, will be given a licence to carry goods to France on condition that he helps a French haulier, carrying goods to Britain, to obtain a load back to France. Bilateral agreements are restrictive in that transit is confined to the two countries concerned, and incentives may have to be given to form an agreement at all. West Germany, for example, is obliged to give two permits to a United Kingdom haulier allowing two journeys into Germany for each back load arranged for the German haulier. Entering into a bilateral agreement will often be the only way for a small haulier to begin operating between the United Kingdom and the Continent, but he will find it very difficult to expand his operations further in view of the EEC permit system. The holder of a Community transit permit is allowed to operate one vehicle at any one time on a two-way transport system between the United Kingdom and any EEC country, or between other EEC countries. Separate permits from individual governments will therefore not be required, but the United Kingdom is at present at a severe disadvantage due to the small number of permits allocated to her mainly for political reasons. Community transit permits are gradually taking over from the TIR system and both methods allow vehicles to travel freely throughout the Community without complicated border checks. Out of a total of about 1600 permits only 114 were issued to the United Kingdom in 1972 and although it was proposed to raise this number to 227 in 1974, out of an increased total of over 20,000 only 129 were in fact granted. Allocation of the United Kingdom quota to haulage firms is undertaken by the Department of the Environment, partly on the basis of previous holdings, and it is this method that tends to allow established companies to grow, while newcomers have to resort to the bilateral system. France and Germany have three times the number of Community transit permits than the United Kingdom, which is forcing United Kingdom hauliers into subcontracting much of the traffic generated by them to other EEC haulage concerns, or to establish subsidiary companies on the Continent in an effort to obtain more permits. Holland has traditionally been active in European haulage, and deserves to maintain, on economic grounds, her 40 per cent share of Europe's road traffic. It will be seen how easy it is though under the EEC system for other countries to block the issue of the required number of permits, and to gradually deplete for example the Dutch road haulage industry. It is this inadequacy of the EEC system that has been the cause of the majority of Community transits between countries unable to obtain sufficient Community permits to take place against bilateral permits, while other countries with an abundance of Community permits are using them for bilateral journeys. Due to the discriminatory and distortive effects of quotas and permits, the United Kingdom is in favor of abolishing the system, which would then make it unnecessary for permits to be forged, and would allow freedom of movement of vehicles of all EEC nationalities within the Community according to the service given and the price offered. Countries having the ability to transport goods economically would then be able to develop their road haulage industry, while other countries laid emphasis on building up industries that they were better suited to.

A 40-foot trailer or container is capable of transporting about 30 tons of cargo, but due to the limitations imposed by the EEC states on the size and weight of vehicles passing through their countries, it will seldom be possible to load more than 20 tons of cargo. The United Kingdom is particularly active in restricting axle loadings and over-all gross weights, and will only allow vehicles with an axle loading up to 10 tons and a total weight of 32 tons to enter the country. These figures conflict with the proposed EEC axle loading of 11 tonnes (10.8 tons) and total weight of 40 tonnes (39.4 tons). Even the EEC figures prohibit maximum utilization of equipment, and national policies of this type, although desirable on environmental grounds, make it impossible to obtain full benefit, not only from domestic road trailers and containers, but also from containers shipped on a deep sea basis by the containerships. To load a container or road trailer to capacity would involve the haulage of a unit with a total weight of about 44 tons, and as rail containers will usually begin and end their journey by road, they too are not being used as was intended. Britain has no intention of accepting the proposed EEC weight limits and it is this rejection at the beginning of 1973 that prompted France into blocking the issue of a larger quota of Community transit permits to Britain.

This veto continued until June 1974, and as future allocation of permits should now be on a fairer basis, and as the United Kingdom must surely accept the inevitability of the heavy vehicle, we should be constructing more by-pass and lorry routes to and from the ports with a view to accepting the proposed EEC weight limits which would not be effective anyway in the United Kingdom until 1980. Such a policy would not restrict the growth of rail traffic, but would instead encourage carriage by rail over long distances of units filled almost to capacity, in the knowledge that final delivery would be permitted by road.

Britain's entry into the EEC has boosted still further the previ-

ous annual rate of growth of roll-on roll-off traffic of approximately 30 per cent, and has led to more international road haulage
firms commencing to trade, and to the growth of existing firms.
The roll-on roll-off share of total unit load traffic between the
United Kingdom and the Continent has increased from 43.9% in
1970 to 47.1% in 1972, and in spite of the current return to favor
of the short sea container, it is expected to rise still further. While
there is a trend toward fewer but larger groups carrying a greater
share of trailer traffic, there is also ample scope for the smaller
concern to play an increasingly active role. The owner driver
is often better able to obtain back loads by offering very competitive rates, while the larger groups, even with their extensive system
of agents, will sometimes be hard pressed to keep trailers loaded
in both directions. The larger concern, who would normally have
no trouble in obtaining back loads, will find it impracticable
to cut rates to the level of the owner driver or smaller haulage
company, who will be working purely on a commission basis
perhaps with a number of freight forwarders. Shippers and importers of groupage cargo also often find that the "regularity" of
the large operator is not that regular after all, and they may
obtain a better service at a cheaper rate by going through a non-
operating freight forwarder who will have up-to-date information
on the service, which will vary as conditions change, offered by
a number of hauliers.

But the problem of the heavy lorry will remain insoluble as
groups said to be environmentalists, and others propounding the
economic advantages of moving goods in ever-increasing quantities, continue to pour forth their protestations. Much of these
disagreements would be obviated if it were realized that it is unfair to expect those people adversely affected to welcome the
lorry into their formerly fairly peaceful surroundings, after being
told that the country as a whole will benefit through lower consumer prices. The international road haulage vehicle will of necessity converge on the roll-on roll-off ports, and lorry routes should
be constructed in the vicinity of such ports, as far as possible
to avoid the town centers and areas of habitation. If the problem
of the ports can be solved in this way, and the lorries can then
be kept on the motorways and by-passes, the problem then broad-
ens out into one dominated not by the international road vehicle

but by the domestic carrier. International movements of cargo, even though more visually conspicuous, as a percentage of total movements within the United Kingdom are quite small, and more attention should be given to those manufacturers who have realized the competitive nature of moving their goods within the United Kingdom in large loads.

Dock Labor

The last major group to be affected by containerization, and the most voluble one, is dock labor. The docker has by tradition been reluctant to accept change, and has shown increasing solidarity when discussing new methods of working. These feelings have developed largely from former exploitation when dockers were hired on a casual basis by the hour, half-day or day. Regular employment did not exist and obligations on the part of employers were minimal. The need arose, which is still apparent today, to rigidly define what work was to be undertaken by casual dockers, in an effort to avoid exploitation, but with a large pool of unemployed non-dock workers only too willing to work under almost any conditions, definition was difficult to enforce. In an effort to keep outsiders away from the docks it was attempted in London to form a nucleus of genuine dockers, but due to union resistance the scheme failed. Meanwhile in Liverpool a registration scheme was introduced in 1912, whereby port employers issued metal tags to genuine dockers who were then given priority over non-dock labor when gangs were formed for the day's work. Casualization though continued, and if a docker failed to find employment his entitlement to, and level of attendance money depended on the particular port or port employer. Guaranteed wages to port workers were not generally introduced until 1947, when the National Dock Labor Scheme was set up. The scheme covered Britain's major ports of the time, and all port labor had to be registered with the National Dock Labour Board. As explained in Chapter Three, the Board controls conditions in the "scheme" ports, and the ports have to pay a levy to the Board which in turn guarantees wage rates and gives security of employment to 34,500 registered dockers. In 1947 ports such as Felixstowe, Harwich, Dover and Shoreham were considered too small to warrant inclusion in the scheme, and it is the subsequent growth of many of the non-scheme ports, which between them now employ about 2,400 men, that has prompted demands for their inclusion. Undoubtedly the introduction of the National Dock Labor Scheme was of considerable benefit to the port worker, who could now rely on a guaranteed income and who was not subject to exploitation by the port employer, but during the 1960's when container and other unit load methods of shipment were being introduced into Britain's ports, a need for dockers with specialized skills arose. To provide such labor was outside the function of the National Dock Labour Board, and indeed the Board was tending to perpetuate a level of employment higher than would actually be required with the introduction of the new cargo handling systems. As jobs were guaranteed, the structure of the scheme itself prevented any change in the size of the registered labor force, and this lack of flexibility was not conducive to initiative being shown by the docker. The Board freely admits that its function is purely to administer the scheme, and that it avoids involvement in other matters. But the need now was to abolish casualization, together with its attendant restrictive practices, and create a highly skilled labor force, working on a regular basis, and willing to accept more flexible working methods as conditions changed. Casualization was finally ended in 1967 following the report of a committee appointed earlier in 1964 under Lord Devlin.

It had been clear to the ports for some time that to remain competitive, without the help of subsidies, it would be necessary to introduce more modern working methods and to provide facilities to cater for containers and other unit load systems. If costs could not be maintained, charges would have to rise, and as the handling of containers was to be less remunerative anyway than handling break-bulk cargo, it was essential that total labor charges be cut. It was clear by 1964 that the new types of port that were envisaged would require a new employment system in order to keep pace with the rapid developments that were to come. It was to ascertain the most acceptable method of implementing these changes that the Devlin Committee of Enquiry into the Port Transport Industry was appointed in late 1964, under Lord

Devlin, to enquire into labor relations in general, and de-casualization in particular. The Committee reported in August 1965 and the proposals of Devlin are now the foundation of a radical approach to port working.

Devlin found that casual labor combined with often casual management led to disinterest on the part of the docker, that piece-work systems of working were a major cause of disputes, and that excessive overtime was frequently a means of wasting time at the expense of the employer. He maintained that de-casualization should be accompanied by higher wages for flexibility in working, that unnecessary overtime should be abolished, and that shift working should be introduced. Devlin therefore proposed that (1) regular employment of all dock workers on a weekly basis was necessary, (2) a substantial reduction in the number of employers should take place, and (3) an improvement in general welfare facilities throughout the ports was overdue. These proposals meant that employers and employees would benefit from a more permanent and personal relationship, and greater stability and security of earnings for the dock workers would follow. It would be necessary, however, for both parties to accept modernization of the industry's working practices in order to obtain more efficient use of manpower, and it was from this sphere that much of the ensuing labor unrest emerged.

The first necessity would be to end the casual system of labor recruitment, which operated alongside the regular employers such as the stevedoring firms and the port authorities themselves, whereby a labor pool existed which was drawn on by the employers to supplement their work force when required. This labor pool was used primarily by a number of occasional port employers, but Devlin pointed out that in Southampton four out of seventeen employers did 98 per cent of the work and in Bristol fourteen out of seventy-seven did 95 per cent. It was therefore clear that the needs of the smaller employers could not support a regular staff of dockers on proper terms and these groups would have to be phased out.

De-casualization would have to be followed by an over-all reduction in the size of the labor force, and by means of voluntary severance payments the number of employees was expected to fall from 60,000 in 1968 to 40,000 in 1970. Severance payments were offered to labor below the age of 65, and to finance the scheme, whereby up to £1,800 could be paid per man, £3.5 million was put aside for distribution in London and Hull alone where overmanning was most severe. The next part of Devlin, now known as Devlin Stage II, was the establishment of a two shift system of working which would be necessary to ensure that labor would be available over a longer period of time per day to handle the container vessels which would have to be turned round in a matter of hours, and not days as previously. It was also envisaged that piece-rate working would be phased out at the container terminals in favor of a structure based on a higher basic wage.

As mentioned above it was the vast modernization programmes of the port authorities that laid the seeds of the present state of unrest, and dock workers were perfectly aware that widespread redundancies would be inevitable. The International Transport Workers' Federation had reported in 1968 that on a container berth 50 men in 20 hours would carry out work previously done by 160 men in a week, and earlier in 1967 the McKinsey Report had indicated a similar situation whereby at a conventional berth 30 tons of cargo was handled per man per week, whilst at a container berth 600 tons would be handled per man per week. The expected decline in the need for labor sparked off a series of obstructions and stoppages, and demands were submitted by the unions whereby most of the advantages of a container system would be absorbed by a higher pay structure based on increased productivity. This was unreasonable in view of the enormous capital expenditure put forward by the shipping industry, which was designed to put the industry on a sounder financial footing, and indeed OCL/ACT threatened in 1969 to move their operations out of Tilbury to Rotterdam on a permanent basis, and many other services were diverted on a permanent or temporary basis to Continental ports.

The OCL/ACT dispute at Tilbury was the first of the container strikes, and was really an attempt at defining exactly what dock work was. It had always been difficult to define dock work, as it was nearly impossible to say which port employers really needed dockers, and which could manage with other types of labor. What was important was whether work should be performed by dockers, and not whether the work was dock work. It had long been a bone of contention that firms could establish premises, apparently within a dock area, and employ their own labor to carry out work that would otherwise have been undertaken by registered dockers. It was often asked, for example, whether a particular dock, used for supplying bulk commodities such as coal and timber to a plant, was an extension to the plant or whether it should be considered as a dock, and as such, liable to employ registered dock labor. The question is still being asked, and as recently as November 1973 the National Dock Labour Board tried to transfer work being undertaken at a riverside timber berth on the Humber from ordinary labor to registered dockers. The Court of Appeal ruled that the work could not be classified as dock work, and that it could be undertaken by the regular employees of the timber firm. An attempt at allaying the fears of the dockers was the appointment of the Bristow Committee, which also brought to an end the strikes of 1969. The Committee's report, published in January 1970 and welcomed by the unions, recommended that a 'dockers only' corridor should be established, stretching for five miles on either side of the Thames from Foulness to Teddington. The unions were in favor of extending the limit to ten miles where container handling was involved, but this rather unimaginative scheme, which would have embraced all manner of industries, was discarded.

The London enclosed dockers agreed to abandon piece work in 1969, in accordance with the recommendations contained in Devlin Stage II, and to accept a relatively high flat rate instead, with overtime and other extra earnings being limited to weekends and to the provision of special skills as required. A high base rate and permanent employment was thus obtained in exchange for flexibility of working and reduced manning, and the way appeared to be clear to raise productivity. Devlin Stage II was finally accepted in London following negotiations between the Port of London Authority and the unions on 29 June 1970. Two shifts would be worked, the first from 7 am to 2 pm and the second from 2 pm to 9 pm each with a 45-minute meal break, the eventual aim being the existence of a small, highly mobile, mechanically-minded labor force. Dockers' average wages had already increased from £23.50 for a 50-hour week in 1967 to £36.00 for 47 hours at the beginning of September 1970, and Devlin Stage II involved a guaranteed wage of £36.50 for a 31¼-hour week, whether or not any work existed, and a guaranteed £39 a week for men actually working. The employers' wage bill would thus be substantially greater than in 1967, and it was inevitable that charges on ships and goods would rise.

It was pointed out by the British Shippers' Council (in a letter of protest handed to the Port of London Authority on 8 September 1970), however, that these higher charges would have to be financed eventually by the cargo owners themselves, and any advantages from Devlin Stage II would benefit the shipowners and consortia using the ports, as well as dock labor. This warning proved to be justified, not because of widespread non-cooperation by port labor, but by the failure mainly of the road haulage industry to realize that they too must change their method of working to enable deliveries and collections at the docks to be made throughout the two shifts of port working. The industry was maintaining its old hours of working, and pointed to the restrictions on drivers' hours which made it uneconomic to have a vehicle and driver standing idle for most of the day waiting to make an evening visit to the docks. Dock employers also failed to deploy their men effectively, and the resulting shortage of labor during the far busier period of the first shift, resulted in delays to vehicles and uneconomic working of vessels. Vehicle delays have now been considerably lessened through the introduction and successful operation of a vehicle appointments scheme, which enables a road haulier to book a time direct with the dock, wharf, or inland terminal, for the handling of consignments.

It will be evident that the situation in the London docks immediately following the introduction of Devlin was verging on the chaotic. Partly as a result of the clashing of work periods of lorry drivers and dockers, productivity fell by one-third during the first nine months of the scheme. This decline is reflected in average weekly hours worked per man dropping from 50 to 31½, while wages rose by 20 per cent. It was taking far too long to turn vessels round, and several owners left London in favor of Continental ports where productivity was far higher and from where feeder services could be operated to the United Kingdom.

Gradually though the new methods of payment and of working were becoming more accepted, and by the end of 1971 the troubles of the docker were more associated with security of employment than with pay and conditions. It was apparent that work opportunities, even for registered dockers attached to scheme ports, were becoming less with the spread of containerization, and the opportunity was grasped by left-wing militants to expose the "precarious" position of the docker. A national dock strike followed during the summer of 1972, which embraced, through union membership, those unregistered dockers working in the non-scheme ports as well. The fact that most registered dockers were in favor of accepting guaranteed wages under the National Dock Labour Scheme during periods when work did not exist, was immaterial to the militants, and a further blow to the competitiveness of Britain's ports was struck. In an effort to avoid the strike the Government had earlier set up a joint employers-trade union committee headed by Lord Aldington, chairman of the Port of London Authority, and Jack Jones, leader of the Transport and General Workers Union, to look into the changing demands for dock labor following containerization, but at the time this action was not deemed positive enough by the strike leaders to call off the dispute, which was eventually to cost the country an estimated £8 millions.

Registered dockers cannot be sacked by law, but the value of voluntary severance payments to draw men out of the industry through payment of a lump sum, had already been appreciated by Lord Devlin. Following his recommendations, severance payments of £1,800 per man were being issued in 1971, which was twice the then national average, but due to the difficulties of re-employment in other industries, and because dockers were earning such a good wage in any case, the scheme did not bring about severance in sufficient numbers. If registered dockers were to feel that their employment prospects were really secure, it would be necessary to remove the labor surplus, and abolish the Temporarily Unattached Register. To this end the Jones-Aldington Committee recommended that severance payments of up to £4,000 be offered to dockers aged 55 and over as an inducement to leave the industry. Whether the size of payment was justified is still under debate, but the effect was that out of a total labor force of 41,000, 11,000 of which were eligible for the scheme, 8,500 applied for severance. In both London and Liverpool over 2,000 men applied and it immediately became apparent that it would be possible to abolish the pool of "unattached" men who were being paid a guaranteed £23 per week.

It was considered by many port employers that the severance payments were far too high, and that too much labor had been drawn out of the docks. The Jones-Aldington estimate of the cost of severance stood at £8-£9 millions, but in actual fact the scheme involved payment by the Government of a total of £30 millions. Of those who left many possessed special skills, which were badly needed, but due to the regular high rates of pay being obtained by dockers working the container terminals, the containership operators were little affected.

Although the burden of guaranteeing jobs was less following the departures, the problem was changed into what looked like an acute shortage of labor. Many port employers found themselves unable to obtain labor, and some had to discontinue trading. It appeared that a labor surplus had been transferred, at enormous cost, into a shortage, and although the 1972 strike had been brought to an end following Jones-Aldington, the scheme was said to have been far too radical. The Government were recommended to allow recruitment to the permanent register, but neither they, nor the National Dock Labour Board were in favor. In actual fact the real problem was not a shortage of labor so much as how labor was deployed. The gang system was still being used whereby a fixed number of men were delegated to a particular job, but while inland container depots, then being manned by unregistered labor, were able to pack and unpack a container using three men, the docks seemed unable to manage with less than six. Set alongside this it should be remembered that at this time the dock worker was earning far more than the inland container terminal employee. The result was a further fall in productivity in some of Britain's ports, and shipowners had to impose surcharges on freight rates to compensate slow turnrounds.

Apart from an over-all fall in the number of dockers required to work a containerized system, the location where some of the work is to be carried out will often change. This is the second fundamental problem, and it will arise principally where LCL containers are packed and unpacked at inland terminals, and to a lesser extent where FCL containers are handled at the premises of the manufacturer or the buyer. Although the Jones-Aldington report solved the problem of too many dockers working at the ports, it did not solve the problem of work being taken out of the port areas and being located at terminals employing non-dock labor. The reaction of the registered dockers' leaders was to refuse to handle container lorries delivering already packed LCL containers, and cases were brought before the Industrial Relations Court and the Court of Appeal involving transport companies and the unions. While the majority of the terminals agreed to employ registered dockers, some refused to do so on the grounds that they were operating quite satisfactorily without the help of dockers, however "specialized" the dockers might be. The immediate result of employing dockers at the Chobham Farm terminal in London has already been examined in Chapter Three, but perhaps the outcome, which is involving a steady movement of registered dockers out of the ports and into the terminals, was inevitable. An additional 400 jobs were found for dockers in container groupage work during the period August 1972 to November 1973, and indeed port dockers will often refuse to handle already packed groupage containers unless a labor agreement exists at the terminal where packing took place. The Jones-Aldington committee found it necessary to recommend the employment of registered dockers at inland terminals, but they also stated that where possible groupage containers should be handled in the docks. While the first recommendation is perhaps unavoidable, the second would appear to indicate a lack of understanding of one of the fundamental necessities of a container system, which requires that handling of container cargo, as distinct from full containers, should be moved out of the ports to less congested areas. Now that the principles of handling LCL containers have had time to settle and be more sensibly reviewed, the attitude of the Transport and General Workers Union is becoming less rigid, and the future may see more non-registered labor working at inland terminals.

The responsible docker is becoming more aware that many of the disputes that affected Britain's ports were groundless, and some of the left-wing extremists have been ousted. Relationships between labor and management within individual ports have become less strained, and the former countrywide feeling of solidarity is lessening. Disputes are more likely to be localized, and are often initiated by unofficial shop stewards for no reason other than a desire on the part of the stewards to obtain more recognition. The docker has for several years been amongst the highest paid of industrial workers, and his minimum wage in 1973 ranged between £41 and £47 per week depending on skills. These were minimum earnings, and actual pay could be boosted to anything between £50 and £100, but the Liverpool labor force saw fit to vote in favor of industrial action in November 1973 in support of a 20 per cent increase. This demand far exceeded the Government's Phase Three limits in force at the time, and there was initially little response from other ports until militants in London and Hull gathered support to lodge a similar demand. The London dockers wanted their basic £41.35 to be increased to £46.00 plus additionals. It is perhaps unfortunate that the dockers working at the Fred Olsen terminal in Millwall Dock, who have their own pay structure, have their two year contracts reviewed in November, and in 1973 they accepted a new level ranging between £47.25 to £52.65 depending on skills. The other unregistered dockers working at London's riverside wharves have a much lower basic wage, but with bonuses and overtime of £30-70 they can lift their basic of just over £30 to a total of between £60 and £100.

It will be apparent that the different groups of dockers, working under different pay structures, are continually watching pay developments amongst themselves with a view to correcting, when they occur, what they consider to be imbalances. As their pay is so high compared with other industries, parity differences are not their concern, but with very high rates being paid to labor manning the container terminals, there is ever present a feeling that the docker working break-bulk wharves is falling behind. In an effort to overcome such sentiments, systems have been introduced which allow a greater number of dockers to have a share in the high container pay, through working at the container berths on a rota system. But this continual upward movement of wage rates in general is bound to have adverse effects unless productivity is also rising, and charges on goods at the ports have risen in an effort to recoup higher wage costs following Devlin and Jones/Aldington.

The flexibility of labor problem is an old one, but with containership working it has become even more important because of the comparatively short period of working on each container vessel. The Devlin Report contained a flexibility of labor clause which stated that labor should move between vessels and that gang sizes should be altered if necessary. It had always been the norm for one shift to work on one ship only, and if the vessel completed loading or discharge prior to the ending of the shift the labor involved would not usually transfer to another vessel. Largely due to this sort of lack of flexibility over manning, the Seaforth container terminal at Liverpool lost over £1M during 1973, and the port authority has now warned the men that it will be unable to finance similar losses in the future. Apart from flexibility within shifts, there is also the problem of offering continuous 24-hour working to those shipping companies who desire it. When three 8-hour shifts are in operation, at least half an hour will be lost each time a shift changes, sometimes for unavoidable reasons, and in an effort to overcome this lost time Southampton is trying to introduce a four shift system to give uninterrupted round-the-clock manning at its container berths. Lack of flexibility on the part of registered dockers working in scheme ports has been one of the most important obstacles, especially in recent years, to the rapid development of scheme ports, and has been an important contributory factor to the rapid development of such non-scheme ports as Felixstowe where labor is more mobile. Owing to the increasing difficulty of defining exactly what dock work is because of the desirability of moving labor, not only between vessels, but also between vessels and adjacent terminals, the whole registration scheme is outdated and perhaps it should be amended to rid it of its rigidity, or even discarded completely.

Hull is a port where labor is largely divided. The port of Hull itself is one of the scheme ports, but its force of registered dockworkers has long been restless largely due to the activities of the several unregistered wharves along the Humber who employ non-registered dockers. The registered dockers' leaders maintain that these other wharves are "poaching" business that should by right go to them, the most recent instance being that of the handling of the BACAT cargo. The barges are loaded at upriver and canal wharves in South and West Yorkshire, before being towed to one of the unregistered wharves on the Humber for loading into the BACAT vessel. As none of this traffic is passing through the hands of the registered dockers working in the port of Hull itself, they have decided to "black" it on the grounds that work is being taken away from registered ports. Originally the Hull dockers had demanded that 20 per cent of BACAT cargo should be handled by them conventionally, but they eventually agreed to forgo this on the understanding that they could transfer 20 per cent of the cargo from one barge to another, and that six dockers would be paid between £75 to £98 per week for doing nothing. It is now maintained by the registered dockers that barge carrying systems are a bigger threat to job security than containerization, and the 2,200 Hull dockers are endeavoring to gather support amongst lorry drivers and other labor groups connected with the ancillary services for BACAT, to spread their "blacking" policy.

The attitude of the registered dockers at Hull illustrates another instance of trying to merge scheme and non-scheme ports, and at the request of the Jones-Aldington committee the National Ports Council submitted a report dealing with the differences between the two types of port in March 1973. The Council recommended to the Committee that while casual labor should be ended at the non-scheme ports there was no justifiable reason for amalgamating them with the scheme ports. Wages and conditions in the non-scheme ports were found by the Council to be as good as those in the scheme ports, but in spite of this the Transport and General Workers Union still pressed for full integration. The Union also wants a new definition of dock work, presumably to allow even more registered dockers to work at the inland terminals, but the underlying aim of the Union would appear to be more closely aligned with increasing the size of its membership and hence its power. It should be pointed out that neither the employers nor the United Kingdom Chamber of Shipping are in favor of extending the scheme, but it was announced by the Government in July 1974 that they were after all planning for the extension of the scheme to all "outside" ports.

Underlying much of the recurrent labor unrest, such as the recent one day strikes at Hull and the troubles at London and Liverpool, is a desire on the part of the docker to revert to a system of incentive bonus schemes. Devlin Stage II had much earlier recommended that piece work be abolished in favor of a higher basic wage, but now that this higher basic wage has been attained there is a feeling that it should be further inflated through the payment of "additionals". The London enclosed docker points to the system of bonuses paid to the London riverside dockers, and maintains that in future these bonus payments, which are in addition to a relatively small basic wage, will be potentially of greater benefit than a high basic wage without additionals. Any such move would be opposed by the Transport and General Workers Union and the official shop stewards, but following a strike in the summer of 1974 in Millwall Dock, London, over the payment of extra money to dockers handling "dirty" cargo, employers in London were forced into conceding extra payments for the handling of "dirty" cargo and awkward loads. Viewed alongside the quite considerable progress made in the docks over the last few years relating to shift working and regular wages for regular working, this move toward the re-introduction of bonus schemes must be regarded as a step backward.

Although recruitment of registered dockers was restricted by the National Dock Labour Board in 1966, and indeed the Board rejected any further recruitment to the permanent register in August 1973, they resumed normal recruitment early in 1974. It was originally thought by both the Board and the Government that a further situation of overmanning, as was evident prior to Jones/Aldington, should be avoided, together with the protection against dismissal which ran parallel, but following advice from the Jones/Aldington committee to the Government in November 1973 it was decided to recruit. The National Dock Labour Board is therefore trying to reduce the number of supplementary workers to ensure that a labor "pool" does not build up again, and to allow a controlled inflow of permanent men as they are required.

It is becoming increasingly recognized that the speed at which vessels are turned round at any world port entirely depends on the attitude of labor to its work, assuming that the facilities provided are adequate, and port authorities are becoming more aware of the value of operating apprenticeship or other training schemes. These schemes have been running for several years on the Continent, and they will be a necessity at all major ports where modern handling methods are being used if the right type of labor is to be attracted to the docks in the future. In addition to practical training in the dock itself, some authorities, notably the PLA, have also started training schemes for middle management which are also open to the docker. While many dockers are in favor of such schemes, neither the National Dock Labour Board nor the Transport and General Workers Union have approved, but it is through schemes such as these that the gap between management and labor might be narrowed. It is to be hoped that the Board and the Union will view the situation more realistically in future.

Dock labor problems in the USA are very similar to those found in the United Kingdom. Unrest over containerization has been growing for several years and it has become more difficult to agree new contracts with the unions as the old agreements have expired. At USA East Coast and Gulf ports longshoremen are members of the International Longshoremen's Association (ILA), while at West Coast and Hawaiian ports the International Longshoremen's and Warehousemen's Union (ILWU) negotiates pay and conditions on behalf of its members. It has traditionally been the practice when formulating new contracts, for local contracts to first be established at each port, prior to discussions starting on a master agreement for the whole area controlled by the union. It could therefore take several months of negotiation before a master contract was established and local grievances would often delay finalization. The strike of 1971 followed disagreement between employers and the unions over wages, the loading of containers at off-pier consolidation points and waterfront terminals, and wage guarantees, and due to lack of a settlement it was necessary to invoke the Taft-Hartley Act which requires that labor returns to work for an 80-day "cooling off" period while discussions continue. While it might be desirable to formulate a single pattern contract for all ports under a particular union's control, as asked for by the ILA, such a contract would strengthen still further the position of the unions as disputes would be spread over a far wider area. The "one port down, all ports down" principle would apply, and because of a localized and possibly quite insignificant grievance, a large part of the USA's overseas trade could be halted.

Work opportunities in North American ports have dropped

considerably following the growth of containerization, and in New York alone the labor force has fallen from 25,000 in 1964 to 15,000 in 1973. The ILA is trying to enforce wage guarantees based on a 40-hour week for high seniority workers and on a 32-hour week for low seniority workers, and it may be that the guarantees will have to be financed directly by the containership companies.

It has already been stated that when container cargo is handled by non-longshoreman labor, the union representing the longshoremen at the port where the container is shipped will often insist on payment of a royalty for each ton of cargo handled, and the ILA have incorporated into their contract a "50 mile rule" governing groupage containers. Under this rule container cargo originating at or destined to points within a 50 mile radius of a port, must be handled at the port by ILA labor, and containers are having to be unloaded and re-loaded again to comply with the rule. The ILA are also insisting that if a groupage container is moved off the piers to a warehouse, the cargo must remain in the warehouse for at least 30 days without being sold. This rule is to avoid importers passing cargo through a warehouse merely with the intention of avoiding ILA intervention, and should not affect cargo genuinely warehoused. If goods are sold within the 30-day period, the warehouse involved is blacklisted, and if a carrier continues to supply containers at the warehouse he is obliged to pay $1,000 to the ILA's container royalty fund. In spite of these penalties the 30 day rule is evidently ignored, and because of this the unions now want all groupage cargo to be handled at the piers, whether for eventual warehousing or not, and the 30 day so-called "good will" gesture to be abolished. In addition to shipowners having to finance a large proportion of the fines, which must inevitably be passed on in the form of higher freight rates to cargo owners, it is becoming necessary for shipowners to reject LCL traffic due to the severe congestion that is occasioned through unpacking and packing the cargo. It may be that schemes similar to those used in the United Kingdom involving the "buying off" of surplus labor, may have to be introduced in the USA and even though the cost of such schemes is enormous, they may be the only way to a long-term solution.

Chapter 8
Development Overseas

Deep Sea Terminals and Feeder Ports

The port is the most important link in through transport systems because the efficiency attained by it will have a direct bearing on the efficiency attained by the shipping company, and any malfunctioning of the port will largely be outside the control of the shipping company. The highly productive port allows vessels to turn round quickly and to spend as much time as possible at sea. It cannot be overemphasized that a vessel in port is a liability, and that it is only able to earn a return on its capital investment while at sea.

Before the advent of containerization it was not uncommon for vessels to wait up to three weeks for a berth, and even today a similar situation exists at many ports where modern handling facilities have not been provided. Shipping companies, desperately trying to become profitable enterprises, will tend to avoid such congestion, and will base their operations instead where delays are minimal. A containerized system working properly will provide an opportunity for shipowners and port authorities to benefit from a rapid throughput of cargo, and ports that provided container facilities during the early years of containerization have generally benefited from increased cargo flows, even though per ton revenues will be less than the revenue earned through handling break-bulk cargo.

Ports working conventional cranes had to either radically change their outlook on cargo handling methods by opting for a containerized system, or they had to try to improve efficiency

158

while at the same time retain their existing cranes. These were not the only alternatives, but were often the only practicable ones open to a port traditionally handling general cargo. Commitment to a fully containerized system, however, will be a hazardous undertaking for a port if firm assurances from consortia are not forthcoming of their intention to use the facilities, and when the container system, and indeed any other system, has not been fully proved as being the 'ideal' method of international transit. The advocates of palletization, for example, maintain that their system is more flexible and involves a fraction of the capital investment required in a containerized system by the ports and shipping companies. The future could thus be in multi-purpose cargo vessels carrying partly containerized and partly palletized goods, or in other combinations involving roll-on roll-off and LASH barges. Although such combinations might lead back to a state of congestion, the ports should be wary before becoming fully committed to containers.

But because of the very large sums of money already invested in containerization, and because of the optimistic views of the consortia, it can be assumed that considerable further expansion will take place. The Europe/South Africa trade is the next major area for conversion to cellular vessels, and much further in the future the Indian and South American trades may be partly containerized. To cater for the larger number of containerships many countries are already building large port complexes, where in addition to the provision of container berths, bulk handling facilities will transfer raw materials directly into plants operating within the port area. While Britain's unsubsidized ports must sound out the market before expanding, her Continental rivals, especially those in France, are taking advantage of subsidies prior to the introduction of a common EEC ports policy which would almost certainly discard all Government assistance, and are building such port complexes at an unrealistically fast rate. These complexes are often regarded today purely as prestige projects, but tomorrow they could well be handling much of the United Kingdom's deep sea container traffic, as well as rivalling established north European ports such as Rotterdam.

It used to be thought that deep sea container ports would be limited in number, and that these ports would act as a transhipment center from where feeder vessels would serve a number of subsidiary ports. While feeders are frequently used to advantage, it has in fact transpired that partly due to regional and national pride, fully equipped container berths have been provided at a very large number of ports, in some cases to such an extent that facilities are needlessly duplicated. If two distinct types of port are to materialize, it is more likely that central "super" ports built along automated lines and serving wide geographical areas will be constructed, while the container ports of today act as collection and distribution points for large feeder vessels. If automated ports are widely constructed the deep-sea containerships, which will use them as a type of "clearing-house", will be able to operate between single terminals in each country or continent, and will therefore spend the greater part of their life at sea. Over a longer period of time the capacity of the subsidiary "feeder" ports should adjust to a cargo throughput equivalent to a volume of cargo generated purely by the area the port naturally serves, and under-utilization will not have to be corrected by the diversion of cargo from other areas. Under-utilization is often pointed to today as being a drawback of containerization, but it should be remembered that container vessels in service at present find it necessary to call at too many ports in their endeavor to provide as wide a service as possible. If deep sea vessels are able to restrict their calls by relying on the feeder vessels to distribute containers, and if the feeder ports are able to contain their growth to a possibly modest degree, the container ports of today, which in turn will be the feeder ports of tomorrow, will continue to thrive, and latent benefits inherent in containerized systems will become apparent.

On average approximately one third of general cargo passing through the world's larger ports is containerized, and according to some forecasts nearly all general cargo will eventually be carried in containers. As the containership consortia broaden their field of operations to include countries not previously served by containerships, port authorities in such countries will have to decide whether to provide containership berths, probably in competition with other similar ports, or whether to limit capital expenditure by possibly continuing to provide bulk cargo facilities, but with the addition of roll-on roll-off berths. Barge carrying vessels will be restricted to ports that are connected to the interior by navigable rivers and waterways.

Less Developed Countries

A scale of investment in capital equipment that may appear to be modest to a developed nation will often present serious problems to an underdeveloped country where the demands on scarce resources are many. Such countries will usually have a surplus of labor, and labor intensive industries will predominate until the country is able to "take off" to a higher state of development through the implementation of a scheme of planned growth. But growth requires increasing returns to scale which in turn requires investment in capital equipment, but as this investment will initially be channeled to light industry to stimulate local demand and create a market, there will be little incentive for funds to be apportioned to port development where the immediate effect would surely be to worsen an already high rate of unemployment. A further argument against port development is that as labor is comparatively cheap it will not follow that a container handling system will reduce the cost of running the port. The only beneficiary would be the shipping company (and possibly cargo owners) if containerization is able to produce the promised rewards. The effect on prices to the consumer would be negligible.

It should also be remembered that underdeveloped countries usually rely very heavily for their export earnings on primary products, and such traffic is not suitable for containerization. The flow of finished goods exported will be at a low level and will remain so until the country is able to compete in overseas markets following the build up of manufacturing industries. Goods suitable for containerization will mainly be moving into the country, and it is difficult to contemplate a situation whereby vessels are fully utilized on a round voyage. Methods of efficient bulk handling will be more important to the country, and the need to develop ports to handle container vessels will not become apparent until overseas markets are entered and a thriving trading relationship with the outside world is built up.

For those countries already into a growth programme where

less dependence is placed on the primary sectors following a move of resources into industry, funds may be available internally or be forthcoming from outside that will permit modernization of selected ports. It is assumed that at this stage of development internal communications will have been built up involving a comprehensive road and, if geographical conditions permit, rail network connecting the ports to the industrial centers. Port authorities will have to decide whether to partially commit themselves to containerization by providing modern container berths incorporating portainers and a back-up area served by handling equipment, or to tread more warily and become initially less committed. If the latter path is chosen authorities may consider renting a semi-portable container crane that can be erected on an existing dockside without prior reinforcement, thus avoiding heavy capital costs. If an extensive back-up area is not available, such a crane can stack containers six high directly underneath its own boom, which reaches back to span the available dockside area, thus providing terminal handling in addition to ship handling facilities. Further flexibility is obtained through the crane being suitable for the handling of palletized general cargo, when a conventional hooking arrangement is used instead of a framed distributed lift necessary for containers. Part container vessels or conventional vessels carrying a limited number of containers can therefore be worked with ease at one quay, in addition to proper containerships. These types of crane will also find their markets in the smaller feeder ports, and will be utilized by shipping companies with limited resources who provide their own shoreside handling equipment.

For several years the less developed countries have maintained that containerization is a "spin-off" from the highly developed economies of the industrialized countries, and even though they want to introduce containerships and build container ports, they are unable to do so because of a lack of finance and because of backward technology. Due to this enforced state of nonparticipation the less developed countries have in the past had little say in the future development of containerization, but during the 1973-1974 United Nations Conference on Trade and Development held in Geneva, the situation of the less developed countries was, if anything, rather hurriedly examined. It was proposed by

UNCTAD that developing countries should carry 40 per cent of their own trade in their own flag vessels, whether cellular or break-bulk, and that as the 40 per cent rule was to apply to cargo carried by conference vessels only, that entry into shipping conferences should be made easier for the lines concerned. While the less developed countries were in favor of the proposition, strong maritime powers such as Britain, Greece, Scandinavia and the USA were not, but doubt was expressed anyway on the ability of the less developed countries to actually carry 40 per cent of their own trade. It is likely that the maritime countries will enter into management contracts with the less developed countries to carry part of the 40 per cent, but if such contracts cannot be arranged some of the existing conference lines might well leave the conference and operate either individually or as rival groups. This move would be justified on economic, if not social grounds, as conference rates are usually drawn up to cover the operating expenses of the line with the highest costs (or the least efficiency), and the more productive lines could operate outside the conference at rates based on their own much lower costs. If this were to happen the gulf between non-conference and conference rates might widen to such an extent that the conference plus the shipping fleets of the less developed countries would collapse. Rigid cargo sharing as proposed by the 40 per cent rule should be avoided as optimum vessel loadings are unlikely to be achieved, and instead the maritime activities of the less developed countries should gradually be integrated with the established shipping conferences.

It will be evident that many questions must be answered and much research undertaken by those parties responsible for overseas port development before they become committed to installing container handling equipment. Where investment is at the risk of the country concerned, the prime consideration should be whether the measures will benefit her own economy, and any tendencies to accept finance from overseas, often originating in Communist bloc countries, should be avoided in cases where it is all too evident that the undertaking will become a "white elephant". Funds in underdeveloped countries apportioned to prestige projects are a waste of scarce resources, and should be channeled instead into investment of benefit to the community at large.

The Europe/Far East Container Service

Undoubtedly the most significant expansion of the principle of containerization has been the establishment of services between Europe and the Far East. To offer regular containership sailings over long distances it is necessary to operate a number of vessels, and to keep freight rates as low as possible large vessels offering economies of scale must be built. This could only be achieved if a number of lines were to come together, not to pool their resources, but to act closely together in the regulation of sailings, and to share common container berths. To this end five shipping companies from three countries formed what has become to be known as the "TRIO" group, with the intention of building up a seventeen-strong fleet of large modern containerships, and in December 1971 the M/V *Kamakura Maru* belonging to NYK, one of the two Japanese members of the group, opened the service by sailing from Japan to Europe.

Each vessel was to be able to carry upward of 1,800 20-foot (or their equivalent) containers, and would have a gross tonnage exceeding 50,000. Cells would be convertible to accept either 20- or 40-foot units, and whereas previously built containerships were carrying approximately 35% of containers on deck, these new vessels would only load about 13% on deck stacked one layer high, while those below deck would be stowed nine high. The greater the ratio of containers below deck to those on deck, the greater the vessel's freeboard (the distance between the waterline and deck) and therefore heavy seas will largely be kept off the deck areas. Turbine or diesel engines would maintain a sailing speed of 26 knots and a transit time between the United Kingdom and Tokyo via the Panama Canal of 23 days would be offered. Vessel dimensions have been somewhat limited by the Panama Canal, and indeed the breadth of the TRIO ships in relation to their length and draught is already too small because of the limited width of the Canal locks. A bow thruster driven by a 2,300 volt 900 kilowatt motor is fitted to some of the vessels, and the need for tugs during sailing and docking is therefore reduced.

A space charter arrangement enables each vessel to carry containers belonging to the other operators within the group, and each member will therefore have an allocation of space on each

FIGURE 14 OCL cellular containership *Cardigan Bay* at Southampton
(Courtesy of Overseas Containers Limited).

sailing. It was thus possible for all the members to take an immediate part in managing the consortium, even though some were not able to introduce their own vessels until later. In addition to this "slotting" of allocations into shared vessels, the terminals and handling equipment are also shared, but marketing the service and arranging the inland haulage within Europe and the Far East is undertaken separately by each member. Co-operation therefore extends to ships and terminals while individual competition in inland services is maintained.

Two of TRIO's members come from Britain, two from Japan and one from West Germany, and they all belong to the Far Eastern Freight Conference. In Britain Overseas Containers Limited (OCL) operate five vessels, Ben Line Containers Limited, a joint venture by Ben Lines and Ellerman Lines in conjunction with Associated Container Transportation Limited operate three, while in West Germany Hapag-Lloyd run four vessels. The two Japanese members, Nippon Yusen Kaisha (NYK) and Mitsui OSK have contributed three and two vessels respectively. OCL is the most heavily committed member of the TRIO group, having invested nearly £80 million in ships and containers, and a further £4.5 million in the United Kingdom terminal at Southampton and a clearance depot at Barking. Ben Line Containers have invested about £40 million in ships, containers, terminals and equipment, and began operating their own vessels a little later than OCL in 1972. Ben Line is able to draw on accounting, electronic data processing, and research and development facilities provided by ACT Services Limited, a service company established to assist both Ben Line and ACT (Australia) Limited.

Hapag-Lloyd and the two Japanese members of TRIO, NYK and Mitsui OSK, have invested amounts in proportion to the OCL and Ben Line share, and both NYK and Mitsui had previously gained considerable experience in operating containerships between Japan, and the Pacific coast of the USA and Australia. They undertook extensive research into the Europe/Far East trade, and along with their counterparts in Japan they have become perhaps a little over-committed to the container concept.

Acting as the United Kingdom terminal for the TRIO vessels, the port of Southampton has considerably benefited from the Far Eastern traffic. This boost came at an opportune time in view of the decline in passenger traffic, and from a total annual through-put of container cargo in 1969 of 80,000 tons, container and roll-on roll-off trade has increased to approximately 2 million tons per year. To accommodate the increased demand for the services of the railways, Freightliners built a second rail terminal at South-ampton, and signed a multi-million pound contract with OCL and Ben Line for the carriage of over 100,000 containers per year for a ten-year period. As an illustration of the current growth it should be noted that during 1972-1973 container throughput doubled at the port, largely due to TRIO, from 74,000 units in 1972 to 162,000 units in 1973. On the Continent container term-inals are used at the ports of Hamburg and Rotterdam by the TRIO vessels.

While terminals as modern as those in Europe have been pro-vided in the Far East, the state of development in some of the countries is limiting the application of the container system in some sectors of the movement. Although Japan has been handling containerized cargo since 1968, she only quite recently decided to initiate a five-year plan to provide facilities enabling containers to be readily transferred between different modes of transport. Rail terminals similar to those in the UK and on the Continent are being built, and inland groupage terminals are being provided. Container berths at Tokyo and Kobe, the former using portainers and a transtainer, and the latter portainers and straddle carriers, are used by the TRIO group for Japanese cargo, and have been operational since December 1971. The East Lagoon container port at Singapore was opened in June 1972 and was used by TRIO shortly afterwards. TRIO also began to serve Hong Kong in the middle of 1972, where the facilities provided at Berth No.1 at the Kwai Chung complex about ten miles out of the city center are used. In both Singapore and Hong Kong severe restrictions have to be placed on the movement of heavy road vehicles to control congestion, which contrasts with the rapid throughput of con-tainers at the terminals, but in the case of Hong Kong the contain-er facilities may in the future be used more for transhipping containers to and from other Asian ports. Port Swettenham (now Port Kelang) was connected in August 1973 and calls at Kaohsiung in Taiwan completed the TRIO link up a little later.

Prior to the beginning of the TRIO Europe to Far East sailings, and in order to give shippers, consignees and the lines experience in operating a containerized service, an experimental period of shipping containers by conventional vessels was started in September 1970. Although the scheme was necessarily limited due to the conventional handling facilities in the ports at the time, several shippers found the method advantageous. Damage to previously vulnerable cargo was considerably lowered, and some shippers and receivers found a cost saving to be evident. The Conference agreed to amend the tariff rules to allow container shipments to continue beyond the original finishing date of 30th September 1971, and many cargo owners preferred the new method even though a container hire charge of $40 per unit was levied.

With the conference system operating in its present form largely as a regulator of freight rates and conditions, the formation of large consortia such as TRIO does not directly affect the already existing limitation of choice imposed on cargo owners. While this limitation of choice does not relate to shipping companies, it does relate to the freight rates they charge, and as these rates are largely determined by the shipping companies and consortia making up the conference membership, any large-scale grouping of shipping companies within the conference into organizations such as TRIO, should be viewed in relation to their possible future monopolization state in the conference. The TRIO group maintain that a better standard of service will follow from a number of lines closely co-operating, and that freight rate increases will be less severe than would have been the case if conventional break-bulk services had continued as the only method of transporting general cargo. The first assumption has materialized, but only after cargo owners have changed, in some cases quite drastically, their method of forwarding goods, and of cargo owners being faced at times with a shortage of shipping space due to the inflexible nature of closely knit sailing schedules which preclude rapid introduction of temporary tonnage. It is difficult to assess accurately how fast freight rates would have risen if the Europe/Far East trade had continued to be served by break-bulk vessels, but recent studies in other trades have indicated that break-bulk and palletized cargo can be shipped at a cheaper cost per ton than containerized cargo. It should not be forgotten, however, that an over-competitive situation with a number of independent container lines scrambling for a limited amount of cargo can only lead to over-tonnaging with possibly worse long-term effects than those caused by controlled collusion.

Competition will not therefore relate to freight charges where conference vessels are concerned, but will be confined to the service given by the lines making up the conference membership. It was originally thought that a rival consortium formed by a Dutch shipping company, Nedlloyd, and a group of lines trading under the name of Scanservice, and representing Scandinavian interests, would join TRIO, but even though it was maintained by the consortium that to operate fast regular services between Europe and the Far East would not be viable unless they could co-operate closely with TRIO, the consortium is now operating as an alternative group within the conference. This type of construction where large rival groupings exist will re-introduce a competitive element to the trade, and conference policy will not be formulated by possibly parochial interests.

The Nedlloyd/Scanservice consortium, which now trades under the group name of Scan Dutch, was originally formed through the coming together of Nedlloyd, the Dutch shipping company, with the East Asiatic Company of Denmark, the Swedish East Asiatic Company of Sweden, and Wilh. Wilhelmsen of Norway. A total of six vessels were put into service, and sailings are maintained between north European and Scandinavian ports, and Tokyo, Kobe, Singapore and Hong Kong. The 79% state-owned line of France, Messageries Maritimes, in conjunction with another French line, Cie. Maritime des Chargeurs Réunis, had applied to join TRIO, but were turned down because they could only contribute one vessel out of a promised two, and because they would not agree to the space quotas proposed by TRIO. The Messagerie vessel *Korrigan*, newly built in 1973, had been prepared for service, but instead of joining the other TRIO ships, had to be berthed in Brest at a cost of £6,500 per day. Eventually, however, Messageries Maritimes were accepted by Scan Dutch in July 1973, but under terms far from favorable to the French line. Only 10 per cent of the group's carrying capacity was allocated to the *Korrigan*, and a condition of membership was that the line would withdraw all its conventional vessels operating in the Europe to Far East trade. Messageries also had to leave a group of shipping companies operating from Mediterranean ports, and had to disband all her agencies in the Far East. These moves were aimed at removing French competition from the trade, and are an obvious blow to France as a maritime power. It has been suggested that TRIO and Scan Dutch should come closer together to avoid the type of instability that follows from the granting of indirect rebates, and from other malpractices contravening conference regulations, and in view of the UNCTAD recommendation that 40 per cent of cargo in particular trades should be allocated to the lines of less developed countries serving the trade, any co-operation between the two groups would favor Scan Dutch, being wholly European based, while TRIO membership is divided between European and Far Eastern interests.

A third group of shipping companies, operating as the Mediterranean Far Eastern Container Service or "Med. Club", is running containership-tonnage from Mediterranean ports to the Far East. Cie. Maritime des Chargeurs Réunis and Messageries Maritimes had applied to the Far Eastern Freight Conference for a share in the Far Eastern trade, but due to the granting of only limited loading shares in December 1972 the two lines discontinued their plans for a joint service. This embargo on the French was partly in retaliation for their earlier refusal in 1970 to reduce their loading shares, when the Far Eastern shipping companies were granted increased shares following a general expansion of trade between Europe and the Far East. The Med. Club started running a container service in November 1972, using medium-sized vessels with a capacity of 720 20-foot units or their equivalent, chartered from one of the members, Chargeurs Réunis. Messageries Maritimes were at this time a member, but as stated earlier they were obliged to leave the group when they joined forces with Scan Dutch in July 1973. The present members of the Med. Club are Chargeurs Réunis of France, Lloyd Triestino and Flotta Lauro of Italy, and NYK and Mitsui OSK of Japan. Sailings conform to the regulations of the Far Eastern Freight Conference and the four vessels maintain services out of Barcelona, Genoa and Fos (Marseilles).

Although groupings such as TRIO, Scan Dutch and the Med. Club control a large percentage of the tonnage handled by the members of the Far Eastern Freight Conference (12.9 million tons in 1972 and 14 million in 1973), there is still plenty of cargo available to the shipping companies acting independently, or in much smaller groups, and indeed some of these lines are so successful that they are now a serious threat to the much larger groups. K Line of Japan, and Maersk Line, part of the A.P. Moller group of Copenhagen, used to have joint membership of the Conference, and operated a joint service to the Far East until the end of 1973, when Maersk decided to pull out of the partnership. K Line applied unsuccessfully to join TRIO, but was accepted by the Far Eastern Freight Conference as a full member, and is running three multi-purpose semi-containerships between Europe and the Far East. K Line adopted the 40-foot container as the unit most likely to maintain costs within its services between Japan, and the USA and Europe, and although the line is operating successfully, it is still pressing for membership of TRIO. Maersk, in common with many other Scandinavian owners, built up a fleet of vessels built to carry palletized cargo, but now favors the container, and is ordering wholly cellular tonnage for introduction into the Europe to Far East trade. This swing to containerships is an example of the more general trend of Scandinavian owners to place less emphasis on the pallet ships, in order to become internationally competitive. Maersk, like her former partner K Line, is also an independent full member of the Conference.

Perhaps the biggest threat to the groups in the Far Eastern trade comes from C.Y. Tung's rapidly growing fleet of vessels. Tung's Formosan Orient Overseas Line, a full member of the Conference, began a new part-container service in April 1973, as a preliminary to the introduction of a completely cellular service maintained by four vessels under the Orient Overseas Container Line flag. While such competition is welcomed by TRIO and Scan Dutch, the possibility of over-tonnaging is not, and in view of the present very large cargo flows maybe being of a temporary nature, and of the future rapid growth of non-conference as well as conference lines, this possibility could well turn into a reality. It is also thought in some quarters that Tung might withdraw his Europe to Far East vessels from the Conference to act independently, or that he would form a third group of Far East shipping lines to directly challenge TRIO and Scan Dutch. If he were to follow the latter course, and if the UNCTAD 40 per cent ruling materialized, he would be in an exceptionally strong position to control a steadily growing share of the Europe to Far East traffic.

Two other Conference members are the Malaysian International Shipping Corporation and Neptune Orient Lines (Singapore) Limited. Both lines want to expand and are trying to persuade the Conference to grant them larger shares of the Europe to Far Eastern traffic. Malaysian International applied to join TRIO in March 1973, and if applications are continually unsuccessful, the company would be ideally placed to co-operate, along with other lines anxious to pool resources, with Tung. Neptune Orient is Government of Singapore owned, and has been running side loading vessels in the trade capable of shipping palletized, break-bulk, and containerized cargo, since June 1973. Two hundred 20-foot containers, together with the palletized and break-bulk cargo, can be carried by each of the two vessels, and because of the constant demand for conventional shipping space between Europe and the Far East the line should prosper.

Non-conference competition is provided by the Zim Container Service, and by landbridge routes over North America and Russia. Zim use Dart Containerline sailings for shipping Far East containers from Southampton to Halifax, where transhipment to Zim's own container vessels takes place. The Zim vessels call at Los Angeles on their way to the Far East, and rates up to 25 per cent below the conference tariff are offered. The landbridge routes in their present form do not constitute a serious threat to the containership companies, but the Russian route which uses the Trans-Siberian railway, and which will be examined later in this chapter, has the capability of developing into a very serious contender for Far Eastern traffic, if all its modes of shipment and of handling are co-ordinated more harmoniously.

Currency fluctuations following changes in a country's internal economic position, and the availability or otherwise of raw materials, will have an effect on the country's terms of trade, and the level of exports relative to imports will change. In the Europe to Far East trade eastbound vessels used to be only about 50% loaded, and the majority of cargo was being carried from the Far East to European countries. Japan in particular was contributing to the imbalance, but as difficulties of selling to the Japanese market became less, and following an effective re-valuation of the yen, the imbalance gradually began to reverse. By the end of 1973 eastbound trade was so heavy that it became increasingly difficult for European exporters to find container space at all. The landbridge routes were unable to absorb the surplus, and in May 1974 some shippers had to wait up to five weeks for space. It became necessary to charter cellular tonnage, but now that the lines have been able to position more containers in Europe the situation is easing considerably. This inflexibility is partly due to the rigidity of the conference system, which precludes newcomers with cellular tonnage having access to cargo of conference shippers, but in view of the peculiar conditions prevailing during 1973-1974, and of the efforts to charter tonnage, the severe criticisms leveled at the conference and the shipping companies were perhaps a little unjust.

It is to be expected that in today's inflationary climate shipping companies will find it very difficult to absorb cost increases, and that rates will continually be spiralling. While rates have undoubtedly risen at an alarming rate, it may be that had the Europe to Far East trade remained as a conventional service, rates would have risen even more sharply. This would have been because of the greater effect of inflation on conventional break-bulk methods of shipment, as variable costs in relation to fixed costs will be more than those found in containership trades. Inflation will have little effect on fixed costs, and indeed the containership itself will probably be appreciating in value, while the more labor-intensive conventional shipping activities will be suffering from higher handling charges. Due to the frequency and severity of rate changes the conferences are finding themselves under pressure to reveal their true operating costs to shippers' councils (representative bodies of the cargo owners), and to examine suggestions put forward by the councils aimed at maintaining costs. The Far Eastern Freight Conference will be following such a course prior to the introduction toward the end of 1974 of a rate increase considerably higher than the usual periodic increase of about 10 per cent.

The Far East is a rapidly expanding market and source of supply of finished and semi-finished goods, and the present volume of cargo carried by container is small in relation to possible future growth. This growth is largely controlled by the rate of development of internal surface communications, and there will therefore remain for some time a need for conventional break-bulk shipping methods. Container cargo accounts for about 70 per cent of total general cargo in the trade, and this percentage will probably remain static for a few years as the over-all tonnage climbs. Semi-containerships will probably continue to serve such countries as the Philippines and Thailand, while the TRIO containerships restrict their area of operation in the Far East to those ports presently served on a direct call basis. In contrast to these direct calls, Scan Dutch are using feeder vessels in both Europe and the Far East, and they maintain that the system allows a far wider area to be covered. They are able to extend their operations as far as Spain in Europe and to some of the smaller ports in the Far East, and will therefore have access to cargo that is not available to the TRIO group.

The Europe/Australia Container Service

Prior to the inauguration of the TRIO group serving the Far East, the principal interest of OCL was in the trade between Europe and Australia. It had been decided to containerize the Australian trade as early as 1965, and OCL together with the other British consortium, Associated Container Transportation Limited (ACT), spent nearly four years planning the service. The first containership sailing to Australia was the OCL *Encounter Bay* which left Rotterdam on 6th March 1969, and during the following year a further five OCL vessels entered service. The OCL ships are each of approximately 27,000 gross registered tons, have a capacity of up to 1500 20-foot containers (or their equivalent) and a service speed of 22 knots. ACT contributed two vessels to the joint service, the *ACT 1* and *ACT 2*, each of 25,000 gross registered tons, a capacity of up to 1400 20-foot containers (or their equivalent), and having a service speed of 22 knots.

Problems which normally befall pioneers were in no short measure during the early years of the OCL/ACT service, and mention has already been made of the labor dispute at Tilbury, the United Kingdom terminal, which resulted in vessels having to load and discharge at Antwerp, and of the problems encountered following the consortium's decision to stack containers at Tilbury five high. But the teething troubles were prolonged due to labor unrest in Australia, and due to the necessity of strengthening the vessels because of the tremendously punishing schedules that had to be maintained. In view of these initial setbacks, and of the heavy investment in vessels and equipment, it was hardly surprising that OCL reported a loss of £9 million up to the period ending September 1970 and forecast an even larger deficit of £13-14 million for the following year. These figures brought forth a new wave of criticism to add to the existing opposition to containerization, and although the figures did make sorrowful reading at the time, it should be remembered that the container principle was still in its infancy.

In order to co-ordinate the sailings of OCL, ACT, four Continental lines and an Australian line, it was proposed that an international joint venture, similar in construction to groups such as TRIO and Scan Dutch, be set up. Accordingly the Australia Europe Container Service (AECS) was formed as a body to rationalize the sailings of the Australian National Line (ANL), Hapag Lloyd, Nedlloyd, Messageries Maritimes and Lloyd Triestino with those of OCL and ACT. It was now possible to offer a sailing from Europe every five to six days through regular positioning of spaced vessels, and cargo flows were spread more evenly over member vessels. AECS members virtually had a monopoly of containerized cargo in the Europe to Australia trade, and its dominant member, OCL, was able to control about two-thirds of the flow. Thirteen vessels were involved, each spending about 75 per cent of its time at sea, and completing between four and five round trips per year.

On 1st November 1971, however, an announcement was made by ACT (Australia) Limited of significance to the entire general cargo shipping industry. ACT together with the Australian National Line (ANL) had decided to break away from the AECS joint operation as from 1st September 1972, to offer a rival independent container service between the United Kingdom and Australia, but with the added facility of also connecting with New Zealand and North America. ACT and ANL were to remain members of the Australian Conference, and would therefore not undercut AECS rates, but through acting independently they would be

FIGURE 15 ACT cellular containership *ACT 2* loading at Rotterdam (Courtesy of Associated Container Transportation (Australia) Limited).

able to offer a more efficient and comprehensive service. By calling at ports in New Zealand, ACT/ANL would be better placed than the AECS lines to maintain a reasonable level of cargo northbound to Europe following any general slackening of European imports from Australia due to the enlargement of the European Economic Community, and would be spreading the risk factor while at the same time taking advantage of future container growth through extending their interests to North America. Europe to Australia and New Zealand traffic was to be shipped by the two ACT vessels and the ANL vessel *Australian Endeavour*, and a third ACT vessel, the *ACT 6* made her maiden voyage out of Liverpool to Australia and New Zealand in January 1973.

While the member lines of AECS principally cater for general dry cargo and serve Continental ports direct, nearly half of ACT/ANL's containers are refrigerated and fewer ports are called at. ACT/ANL omit Freemantle from their sailing schedule to concentrate more on the meat and fruit handling ports, and they now run the largest refrigerated container fleet in the world. London and Liverpool in the United Kingdom are the only European ports served direct, and a quay refrigeration system has been installed at both locations to reduce the problem of storing refrigerated containers following discharge. Although ACT has effectively broken away from its former partner, OCL, an arrangement exists for chartering container space in AECS member vessels, and vice versa.

A third independent group in the Europe to Australia trade, and like AECS and ACT/ANL a Conference member, is the Scandinavian consortium Scan Austral. Scan Austral was formed by Wilh. Wilhelmen Lines of Oslo, Transatlantic Steamship Company of Gothenburg and East Asiatic Company Limited of Copenhagen, and although running a fleet of five roll-on roll-off vessels is competing for cargo with the other groupings. The Scan Austral vessels are very flexible with regard to cargo types, and in addition to, or in place of unitized roll-on roll-off traffic, are able to accept up to 1,400 containers. Refrigerated space has recently been provided through installing cold chambers in the five vessels, and this method of shipping perishables may indeed be preferred to refrigerated container movements.

Ports in Australia used by the containership lines were selected on the basis of facilities offered, or capable of being provided, their proximity to areas of production or consumption, and whether good rail links existed. The industrial regions are principally situated along narrow coastal strips, and because a long overland haul would not be necessary to reach these regions, it would not be possible to fully exploit the latent benefits of through container movements. Perhaps it may have been better to utilize the already existing railway system, which had been handling container vans for the previous twenty years, to complete the link to the industrial regions along the south and east coasts by using the west coast port of Freemantle as a terminal for moving containers between vessel and rail flats. Voyage times would then have been shorter, and sorting containers to a number of different ports would not have been necessary. The through transit time to Sydney would have been less as a rail landbridge linking the 3,000 miles between Freemantle and Sydney would take four days, while the containerships take ten days by sea. This sort of operation would not be economic for all cargo moving between Europe and Australia, but over selected routes, and in close cooperation with the railways, use could have been made of an internal system already familiar with transport of unit loads over long distances. It was decided, however, during the planning stage of the initial OCL/ACT service to make direct calls at Freemantle, Sydney and Melbourne, and to serve Brisbane and Newcastle by rail link from Sydney, and Adelaide by rail link from Melbourne. Freight rates from Europe to all three Australian ports of discharge were to be the same, and cargo owners were not therefore encouraged to make a possible cost saving through shipping Sydney cargo through Freemantle, and completing the journey overland by rail. Seatainer Terminals Limited were appointed to operate the container facilities at Freemantle, Sydney and Melbourne, and twin-lift portainers and transtainers each with a capacity of 45 tons were installed.

Freemantle has a forward looking outlook regarding container development, has been able to update the original facilities of 1969 as traffic has grown, and has plenty of room to expand further if need be. It does not handle the increasing flow of traffic to and from New Zealand, Japan, and North America, and has therefore been able to avoid the serious congestion to be found at Sydney and Melbourne. Sydney is generally the second port of call, and in contrast with Freemantle the port facilities have had to be provided in very congested areas. The AECS vessels use the White Bay terminal, which is leased to Seatainer Terminals by the harbor board, and which has three container berths on a 21½ acre site. Due to limitation of space at White Bay the terminal purely acts as a loading/discharge medium, and is served by two container depots fourteen miles away at Chullora and Villawood by a rail link. A second container terminal in Sydney, originally intended to handle vessels in the North American and Far East trades, has been provided at a cost of A$13 million at Glebe Island on a 25 acre site. The terminal was opened in February 1973, is worked using two portainers and five transtainers, but has had a persistently poor throughput of cargo due to inefficient management on the part of the Maritime Services Board who were running it as a common user berth. The terminal was also opened before it was capable of efficient operation, and the surrounding road congestion made it difficult to maintain a smooth flow of containers. The handling speed at Glebe Island was half that at White Bay, and the Maritime Services Board had no alternative but to lease the terminal out in a similar way to White Bay. Eventually a group of shipping companies comprising Farrell Lines of the USA, Columbus Lines of West Germany, and Australian Liner Services, in conjunction with the stevedoring firm James Patrick, accepted responsibility for the future operation of the terminal, and they will continue to run it along common user lines. In addition to their own vessels, Glebe Island is also used by the vessels of the ACT/ANL partnership. While expansion of container throughput at Sydney has been very fast, it has become the slowest container handling port in the world, and the Conference lines found it necessary to impose a 6.5% congestion surcharge in July 1974 on cargo passing through Sydney. The present facilities will obviously not be adequate to cope with future throughputs, and it has been decided to construct a third terminal at Botany Bay to accommodate the larger vessels of the future at five berths where an alongside water depth of 50 feet will be provided. Although the river port of Melbourne has also become congested, it does not have to cope with problems on a scale faced by Sydney. Container handling facilities have been provided at Appleton Dock where a back-up area is capable of accommodating 3,500 units, and at Swanson Dock an 800-foot long berth is worked using a Paceco twin-lift portainer. Major expansion is to be undertaken at Melbourne principally involving the provision of more roll-on roll-off berths to supplement the present four container berths and the four coastal shipping roll-on roll-off berths.

The remainder of the Australian ports, some of which enjoyed comparatively large throughputs of general cargo before the opening up of container services, have not fared as well as Freemantle, Sydney and Melbourne. Adelaide has no container facilities at present, and containerized cargo is fed via a rail link through Melbourne. It is proposed though that a A$5 million container berth should be built at Adelaide, and although there are no assurances that containerships will in future use the port, it is hoped that the scale of future growth of container shipments will warrant direct calls by 1977. The port is losing over 200,000 tons of cargo per year to Melbourne, and desperately needs a return of the revenue being lost. Brisbane has limited container facilities, and OCL container cargo is fed by rail over Sydney. Any very large-scale port expansion would be difficult because of the large quantities of silt deposited by the Brisbane River in Moreton Bay, which has to be frequently dredged. Newcastle and Port Kembla, along with other bulk cargo ports, will be little affected by containerization, and the service advertized by the consortia to Newcastle is again maintained by a rail link from Sydney. These rail feeder ports have had to develop inland depots where containers may be assembled, and the 24-acre facility at Newcastle is connected to the Pacific Highway by a private access road. While Townsville installed a portainer in 1974, to be used either for container cargo or more conventional handling, and is building container berths, Portland seems undecided whether to continue as a predominantly bulk handling port, or to invest in container handling facilities. Portland seems intent on raising as much revenue as possible from a high throughput of vessels, partly to meet interest payments on a A$19 million loan, and provision of more modern equipment is being overlooked. Ports in Tasmania are connected to Melbourne by a feeder service, but the long-term position of Tasmania could be drastically altered if plans to construct a huge deep sea container terminal at Port Huon on the D'Entrecasteaux Channel materialize. The terminal, which could handle containerships of up to 100,000 tons, would be fully automatic, and would act as the southern base for the trade between Europe and Australia. Australian ports, and maybe those in New Zealand as well, would be connected by fast feeder vessels, which would allow the deep sea containerships to turn round and be sailing back to Europe a few days after arriving.

During 1973 it became increasingly difficult for European exporters to obtain space in container vessels sailing out to Australia. A number of factors contributed to the space shortage, and even though the consortia were severely criticized by some groups for allowing the situation to develop and worsen, it is now generally recognized that there was little the consortia could do other than what they did to remedy the situation. Following France's nuclear test in the Pacific, the AECS vessel *Kangourou* belonging to the French line Messageries Maritime was blacked in Australian ports, and an immediate drop in capacity of 10 per cent occurred. While the *Kangourou* was chartered during the blacking to Atlantic Container Line for service in the North Atlantic, it was not possible to immediately charter a replacement for the Australian trade, and some containers had to be re-routed by the consortia via America and Japan at considerable extra cost. The other main reason for the shortage was the rapid growth of imports from Europe following Australia's changed trading policy of late 1972 when the Labour Government took office. Tariffs were reduced by 25 per cent in an effort to make Australian industry more competitive, and southbound trade increased by 25 per cent during mid-1973 to mid-1974. A further source of trouble was the persistent labor disputes in Australian ports which meant that round voyages were taking longer. Whether or not the consortia wished to introduce more vessels to the trade, the Conference was forbidden by Australian law to create a situation of over-tonnaging, and in view of the possibly temporary nature of the situation, a better alternative was to divert vessels from other trades, or to time charter tonnage. It was thought at one time that OCL might take one of its vessels off the Far Eastern run to supplement the Australian trade, but instead the *Manchester Vigour* capable of carrying 296 containers was chartered from

Manchester Liners, and sailed for Australia on 30th July 1973. At this time it was not unusual for cargo owners in Europe to have to wait for five weeks for a container, and only if additional vessels were chartered could the backlog have been cleared. But further charterings by AECS members were hampered by the shortage of cargo moving between Australia and Europe, and would have meant substantial operating losses for the lines. The problem was an insoluble one unless the consortia, the Conference, and the various shippers' councils agreed that all outward freight rates must rise to subsidize the cost of diverting part of the southbound cargo to alternative routes. The rate rise could have been collected as one of the now all too common "temporary surcharges", and the over-capacity problem in the homeward trade would have been avoided. But Conferences are under an obligation to provide regular sailings in their particular trades, and are also obliged to discuss rate changes with the shippers' councils. A rate increase caused by an inability to provide sufficient tonnage would not have been readily sanctioned by the shippers' councils, and the Conference decided to increase the number of conventional sailings from Europe during May and June of 1974 instead. At the beginning of 1974 there was an eight-week waiting period for space, and some owners maintained that the demand for space had increased by 70 per cent over the previous year. OCL again entered the charter market in May 1974, when two more Manchester Liners vessels were put into the Australian trade. The vessels, which were each able to ship 586 containers, were taken on a two-year time charter, and were initially used to move cargo southbound and empty containers northbound for re-positioning quickly in Europe. They may be switched to the Far Eastern trade if the imbalance between Europe and Australia rectifies itself. It is unjust to place the responsibility for space shortages in the southbound Australian trade with the Conference and the consortia, and the action taken by AECS members since September 1973 which resulted in the chartering of three cellular and nine conventional vessels should be given its just due.

In spite of the 12 per cent devaluation of the Australian dollar in September 1974, which will make imported items more expensive and exports more competitive, the trade imbalance will be further aggravated due to the distortive effect on trade between

Europe and Australia caused by the enlargement of the European Economic Community. Trade diversion, whereby the supply of goods is diverted from a low cost source to a high cost source, will result in much of the traditional trade from Australia to the United Kingdom being switched to European suppliers. The EEC's common external tariff, coupled with the abolition of Commonwealth Preferences, will cause prices of imported goods from Australia to rise, and prices of similar goods produced within the EEC will fall as internal tariffs are abolished. This trade diversion, which operates irrespective of the comparative costs of producing one item of goods between two countries, will, according to some estimates, cut northbound traffic by as much as 50 per cent. It is clear that the troubles of the consortia are not over, but if current experiments in the carriage of alternative cargoes are successful, coupled with a more general alteration of schedules to include calls at New Zealand, and maybe even at ports in other countries, these difficulties might in part be obviated.

If containerization of the Europe/Australia trade had not occurred when it did, the effects of inflation on the costs of running conventional ships coupled with the limited carrying capacity of the ships, would surely have meant that freight rates would have been higher than today's level. Palletization may be pointed to as an even greater source of cost saving, but where very long overland hauls take place, as in Australia and the USA, palletization becomes less attractive. The containerships being used in the Australian trade today are capable of moving eight times as much cargo over a year as conventional vessels, due not only to their size, but also to the speed of turnround. During the early years of operation the consortia were incurring heavy losses, but following repayment of much of the capital debt, and a rapid build-up of cargo to a level of 85 per cent of UK/Australian cargo being carried in containers, OCL reported a 13 per cent return on capital employed during 1973 representing an £18 million operating profit. This compares with a £4.75 million profit in 1972, a loss of nearly £1 million in 1971, a loss of £1.87 million in 1970, and a loss of £3.87 million in 1969. For future operation the ACT/ANL partnership have ordered a 29,000 ton A$32 million containership to be delivered for their Europe/Australia/New Zealand service in 1977, while OCL have ordered two 42,000-ton vessels for the Europe/Australia trade for delivery in 1977/78.

The Problem of New Zealand

In 1969 the next step toward containerizing the world's seaborne trade seemed to be the provision of a Europe/New Zealand service, and four British lines belonging to the New Zealand Conference announced in March of that year that such a service was planned. The lines involved were P & O, Furness Withy, Cunard and Blue Star who agreed to invest a total of approximately £50 million to enable operations to commence in 1973. The scheme was possibly a little over-ambitious in view of the relative smallness of New Zealand's market for industrial and consumer goods, which combined with a changing pattern of trade following the United Kingdom's probable entry into the EEC, would surely lead to over-tonnaging even with only the British container vessels operating. Orders were, however, placed in 1969 in Britain for the building of four vessels, each of 41,000 gross registered tons, each carrying 1,420 containers, and costing a total of £44 million. It should be remembered that at this stage OCL and ACT, who were co-ordinating the container interests of the four lines, were in a far from favorable situation, and even though the operating costs of a container service between Europe and New Zealand would be less than the cost of the conventional service, it had to be announced in May 1971 that the container service had been cancelled. The reasons for the cancellation as stated by the lines were: (a) rapidly rising capital and operating costs, (b) the unwillingness of New Zealand shippers to accept a substantial rise in freight rates, and (c) the reluctance of New Zealand to provide investment to finance the port facilities. These three aspects were certainly in evidence, and the original investment figure of £50 million had in fact spiralled to £80 million, but considering the lines' existing involvement in OCL and ACT together with the EEC implications, additional reasons affecting the cancellation are not difficult to find.

When the cancellation was announced the building of the first of the containerships, the *Remuera*, for P & O was so far advanced that it had to be completed, and $8 million had been invested in terminal facilities at Wellington, and work was proceeding at Auckland. The smaller port authorities were glad to hear of the news and looked forward optimistically to continuing to handle their share of New Zealand's trade, particularly meat and dairy products coming forward through the various producer boards. While some of these ports were stating that the boards would have been at a disadvantage had they switched to container shipping, due to the relative smallness of such vessels which would have kept freight rates high, the boards themselves appeared initially to be greatly shocked at the announcement. They were quick to state, however, that they were far from dependent on shipping by container in the future, let alone by British lines, and the Apple and Pear Marketing Board drew attention to their own policy of using Danish and Israeli lines. The New Zealand Meat Board denied negotiating with foreign owners, but much later in May 1974 they were threatening to use non-British lines if the consortia failed to increase containership tonnage between New Zealand and the United Kingdom by 1977. The optimism of the smaller port authorities though was short lived. Wellington and Auckland continued with their building programmes, and the facilities were soon being used by cellular or semi-container vessels linking New Zealand to Japan and North America. Today about 12 per cent of general cargo passing through Wellington is containerized and one portainer is in use. A second has been ordered and should be operational by March 1975. Auckland also has one portainer but a second is planned when the existing container berth is lengthened.

In August 1971, just prior to ACT's announcement of November 1971 of the ACT/ANL intention to withdraw from AECS, the two lines had begun to operate a containership service between Australia and New Zealand, and the east coast of North America. The line was to be known as Pacific America Container Express (PACE), and would bring a limited amount of traffic to New Zealand ports. The majority of the containers in the trade were to be refrigerated, being suitable for the carriage of meat from Australia and New Zealand to the USA and Canada, and wool and other primary products together with some general cargo were also to be carried. Similar services were also being provided by Columbus Line of West Germany and Farrell Line of the USA.

But New Zealand still remained unconnected by a container-ship line to the United Kingdom, and New Zealand shipping inter-ests were looking in August 1971 at the possibility of operating a feeder service to Australia to link up with the joint Europe/Aus-tralia service run by OCL—ACT. Thomas Nationwide Transport and Associated Steamship Proprietary Limited were both inter-ested and Associated Steam said they might be able to operate a service every 14–16 days using the 5,976-ton container vessel *Kooringa*. But following the ACT/ANL announcement of with-drawal from AECS to operate independently between Europe, and Australia and New Zealand, it became evident that at last New Zealand would be connected with Europe by containerships, and the proposed transhipment at Australian ports would not be neces-sary. The new service was to commence in September 1972, and would provide in conjunction with the PACE sailings the first round-the-world containership service.

Columbus Line was the other pioneer of containership sailings to New Zealand, providing a partly containerized service from the east coast of the USA in 1971, and a containership service, initially using three small chartered vessels, from the west coast of the USA in 1973. Following the success of Columbus, their parent company Hamburg-Sud of West Germany containerized its conventional Europe to New Zealand service in April 1974 by introducing two containerships, and the major consortia at present in the Europe to Australia trade are now to extend their opera-tions to New Zealand. While the initiative for these developments is principally coming from Europe, New Zealand herself is to join the container build-up, and has recently formed her own state shipping company. The company, which will start opera-tions by chartering vessels, has appointed as chairman a former head of the New Zealand Meat Board, and will function as a Con-ference member within AECS. A containership with capacity for 1,814 containers has been ordered for delivery in 1978, by which time AECS will have extended its services to New Zealand.

OCL, as a member of AECS, has so far only been involved in shipping container cargo to New Zealand through a space alloca-tion agreement with ACT. ACT has on charter from P & O the *Remuera*, which was to have been the first of four vessels to operate within the proposed but futile link-up between P & O,

Furness Withy, Cunard and Blue Star, and OCL will continue to ship containers through ACT by the *Remuera* until 1976. The vessel will return to her owners, P & O, in January 1977 to be operated by OCL within the extended AECS service to New Zealand. OCL had been considering the full containerization of the Europe to New Zealand trade for several years, and eventually announced in 1974 that two containerships each able to carry 1,814 containers had been ordered for delivery 1977/78. These vessels will allow AECS to extend to New Zealand, but the cost of this extension in comparison to prices for new tonnage in 1971 when the original proposals were announced, is to be enormous. In 1971 the *Remuera* was built for just over £11 million, but the cost of building a similar vessel at the time the OCL orders were placed in 1974 had risen to £25 million. ACT/ANL has already ordered a further two vessels, both able to carry 1,788 containers for delivery in 1977, but with the return of the *Remuera* to P & O (OCL), the ACT/ANL fleet will only be effectively increased by one vessel. These five new vessels, in conjunction with the present ACT/ANL vessels, and a modified AECS fleet, will enable approximately 75 per cent of cargo moving between Europe and New Zealand to be containerized, and will allow far larger carryings of meat and other perishables northbound by container. At present only about 18 per cent of New Zealand meat is containerized, and the expanded container capacity should go a long way to satisfying the demands of the New Zealand Meat Board for more containership sailings. The extension to New Zealand will also help to ease the trade imbalance between Europe and Australia, as New Zealand exports to Europe, and to the United Kingdom in particular, far outweigh her imports from the area. The surfeit of empty northbound boxes will therefore be filled, while at the same time the extra vessels will be able to cope with the large flow of European exports bound for Australia.

The United States of America

The United States of America is regarded as the birthplace of containerization following the establishment of Malcolm

McLean's container services of 1956, and progress since that time has been rapid, but often lacking in co-ordination. Since 1959 the USA has invested approximately $7.5 billion in containerization, which has to some extent checked the decline of the American merchant marine, and which has contributed to ten million tons of general cargo, representing 73 per cent of the total, being containerized in 1971, as compared with less than two million tons, representing 28 per cent, in 1968. The influx of container vessels that made this radical change possible has had its own effects on the shipping industry serving the USA, and paramount among these is the problem of over-tonnaging. Prior to containerization the United States merchant fleet was used predominantly to ship war supplies, but during the mid-1960's the opportunity presented itself for greater general cargo shipping in the new American containerships, and this stimulus subsequently led to over-rapid growth of container capacity and to a gradual widening of the gap between capacity and cargo offered.

This over-tonnaging first became apparent on the North Atlantic, and was later to be accentuated by the run down in military traffic. No container line on the North Atlantic made a profit during 1970 and 1971, and a casualty was Moore McCormack Lines who were forced into selling four of their container vessels, while American Export Lines lost almost $29 million in 1971. United States flag vessels were at one time carrying over 70 per cent of the available containerized cargo in the trade, and many container ships were crossing the Atlantic with a majority of empty boxes. In trying to attract cargo to their particular lines, practices were adopted by some shipping companies contrary to conference rulings and apparently in contempt of FMC/ICC policy. Mention has already been made of the "unhealthily competitive" nature of the spate of rate adjustments whereby through rates from and to inland points were being offered as a way of reducing the conference controlled ocean freight rate. Another way of raising cargo tonnage would be to divert cargo away from its natural port of shipment or entry and move it across the quays of a port possibly several hundred miles away. Such practices would allow the containership company to limit the number of ports it served, thus reducing its costs and making it possible to subsidize the extra cost of the longer inland haul. But this type of action, while benefiting the shipping company concerned, is harmful to the ports who are losing cargo in their hinterland, and will mean that less cargo will be available to other lines serving these ports. Philadelphia and Boston were hit very hard because of diversionary activities, which were contrary to the US Shipping Act 1916, and the Merchant Marine Act 1920, and in a case brought before the Federal Maritime Commission it was ruled that American President Lines should discontinue diverting traffic emanating in the Philadelphia area to New York. Eight other lines had meanwhile suspended their own diversionary activities in the area. If cargo is lost by a port, the labor force will also be affected, and in an attempt to obtain compensation the International Longshoremen's Association sued four American containership companies for loss of wages due to diversion of cargo away from Philadelphia over a six-year period. Cargo is currently being lost to Canadian ports in larger volumes than diversions from Canadian to USA ports, and in view of the strong economic ground upon which diversions take place it is likely that the practice will grow. It is argued in several influential quarters that the Acts of 1916 and 1920 are badly in need of amendment in view of the changed basis upon which container movements are costed, and the signs are that the necessary alterations could be forthcoming. In November 1973 it was mooted by the FMC that shipping companies could after all move cargo to and from any area through whichever port they choose, therefore apparently allowing diversion and making it possible for shipping companies to legitimately absorb additional inland haulage costs.

Although much of the blame for the unsatisfactory situation to be found in the North Atlantic trade during the early 1970's has been placed on rate cutting activities, it should be remembered that this cutting would not have been necessary if investment in new vessels and equipment had not taken place on such a grand scale. The shipping companies are now trying to make this over-investment economic by keeping rates high, and have ceased to grant unofficial rebates, through a self disciplinary system rigidly enforced by the conference, pending the outcome of an attempt at formulating a system of cargo and revenue sharing. It is intended that a revenue pool be established by seven of the North Atlantic containership lines whereby freight is pooled before being

apportioned to each member line in accordance with a predetermined percentage. The lines would therefore retain a degree of
competitiveness up to the point where they reached their permitted "ceiling", and rate cutting would not be necessary. A fixed
range of ports would be served on a regular basis, not through
each line calling at all the ports, but through each port being ade-
quately served by one or a number of the lines. Some ports would
therefore be assured of a steady throughput of container cargo,
while others would lose much of their present share of North
Atlantic traffic. Such a system precludes calls at ports that may
have already embarked on an expensive modernization programme, and does not offer any incentive to call at smaller ports
either direct or using feeders. Larger companies such as Sea-Land
would therefore ideally be placed, if they were to decide not to
co-operate with the pooling system, to make full use of their
existing very comprehensive network of feeders and ocean vessels
to control much of the cargo presently passing through the smaller
ports and those not included in the range where pool members
intend calling.

The need for a revenue pool is probably exaggerated in view
of the current stable nature of rates, and if it is accepted that any
over- or under-tonnaging situation is usually of a temporary
nature, and will be self-adjusting if the conference regulates the
trade as it should do. Shipping companies in a pool would be
assured of a regular income, and there would be no incentive to
provide specialized containers and other equipment to cater for
a minority of cargo owners. A revenue pool would therefore favor
the shipping companies, and if the Federal Maritime Commission
were to sanction it, they would in effect be changing their policy
of shipper protection to one of shipowner protection. A pool as
proposed would also be contrary to the American anti-trust laws
formulated to control monopoly situations. While a pool would
maintain stability, it would not solve the over-tonnaging problem,
as any exodus by conference lines would surely be cancelled out
by the introduction of additional non-conference lines only too
eager to gain a foothold in the potentially lucrative North Atlantic trade. Even though it is felt in some quarters that a rate war
will begin again if a pool is not introduced, the FMC is not convinced that one is necessary, and points to the potential monopo-

listic position of pool members. The possibility of a fall in rates leading to some lines leaving the trade and allowing greater dominance by a smaller group, who would then be able to raise rates to inflationary levels, is not taken seriously by the FMC, but port discrimination is. It appears that the FMC may be in favor of shipping companies deciding for themselves purely on economic grounds which ports they should serve, and even though this will involve some cargo diversion, it is considered to be a far lesser evil than a policy of collusion among the shipping companies whereby some ports are entirely ignored. It is not considered that ports should be encouraged to wastefully duplicate facilities, but they should still have an opportunity to compete for traffic on an equal footing, if only to ensure that service given is not allowed to suffer through complacency setting in.

The major North Atlantic containership companies then have agreed amongst themselves to halt practices that can only be harmful to themselves, as well as to cargo owners, pending a decision on a pool by the FMC, and until the legalities can be sorted out. The conference was unable to discipline its members during the build up of North Atlantic containership tonnage, and from a position of relative weakness the conference has changed its attitude into one penalizing the cargo owner. Demurrage is levied on containers irrespective of whether the cargo owner was the cause of the delay, and this type of inflexible attitude, especially when it is difficult to ascertain the legal powers of the conference, is not conducive to a satisfactory shipper/shipowner relationship. A pool would almost certainly maintain rates at a higher level than they otherwise would be, in order to finance the shipment of many empty boxes, and would not have the desired effect of adjusting vessel tonnage to the quantity of cargo on offer.

In spite of the undesirable nature of a revenue pool, the FMC was recommended in March 1974 by the US Justice Department to approve one, but with certain conditions attached. Shipping companies in the pool would be obliged to submit "confidential" information from their home and overseas offices when requested, and the initial period of operation would be limited to three years, and not six years as proposed by the lines. Non-pool lines should be allowed to ship containers in pool vessels, and a weekly direct service should be provided for Boston. The stipulation that Boston be served direct could be taken as a precedent for other ports to have special treatment, and is not really necessary anyway as a considerable volume of diverted cargo is in fact being shipped by feeder vessel through Boston, and is therefore earning revenue for the port. A condition that may prevent the establishment of the pool at all is a penalty of $2 million for withdrawal by any member line within six months of formation of the pool. Atlantic Container Line, one of the initial group that advocated the need for a pool, informed the FMC in April 1974 that it could not be a party to any agreement containing such a penalty clause, and as ACL would be entitled to the largest share of revenue, the chances of the pool materializing without their co-operation are slender.

While all this discussion has been going on concerning a revenue pool, the fluctuating nature of cargo throughput has vividly been shown by the state of over-tonnaging in the North Atlantic being converted to one of severe under-capacity. During 1973 the United States was able to change a trade deficit to a trade surplus, largely through the decline in the value of the dollar since December 1971, and other significant factors contributed to cargo owners having to wait for up to four weeks for a container during the first six months of 1974. A world shortage or raw and semi-finished basic commodities prompted many firms to stockpile, and the threat of a USA dockstrike added to the upsurge in traffic. Price controls within the USA made exporting more profitable and the energy crisis of 1974, which hit the United States less than most other countries, placed them in a favorable position to fulfill orders that other countries could not cope with. It is appreciated that all these conditions arose at the same time, and combined to raise cargo throughput, but it should be remembered before the lines become committed to a revenue pool, that other factors outside the control of a pool will continue to affect cargo tonnage and that natural regulation is often better than artificial regulation.

The North Atlantic non-conference lines are not yet sufficiently strong enough to have any significant effect on the trade. Maritime Container Lines began their non-conference service between the continent of Europe and the United States in 1972 despite the over-tonnaging situation. A ten-day service was offered using three vessels each capable of shipping approximately 300 20-foot containers. The containers were part owned and part leased, and even though costs were kept to a minimum by avoiding expensive overheads such as computers, the line found it necessary to withdraw from the North Atlantic in early 1974. New England Express Line is maintaining a weekly service between Europe and the United States using three time chartered vessels formerly belonging to Seatrain which have a capacity of 490 20-foot containers each. Sailings are under conference jurisdiction from the United Kingdom to the United States, but outside conference control from the Continent to the United States. New England Express has succeeded largely due to flexibility attained through not having to cope with conference conditions regarding sailing frequency. If sufficient cargo is not offered sailings can be delayed, and through running to near capacity, revenue will be maximized and will not have to subsidize the movement of many empty containers. All containers are leased and as initial capital outlay has been small, rates up to 10 per cent below the conference tariff are offered. Although the non-conference lines are having only a limited effect in the trade at present, a situation could arise later that might be considered by the conference membership detrimental to the running of a revenue pool. While a pool would tend to keep rates at a high level, non-conference lines would be operating at rates below those of the pool, and steps could be taken by the United States government through legislative channels to curb the development of non-conference competition to allow a revenue return to pool members sufficiently large to cover their inflated operating costs.

United States government interference with the free running of US flag vessels, as well as with non-US flag vessels calling at American ports, has been evident for many years, and stems from the subsidies handed to United States shipping companies. Much of this government policy obstructs development, and would be better employed in trying to co-ordinate the functions of the Federal Maritime Commission and the Interstate Commerce Commission in areas such as the establishment of through rates. Harmony between the FMC and ICC is rare, and because of its absence a containership company wishing to file a through tariff rate between an inland point within the United States and Europe will find it difficult to obtain both FMC and ICC approval. Recent examples of excessive interference are the freeze in June 1973 on rates charged by shipping companies using United States ports by the FMC, irrespective of the vessel's flag and contrary to conference intentions of the time, and the condition that the FMC be provided with statistics and other asked for information on the setting up in London in 1974 of the International Council of Containership Operators. The condition that subsidized lines must undertake a minimum number of voyages annually, however, would appear to be justified in view of the involvement of public money.

The largest container port in the United States is New York where container handling is centered at the Elizabeth Port Authority Marine Terminal. Construction of the terminal was begun by the Port of New York Authority as far back as 1958, and it opened in 1962. $143 million had been invested in the terminal by the end of 1972 in providing seven berths and eleven portainers, and current annual throughput of containerized cargo exceeds 10 million tons. New York has long been a high cost port with an inflexible labor situation, but was favored by break-bulk vessels who would usually make the port their first call in the United States, prior to working down the East Coast and returning to collect cargo bound for Europe. But containerization has had the effect of making the port more equal with its East Coast competitors, as containerships will often restrict their ports of call on each continent, and in the case of the United States where most of the other ports are able to offer a service at least equal to that provided by New York, the lines will often base their United States activity at one of the other ports. New York has therefore partially lost its unique services. Part of the Elizabeth terminal is leased to Sea-Land, and many other leased and private terminals exist at New York including those at Port Newark, Port Jersey, Weehawken and Howland Hook. Weehawken, a private containerport across the Hudson River from Manhattan, was built by Seatrain and incorporates an electronically augmented container control system. The terminal at Howland Hook was begun by American Export Lines, but had to be purchased by New York City in March 1974. It is currently being developed by US Lines at an initial cost of $2.9 million, and will be used principally by US Lines with American Export Lines as a subtenant.

The port of Boston, controlled by the Massachusetts Port Authority, was slow in catering for containerships, the Mystic Public Container Terminal not opening until late in 1971. Two portainers have been provided, and in view of the port's recent rapid increase in container cargo which now accounts for 50 per cent of total general cargo, facilities may be increased two-fold. A lot of cargo has been lost to New York through diversionary activities, but Boston has been fortunate in being provided with an FMC approved feeder service from Halifax operated by Maritime Coastal Container Line. As charges at Halifax are much lower than those at New York, Halifax-generated cargo passing over Boston quays is of immense benefit to the Massachusetts port, and has largely contributed to the trebling of container throughput during 1972/1973. Labor relations are good, and Sea-Land in accordance with their policy of owning or leasing their terminals, have their own facilities at Castle Island.

Philadelphia and her neighboring ports on the Delaware River are collectively known as Ameriport, and are controlled by the Delaware River Port Authority. It has already been mentioned that Philadelphia was losing some of its cargo to New York, but facilities at the Packer Avenue Marine Terminal together with those at the Tioga Marine Terminal have enabled much of this diverted traffic to return following a directive from the ICC forbidding Philadelphia's rightful cargo being channeled through other East Coast ports. Container traffic passing over the Packer Avenue and Tioga terminals, each served by two portainers, doubled during the period 1972/1974, and a third terminal is now being planned.

Rivalling New York as the second largest container port on the United States eastern seaboard is Baltimore. Over a quarter of Baltimore's throughput is containerized and about 75 per cent of it is handled at the Dundalk Marine Terminal. $25 million will have been invested at Dundalk when it is finished in 1977 and currently seven portainers are in service at six berths. The terminal was originally built on 360 acres, but the comparative abundance of land in the area is allowing an additional 180 acres to be

FIGURE 16 Packer Avenue Marine Terminal at Philadelphia
(Courtesy of Delaware River Port Authority).

included in the scheme. Dundalk is a public facility operated by the Maryland Port Administration, and a similar terminal is to be provided partly on reclaimed land across the harbor at Locust Point. Locust Point is at present principally handling general break-bulk cargo, but $16.3 million is being invested in the provision of three container berths. It has yet to be decided whether the terminal will be exclusively for container cargo, or whether there will be a mixture of container and break-bulk. In the Canton area of Baltimore harbor the port's oldest container customer, Sea-Land, has been using the private Canton Marine Terminal facilities since April 1963. The portainer at Canton was the port's first, and Sea-Land make use of the extensive back-up area to operate their chassis system. One of Baltimore's principal selling points is her nearness to the eastern and central industrial areas of the United States, which means cheaper inland haulage rates will be levied on Baltimore cargo in comparison with other ports, which coupled with the fact that ocean rates from Europe to ports north of Cape Hatteras are the same, means that through costs will be less. Container throughput at Baltimore rose by about 25 per cent during 1971-1972, while a 55 per cent increase was registered during 1972-1973.

Near the entrance to Chesapeake Bay the predominantly bulk handling port of Newport News is being provided with a $17 million combined container and break-bulk complex, and one portainer became operational in February 1973 at Pier C. Newport News together with Norfolk and Portsmouth are controlled by the Virginia Port Authority, and collective throughput in 1972 rose by 32 per cent over 1971's figure. Further south the port of Wilmington in North Carolina has one crane capable of handling containers, while the South Carolina port of Charleston has four portainers and two terminals. Charleston commenced container handling in February 1971 with one container berth, and since then $90 million has been invested. The port is growing rapidly, and its current annual one million ton container cargo throughput will grow rapidly during development of a $68 million third terminal at Wando River, where eventually seven berths are to be provided. In the state of Georgia LASH and bulk vessels used to predominate at Savannah, and the port was slow in providing facilities for containerships. A container berth was eventually constructed though at Garden City serviced by a portainer and two transtainers, and the port has grown steadily since then. Increasing demands from container lines to call at the port prompted development of a second berth which was opened in 1973, and the port is about to embark on a $66 million five-year expansion programme that will include a third container terminal and two more portainers. Another rapidly growing port is Jacksonville in Florida. Jacksonville is in the midst of a $100 million rebuilding programme which will allow the expansion of the twelve-acre container terminal at Blount Island into a major complex serving the southern states. Sea-Land are active in the port, and have been renting the Talleyrand Terminal since 1966. As the more northern ports become congested, both Savannah and Jacksonville will play an increasingly important role in the transfer of containers between ship and shore.

Containership services in United States waters have grown rapidly, and have prompted the re-evaluation by most port authorities of their role in the container age. In spite of the lines' early indications that fewer ports would be called at by the container vessels, and more use would be made of internal transport systems to distribute and collect container loads, development programmes were quickly formulated by a number of port authorities with the result that funds have been strained and container facilities are sometimes needlessly duplicated. Government assistance to United States ports has always been restricted to dredging costs, and any other direct aid has been vigorously rejected by the ports on the ground that local control is preferable to any form of state control. But it is now felt in government circles that more co-ordination of future port development is desirable, and substantial subsidies to help with terminal construction costs may be offered in return for partial control. Although government money has been trickling into the ports indirectly, when for example a port forms part of an area where a grant has been given for the construction of ancillary facilities, more direct aid on a massive scale will be difficult to reject, and if accepted will allow the government, in association with the Federal Maritime Commission, to determine which ports should be further developed and how far cargo diversion should be allowed to progress. Although state interference should be resisted, state guidance should be encouraged if only to avoid expensive duplication of port facilities during a period when shipping companies are planning larger vessels, and ports of call are almost certain to be restricted. Perhaps the future of many of the USA's container terminals will lie in the provision of facilities for coastal feeder vessels.

Another trade where over-tonnaging has become a problem is that between the Far East and the Pacific coast of the United States. Several American lines entered the trade during the escalation of the war in Vietnam to secure their share of the military traffic, but partly due to the subsequent rundown of military shipments, and partly to the influx of Japanese and other foreign tonnage, too many container vessels were soon chasing too little cargo. Of three American lines deeply involved in the trans-Pacific trade, American President Line and American Mail Line are operating about twenty vessels between them, while the Pacific Far East Line have invested over $100 million on six LASH vessels. The combined effect of the American and Japanese lines' tonnage led to the withdrawal in 1970 from the trans-Pacific trade of Matson Navigation, the pioneers of Pacific cellular containerships, who decided to concentrate instead on the US west coast to Hawaii run.

It has been estimated that by 1975 there will be three times the amount of potential container space as cargo offered and even though the containerships are attracting more and more cargo previously carried by the break-bulk operators, the tonnage shipped by United States flag vessels is falling relatively to other lines, and because public money is involved through the granting of subsidies, the Federal Maritime Commission is treating the matter as urgent. Currently there is a 35% surplus of capacity, but over-tonnaging first became a real problem in the Pacific in 1972, and affected United States flag vessels in particular because of their previous heavy dependence on contracts for the carriage of war supplies to Vietnam. Foreign flag vessels had already built up a regular commercial custom, and were barely able to maintain their freight revenues at a time when US flag vessels found themselves with very little commercial cargo. Vessel operation in the North Atlantic trade up to this time had not brought forth the expected profits, and the part subsidization of the one trade by the other was not possible.

While the FMC were in favor of rationalizing the Pacific trade in an attempt to avoid the granting of rate rebates, as had been found in the North Atlantic trade, the fundamental problems were different from those in the Atlantic, largely because of the varied outlook of the containership companies and of the conferences. Common ground could not be found, the shipping companies were desperately trying to attract more cargo to their particular lines, the conferences were unable to regulate the activities of their members, non-conference competition was becoming more severe, and inevitably unofficial freight rebates began to find their way to cargo owners. Just as the trade was becoming vulnerable, non-conference lines such as rapidly growing Orient Overseas and Zim entered the trade, and they were soon to be followed by the unsubsidized American line Sea-Land. Meanwhile the heavily subsidized Russian line, the Far Eastern Shipping Company (FESCO), were offering rates up to 20 per cent lower in the Pacific than conference tariff rates, and from their one fully cellular vessel which began operating in May 1973, the line is planning to increase its fleet running between Japan and Hong Kong, to the United States west coast, to a total of six fully cellular vessels. Approximately one-third of all general cargo moving between Japan and the US west coast is carried by non-conference lines, and much of this is made up of high-value, high-revenue freight, while the lower-revenue freight is being left with the conference vessels. Although large discounts are being offered by the non-conference vessels, returns per sailing may exceed the revenue being obtained by conference vessels, because of the highly rated nature of the non-conference cargo, and because of the lower overheads of operating outside the conference structure. FESCO has been particularly active in cutting rates, sometimes to apparently uneconomic levels, and the absence of any profit motivation would indicate that the intention is to deprive the more commercial lines of any long-term security in the Pacific. This sort of practice, which was not evident in the North Atlantic in such extremes, can only distort the trade even further and make the job of the FMC more difficult.

Because of non-conference rate cutting the American conference lines threatened to withdraw from the Pacific conferences in November 1973. They pointed to the weakness of the conferences, who were unable even to regulate their own members' activities, and the threat was in fact carried out in December 1973. Rates were being unduly cut on such highly rated items as electronics, toys and textiles, but following an undertaking by three of the non-conference lines to discuss future rate levels with the conferences, the American lines re-joined in January 1974. One method of curbing non-conference rate cutting would be for the FMC to ban entry to United States ports on vessels said to be operating at below cost, but due to the complexities of ship management costings, and to the hostile nature bound to be taken by those countries involved in running heavily subsidized fleets, such action is unlikely. A more realistic approach would be to introduce a system of dual rates into the conference tariff, whereby conference signatories were granted a rate rebate while other shippers would be charged the full rate. A spread of 15 per cent had been asked for by the conferences, but because of objections by the Japanese authorities, the FMC had to settle for a 9.5 per cent spread between the two rates. Following the adoption of the dual rate system by two of the Pacific conferences at the end of 1973, the non-conference lines were quick to state that they would be little affected but they were willing to discuss the possibility of formulating a revenue pooling system, as well as exchanging views on rate levels as mentioned above. They went so far as to say they might even join the conferences if a satisfactory revenue-sharing formula could be worked out, and it may be that the non-conference lines are becoming concerned about their future role in trans-Pacific shipping. To add to the rate disparities in the Pacific, the Scandinavia line Star Shipping introduced a non-conference service in May 1974 based on the FAK (freight of all kinds) system of assessing charges. Under the FAK system the shipping company charges a uniform lump sum per container, irrespective of the contents of the container, but with a discount where several units are moved at the same time. The FAK system will obviously not be attractive to owners of low-value cargo, and will act as a further blow to the conferences who will find still more potentially highly freighted cargo slipping away.

The troubles within the conferences stem mainly from an inherent weakness in controlling their own members, and from rating disparities. The FMC has been unhappy about the activities of four of the Pacific conferences for a number of years, especially in view of reports from shippers which indicate that rates are fixed in accordance with what the traffic can bear. The conferences say that rates are based on demand, but it has been shown that an item travelling in an east-west direction will often be rated far higher than an identical item moving from west to east. In some cases westbound rates were said to be 70 per cent higher than eastbound rates, and United States exporters were finding that their products were becoming less competitive in overseas markets. Such rating disparities are probably an attempt to raise traffic flows from Japan to the United States, which are lower than westbound flows, and have followed the reversing of the former situation in which trade from Japan used to be the heavier. Additionally the majority of Japanese exports consist of manufactured items and are easily carried by container, while a significant proportion of her imports are raw and semi-finished products which are not so easily containerized. As different conferences regulate westbound and eastbound movements, and as differences in outlook exist between the two groups, the FMC is finding it very difficult to assemble accurate statistics. In addition to basic rates, such additionals as bunker surcharges, currency surcharges, and congestion surcharges have proliferated over recent years following oil shortages, currency fluctuations, and labor and other problems in port. Whether these surcharges accurately reflect the extra costs incurred by the conference shipping lines might be open to debate, but it is considered in some quarters that the surcharges are in part being used by the conferences to manipulate the basic rates. It could be convincingly argued that in view of the activities of the non-conference lines, a degree of rate adjustment is warranted, but the effect on vessel operation in the North Atlantic trade following rate rebates not from the conferences, but merely from some of the member lines, should not be forgotten. Because of dissatisfaction with the Pacific conference structure, Seatrain withdrew its membership in May 1974, and intends to join the ranks of the unencumbered non-conference lines.

In order to bring these malpractices to a halt, and prior to the setting up of a revenue pooling system, an attempt is being made to introduce a system of self-policing both within and outside the Pacific conferences, similar in format to the voluntary restraint on rate cutting in the North Atlantic trade. It was proposed during talks held in Tokyo in April 1973 between Japanese merchant shipping interests and the FMC, that observation should be kept on the self-policing system in the North Atlantic trade. By November of the same year the United States containership companies were actively pressing for the setting up of such a system to include all the Pacific conferences, and they were strongly supported by the FMC. But the four major conferences, together with the Japanese government, were opposed to the scheme on the grounds that sufficient control was already being exerted by the conference system. Meanwhile a freight pooling system had been introduced by the Japan and South Korea/North America Freight Conference, and it was agreed by the remaining conferences that the effect on the trade of this pool should be observed. The United States container lines were losing money in the Pacific, and they were in favor of a pool to include all vessel nationalities, which would act to co-ordinate sailing schedules and more fairly apportion cargo carried. But during the months leading up to the time when these discussions and decisions were taking place the Japanese merchant marine found itself entering a vulnerable period. In February 1973 the United States dollar had been devalued by 10 per cent, and the Japanese yen was allowed to float upward. Freight returns therefore fell following effectively higher operating costs, and Japan's earlier commitment to conserve as much foreign currency as possible by carrying as much of her overseas trade as possible began to crumble. The very rapid growth of the Japanese merchant marine had been made possible partly through government assistance, but it was still necessary to enter the very expensive charter market to supplement tonnage.

Action was therefore necessary to check the slide, and to try to retain the inroads already made in the Pacific trade into American containership operations by the six major Japanese lines. This move toward Japanese dominance had been assisted by space charter agreements with United States owners, whereby the

Japanese lines were able to ship a number of containers in American vessels, and even though co-operation of this sort could be regarded as the foundation for a more comprehensive sharing system later, it soon became evident that Japanese intentions regarding a revenue pool involved the "big six" Japanese lines only. It was announced in January 1974 that the Japanese wished to form their own Pacific pool and it was hoped that early FMC approval would be given. Rate discussions among pool members would be encouraged, and individual members would be free to make their own rate changes if 48 hours' notice was first given to the conference. Whether the FMC approves the pool remains to be seen, but in view of it being wholly Japanese, and considering the effect it could have on cargo volumes carried by American flag companies, approval in its proposed form is unlikely.

Admittedly a pessimistic view had been taken of the outcome of the talks held between Japan and the United States in San Francisco in January 1973, and in Tokyo in April of the same year, when over-tonnaging, non-conference competition, and rate rebates had been discussed. The United States had expressed a desire to carry more of its overseas trade by its own flag vessels, and alleged that Japan was discriminating against American vessels. In view of Japan's feelings following her less favorable currency situation, and her desire also to raise cargo levels, it was not unexpected that the outcome of the talks was negative. Japan could possibly have adopted a more flexible attitude especially as the United States had put a halt on any immediate growth in American flag container vessels in the Pacific through temporarily withdrawing new subsidies, but the entry to the trade of Sea-Land's three fast unsubsidized "SL-7" class vessels could not be ignored. Sea-Land's vessels began their service between Kobe and Oakland in May 1973, and are making the crossing in only eight days in comparison to the more usual containership time of ten days. The only current hope for the setting up of a regulating scheme to cover virtually all the Pacific carriers lies in the outcome of a further round of talks held in Oslo in May 1974. Twenty-eight conference and non-conference lines, including the Russian FESCO, discussed pooling and particular emphasis was placed on a possible points system of sharing cargo revenue.

Containerization of the Pacific has had its effect on a number of groups, not least of which are the former American break-bulk operators whose vessels are now largely redundant, and are having to be converted into parcel tankers and other vessel types. It was thought there would always be a place for the break-bulk ships, but much of the cargo they were relying on, such as awkward loads and long lengths, are now being adapted to conform with intermodal shipment requirements, and are being carried in increasing quantities by the container lines. But running parallel with the containership there is a slowly growing tendency to introduce more flexible tonnage into the Pacific trades. Matson Navigation, the pioneers of containership operation in the Pacific, put into service in August 1973 the first roll-on roll-off vessel in the Pacific, which is being used on their United States west coast to Hawaii run. Two roll-on roll-off ships will maintain the link alongside two containerships. While the Pacific Far East Line have been running LASH vessels in the trade for several years, and other United States companies have been active in the container field, the roll-on roll-off concept is new to the Americans and it may be seen as a way of cutting costs and making trans-Pacific vessel operation more profitable. The method is of course flexible in cargo types carried, and range of ports served, and avoids costly involvement in the provision of advanced shore handling techniques. States Steamship Company of San Francisco has ordered four roll-on roll-off vessels for the United States west coast to Far East trade, some of which will be in service by 1975.

The situation the ports on either side of the Pacific Ocean have found themselves in following containerization of the trade is very different. Japan's ports were not constructed with a view to handling any great volume of imported goods, other than raw materials in bulk, and warehousing space is in short supply. The ports have traditionally been export orientated, in the wake of the country's rapid development into a manufacturer of consumer goods, and congestion has built up following an inability to quickly clear and dispose of increasing numbers of containers. The terminals have become choked, and vessel turnround times are badly affected. To make matters worse there is a shortage of trailers and tractor units suitable for hauling containers, and much of Japan's internal road system is not capable of absorbing this sort of heavy traffic. In contrast the United States Pacific ports, while not being directly affected by the containership over-tonnaging situation, have their own problems. Clearance and delivery from the port area will not usually be delayed, but it has been estimated that needless duplication of facilities will result in a 570 per cent over-capacity situation arising by 1975. Ports are vying with each other for the custom of the containership lines, and some are encouraging the growth of the mini-landbridge concept which in effect takes business away from Atlantic and Gulf ports. The American Pacific coast container ports are in three sets of pairs, and it is within each of these pairs where competition is at its strongest.

Seattle was a leader in the provision of container handling facilities, and developments have been proceeding over a period of eleven years. Several container berths and portainers have been provided, and many lines have been attracted to the port including Sea-Land. A lot of military cargo used to pass over Seattle, and through being linked to Halifax by landbridge, a steady flow of containers passing between Europe and Japan are handled at the port. Seattle is only 100 miles south of Vancouver, and due to the superiority of handling facilities at Seattle, and a better labor record, a lot of potential Vancouver cargo is being diverted through the port. In common with some of the United States east coast longshoremen, the labor force at Vancouver is not helping matters by insisting that containers are unpacked and re-packed at the terminals. But the relative position of the two ports could soon be changing following large-scale expansion at Vancouver, but as Seattle has already invested nearly $70 million in port facilities she will be closely watching developments. Watch will also be kept on Portland in Oregon, another port dominated at present by Seattle, where three container terminals have been provided at a cost of $40 million since 1963. It was thought at one time that Portland would act principally as a feeder port for Seattle, but throughput is expanding fast and the port could develop into a major container center.

San Francisco, like Vancouver and Portland, feels dominated by an almost adjacent competitor, and in spite of $55 million having been invested to date, much of the port's cargo is being drawn away to the rival terminal across the bay at Oakland.

Although San Francisco's net income is falling rapidly, and a deficit may indeed be recorded in 1975, development plans are proceeding, and include the spending of $20 million at pier 94 largely for use by American President Lines, and an even larger sum for a 314-acre Multiport complex where container, LASH and break-bulk facilities will be provided. Whether these projects are able to check the increasing flow of containers draining away to Oakland will largely depend on improvements in the management of the port, to allow her competitive position to be raised. The first MACH portainer system (see page 32) in the United States was installed at Oakland's $32 million Seventh Street terminal where currently four berths, three portainers and a giant 170-ton crane are being used. A total of twelve container berths, fourteen portainers, and a roll-on roll-off berth have been provided at Oakland, and the port claims to be the biggest on the United States west coast with the largest number of container ships passing through annually. Sea-Land have their own 70-acre terminal at Oakland and United States Lines are to base their own terminal in the Middle Harbor area. Oakland had far more insight than San Francisco during the 1960's into how containerization would develop and progress since then has been very rapid.

The third pair of competing ports are Los Angeles and Long Beach. At Los Angeles the 30-acre East-West container terminal was opened in 1969 principally to serve the Japanese lines, but expansion will increase the terminal's size to 120 acres. Prior to the East-West development, the world's first container terminal had been built at Terminal Island in 1958 for Matson Navigation at a cost of $20 million. A new container wharf is to be built at Terminal Island and a ten-year expansion programme has been announced. It was at one time thought that Los Angeles and Long Beach might amalgamate, but fortunately for Long Beach the merger never took place. Long Beach is growing rapidly as a container port, and three times more containers were handled in 1973 than in 1972. Ten container berths and twelve portainers have been provided, and a total of 300 acres of storage area is in use. Over $30 million has been invested in three terminals. Sea-Land have been port users since 1963 and a new terminal for their exclusive use was opened in early 1973 on a 66-acre site. Long Beach, which will eventually be able to offer eleven con-

tainer berths at four terminals, is not in favor of linking-up with
Los Angeles, and is well on the way to being one of the few fully
automated deep sea container terminals on the West Coast.

Further south in the Gulf of Mexico, LASH and Seabee barge
facilities have been developed almost as quickly as container terminals. As explained in Chapter Two, barge carrying vessels were
attracted to the area largely because of the extensive system of
rivers and canals that connect some of the Gulf ports with areas
far into the industrial hinterland of the United States. Services
were established with European ports such as Rotterdam, Bremerhaven and Sheerness (Thames estuary), which were also linked
by rivers or waterways to inland points. Use was therefore being
made of the Mississippi River, the Rhine, the Weser and the
Thames, and because of hoped for quick turnrounds by the deep
sea vessel, cost savings were expected. It is estimated though that
to keep a LASH vessel operational costs in the region of £7,000
per day, and in view of slower turnround times than were envisaged, several of the LASH lines have been losing money.

The switch from conventional to LASH and container vessels
can be illustrated by Combi Line, the Hapag Lloyd/Holland America consortium, who used to operate ten break-bulk vessels between European ports and the Gulf. Combi now operate two
cellular containerships, which have given them 25 per cent more
capacity, coupled with faster sailing times. Total commitment to
a barge carrying method of shipment is now considered as unwise,
and where Combi obtain flexibility between barges and containers
through operating different types of vessel, Delta Steamship
Lines of New Orleans have obtained even greater flexibility by
introducing vessels on their Gulf/South America run able to
carry barges and containers in any combination. Their vessels are
therefore able to accommodate an all barge loading, a part barge
and part container configuration, or a complete container loading
of up to 1,740 units. As demand in the trade changes, and as the
South American ports and the inland transport system are further
developed, Delta will be well placed to cater for the differing
requirements, and will not be faced with the possibility of
subsidizing the operating costs of an underused LASH vessel.

But while Delta appear to have made provision for the future, and Central Gulf Contramar Line are showing perhaps too much confidence in the LASH system, other operators have been less fortunate. The trans-Pacific LASH service, the first LASH service in the world, run by Pacific Far East Line has been losing money for several years, while in the Gulf both Prudential Grace and Combi Line are having their own problems. Prudential Grace had to sell its vessels to a finance house to remain solvent, and then lease them back, and Combi Line is suffering from a shortage of cargo due to the effect of the falling value of the US dollar and of the upward movement of some European currencies. Lykes Lines, the largest of the United States flag shipping companies, is the operator of the Seabee barge system described in Chapter Two, and runs in addition to three Seabee ships, twelve part container vessels. Lykes Lines is therefore going for the two extremes of cargo, i.e., bulk commodities to fill the 850-ton capacity barges, and general cargo capable of being containerized. The expensive practice of loading a high-cost container into a high-cost barge, as so often happens in the LASH system, can therefore be avoided if the two cargo types are offered in the required proportions.

Of the cellular container lines associated with the Gulf, mention should be made of Gulf Container Line who were the first in operating fully containerized vessels in the area. Gulf began their service from Europe in July 1970 with chartered vessels capable of shipping both 20- and 40-foot units, but due to the rising cost of chartering its ships, and of the adverse movement in currency values, the line had to withdraw from the trade in August 1973. Atlantic Gulf Service is running part cellular/part break-bulk vessels between Europe and the Gulf direct, while Seatrain recently decided to withdraw its direct service, and operate over Charleston instead. Containers are shipped between Europe and the South Carolina port by cellular vessel, and a rail link from Charleston to New Orleans, Houston, and Galveston completes the link.

As the vulnerability of the barge carrying system has become more evident, the Gulf ports are realizing the importance of providing more facilities for container and semi-container vessels, which may also have the effect of bringing back to the Gulf some of the container cargo being lost to the West Coast ports through the mini-landbridge system. America's second largest port, and the third largest in the world, is the Mississippi port of New Orleans. New Orleans, sometimes known as Centroport, is ideally situated to act as a base for the collection of barges from the hinterland of the United States eastern industrial area, prior to loading to the deep-sea LASH and Seabee ships. Barges can also be loaded at canal-based terminals, and Delta Steamship Lines opened their own $6 million terminal in September 1973 at the Milan Street wharf for their South American LASH service. Container facilities are being expanded at the France Road Container Terminal following the opening of the first berth in 1972, and a second berth was completed in 1973. $64 million is being invested at France Road, and four portainers are in use. Sea-Land have been active in the port for several years and contributed to the 50 per cent increase in container throughput in 1973 over the previous year. Development at New Orleans really got going in 1972, and a total of $400 million is to be spent on the provision of new container and barge facilities, as well as on the port's more traditional bulk and break-bulk wharves. Increasing interest is being shown in the operation of semi-container ships in the area, and New Orleans will be well able to offer quick turnrounds.

Houston is currently the second largest port in the Gulf, but following completion of a massive $100 million development at Barbour's Cut, the port could well become the largest. In the old port confines Sea-Land have their own 17½-acre terminal, adjacent to common user container berths along the Ship Canal. But 25 miles downriver the 600-acre Barbour's Cut development will by the 1990's be able to accommodate twenty container and LASH ships at once. Land in the area is abundant, and the provision of extensive storage areas will be no problem. Deep water channels exist, and phase 1 at Barbour's Cut has involved the provision of two piers alongside which containerships can be berthed. The first LASH vessel was handled in June 1972, and more floating area for LASH and Seabee barges will be provided under the development programme. Phase 2, which involves an investment of $40 million is progressing, and includes the construction of two additional container berths to be serviced by two portainers. Houston's container cargo throughput in 1973 was

80 per cent higher than in the previous year, and this increase was in part accounted for by landbridge traffic moving between Europe and the Far East via the Gulf and West Coast. Barge traffic is drawn to the port along the Gulf intracoastal waterway and canal systems which link up with the Mississippi River, in addition to being generated by the port's immediate hinterland.

While Houston is well positioned to attract general cargo, Galveston Island, connected to the mainland by a causeway, has traditionally been a bulk handling port. But general cargo is growing, and over $20 million is being spent on the expansion of container and barge handling facilities. Two container berths are already in operation and a 15-acre floating area for LASH barges is being provided, together with a berth for Lykes Lines Seabee ships. Following construction of additional container berths, Galveston could be accused of causing an over-capacity situation in the Gulf, but in view of the uncertainties surrounding the future viability of barge carrying ships, there may well be a real need for further container terminals if only to handle semi-containerships.

Mobile is another mainly bulk handling port, where grain and coal predominate, but 10 per cent of total throughput is in containers, and it is hoped that facilities will be provided for LASH and Seabee vessels. Mobile's real hope of developing into a general cargo handling port, however, lies in the construction of a complex system of canals that would connect the port via the canals and the river system to a large area of America's industrial hinterland.

Although considerable advances in the provision of container handling facilities have been made in the United States, developments at Great Lakes ports have been slow due to the reluctance of containership companies to penetrate very far into the St. Lawrence Seaway and Lakes system. Many interests in the Chicago, Detroit, Toledo and Cleveland areas have cargo available suitable for shipment by container, but it often has to be railed to a United States east coast port to meet up with a containership, or it must be shipped by break-bulk vessel. The fundamental problems are that the size of the locks in the St. Lawrence Seaway prevent entry to vessels having a beam exceeding 75 feet, that the Seaway itself is closed for about four months of the year, and that the round transit Montreal/Chicago/Montreal takes too long. These factors combined mean that operating expensive containerships within an area such as the Lakes, where controlling influences must of necessity intrude, will often be prohibitively costly, and the majority of lines have opted to stay clear of the area.

Prior to 1952 most general cargo destined for the Lakes ports was railed from Montreal, or from one of the Canadian or United States east coast ports. During 1952 though Manchester Liners put into service three small break-bulk vessels capable of negotiating the narrow canals and locks that linked the St. Lawrence River with Lake Ontario, prior to the construction of the St. Lawrence Seaway. The service was later extended via the Welland Canal to include Lake Erie, and in 1956 it was extended still further to include Detroit and Chicago. The St. Lawrence Seaway was opened in 1959, and during this period the concept of shipping by container was spreading in the United States. Although Manchester Liners carried some containers in the early 1960's on their conventional vessels, the trend that was later to prevent sizeable throughputs of container traffic at the Lakes ports, had already started. General cargo was returning to the overland routes as the railways found the container an ideal unit to move over medium to long distances at competitive rates. Manchester Liners though were by now firmly committed to the Lakes trade, and in 1971 they started the first direct containership link to Detroit and Chicago. But it was soon found to be too costly to operate deep sea containerships on the Lakes, and it was decided to turn the vessels round at Montreal, and serve the Lakes ports using feeder vessels. In spite of the continuing lack of a purpose-built container terminal and gantry crane, and of practically all other operators utilizing the rail links, Manchester Liners continues to use feeders out of Montreal, even though profit margins must be narrow. The Lakes ports are currently asking for Government aid in an effort to attract some of the lost cargo back, and the International Association of Great Lakes Ports, a body made up of representatives from seventeen United States and five Canadian ports, has recently undertaken trade missions to Europe and the Far East with a view to promoting

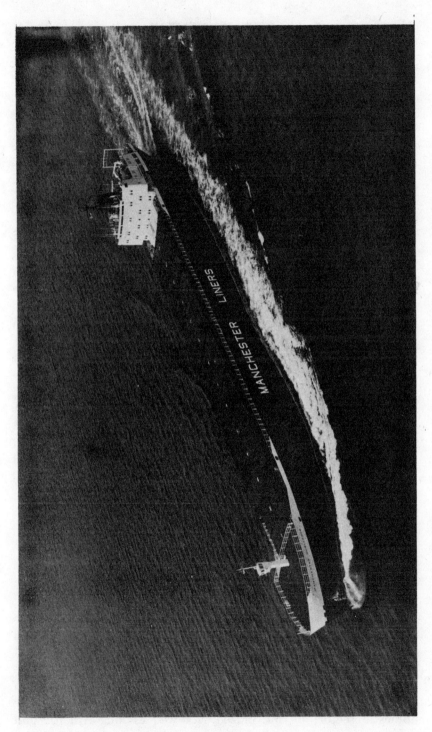

FIGURE 17 Manchester Liners' cellular all-under-deck stowage containership *Manchester Challenge* (Courtesy of Manchester Liners Limited).

their ports. Several European lines have recently withdrawn their services, but the Russians have decided to enter the trade and will be calling at Lakes ports on a direct basis.

Although no United States flag vessels serve the Great Lakes they are in a more competitive position than Canadian shipping companies, because of the subsidies they receive. They are encouraged to draw cargo from the Lakes for shipment out of the United States ports, and the Lakes are therefore trying to cope with yet another problem. Apart from the East Coast exits, some cargo is being grouped at Chicago prior to making up into barge loads for transit down the Mississippi and subsequent shipment by Lykes Lines Seabee ships at New Orleans. It is hoped that a LASH service might be introduced into the Lakes, with loading/discharge of barges taking place at Montreal, but the quicker transit times offered by the sea/rail route may prevent widespread acceptance of the relatively slow movement of barges from Montreal, through the Seaway lock system, and on into the Lakes.

The future of containership operation in the Lakes is uncertain but several of the ports have already decided to provide purpose-built container facilities in the hope that either feeder ships will become more prevalent, or that deep-sea vessels will make direct calls. The construction of a new canal parallel to the Welland Canal linking Lake Ontario and Lake Erie would make vessel operation in the area more attractive, and as the rail links via Montreal and the East Coast ports become less competitive as vessels are able to penetrate further into the Lakes without being delayed, a slightly more favorable period for Lakes general cargo shipping might emerge.

Canada

In comparison with the United States of America, Canada has so far adopted a more liberal attitude toward containerization, and her policy of comparative non-interference has led to rapid railway and port development. Like the United States, Canada is an ideal country within which benefits following the introduction of maritime containerization can, through extension into the domestic sector, be maximized. As well as long Atlantic and

Pacific sea voyages, overland rail distances are extensive, and the use of intermodal transport equipment will allow cost savings to be achieved, not only on overseas cargo, but also on containerized domestic traffic which is able to use the already provided container terminals as rail interchange points. The enormous size of Canada has meant that efficient rail links must operate, and the rail links in turn have helped to promote trade through certain ports. The National Harbors Board, the federal agency controlling all the major Canadian ports, has encouraged substantial investment, especially at the ports in the eastern provinces, and regular containerized traffic flows have been built up to and from areas within the United States as well as in Canada. It is quite usual for goods destined for the Chicago and Detroit areas to pass over container berths at Halifax, Saint John, and Montreal, prior to onward carriage by rail or feeder vessel. Because of federal control of intermodal movements through United States ports, and because of sometimes poor labor relations in the ports, a lot of United States cargo is being diverted through Canadian ports via the rail links or via such coastal feeder services as that plying between Halifax and Boston operated by Maritime Coastal Containers. If the trans-Canadian landbridge linking Halifax with the United States Pacific port of Seattle is developed further, Canada's actual, although not admitted, dependence on the Panama Canal would lessen, and East Coast port container throughputs would be boosted still further.

The trade between Europe and Canadian ports, in relation to trades in adjacent and distant areas, remained relatively stable following the first containership sailings in 1968. The two major lines of the time, Manchester Liners and Canadian Pacific, were quick to establish their mode of operations and their format is little changed today. Atlantic Container Line, Dart Containerline, and Cast Europe (Containers) Limited have similarly become established, and have managed to maintain a peaceable relationship with each other. Although increasing cargo flows will very likely bring newcomers into the trade, present scope for change is largely confined to improvements in service. But competition will become more intense following the beginning of profit taking during 1973-1974, and it is to be hoped that over-tonnaging will, either through conference regulation or through some other type of control, be avoided. Even the less lucrative eastbound containers, which carry low-rated semi-finished and raw products, are making money, and it is ominous to note that already rate cutting is becoming rampant, especially in the heavy trade flows with the Continent, over which the relevant conference is exercising little control.

Prior to the short-lived direct containership sailings to Detroit and Chicago by Manchester Liners in 1971, it has already been described how the company became established as a carrier of cargo between the United Kingdom, and Canada and the United States. Manchester Liners had begun their containerized service to Montreal in 1968, offering a 6½-day crossing from Manchester, and a year-round service by using ice strengthened vessels capable of navigating the partly frozen upper reaches of the St. Lawrence River in winter. Manchester Liners have exclusive use of the Furness Withy operated Berth 68-70 at Montreal, and have now settled for a system of using three 4,490-ton feeder vessels to complete their contracts of carriage from Montreal to Great Lakes ports. When the Lakes are closed because of ice, the rail services run by the Canadian National Railways are used to convey the majority of containers from Montreal onward. Prior to the general use of ice strengthened vessels, Montreal suffered from a restricted season, but the steady year-round trade brought by Manchester Liners and Cast has helped to stabilize throughput. Cast have their private terminal at Berth 77-78, and a further two common user berths have been constructed. But Montreal has become an inflexible port with a surfeit of labor, and rates on cargo handling have had to be raised partly to finance redundancy payments. The introduction of a computer system to control employment of labor caused an illegal strike in 1972, and the diversion of cargo over Halifax and Saint John to take advantage of economical through rates offered by other container lines, has meant that some cargo has been lost that may never return. It must be admitted that container shipping has been the cause of the decline of Montreal, but it is to be hoped that the Government's warning that the port might have to be closed down, because of high wage rates and poor productivity, will not turn into reality.

The Canadian Pacific Railway Company began operating rail services one hundred years ago, and changed its name, following diversification into shipping and other forms of transport, to Canadian Pacific Limited in 1971. The group is divided into independently operated subsidiary companies, and sometimes CP Rail for example will find itself in direct competition with the road haulage division where cargo moving over medium distances is involved. The shipping division of Canadian Pacific has grown rapidly since the days when break-bulk ships were operated, and currently five cellular vessels maintain a service between European ports, and the company's own terminal at Wolfe's Cove, Quebec. The Wolfe's Cove facilities are looked upon purely as a means to achieving a smooth flow of containers between the vessels of CP Ships, and the domestic facilities of CP Rail and of the road haulage division. A large majority of CP's traffic is made up of full loads, especially those travelling from Canada to Europe, and it was found unnecessary, in order to maintain profitability at an acceptable level, to construct a number of inland terminals where groupage cargo could be consolidated into full container loads. Instead of offering expensive LCL facilities, CP use seventeen different types of container, and maintain that at least one of these must satisfy the needs of the majority of cargo owners. The company is obviously not in favor of using waterborne feeder services, in view of the dominance of CP Rail, and a daily rail link between Wolfe's Cove and Toronto is maintained. Cargo for delivery in the Toronto area passes over CP's rail transfer terminal, and on carriage by road is usually through a CP haulage company. Over the shorter distance between Wolfe's Cove and Montreal, it is usually more economic to use the road connections instead of the rail link. The terminal at Wolfe's Cove, Quebec, initially cost over £2 million and was opened in 1970, and now occupies an 18-acre site and makes use of two portainers and a transtainer. Quebec has also been provided with a container terminal at Beauport Flats, where one portainer is in use, and the port's main source of competition, apart from that presented by the East Coast ports, comes from Montreal where as stated above Manchester Liners and Cast are active. Canadian Pacific have the advantage over Manchester Liners and Cast of a marginally shorter steaming distance, and of an ability to include links with both Montreal and Toronto in addition to points further west, while Manchester Liners and Cast will be able to offer competitive

FIGURE 18 CP Ships' cellular containership *CP Voyageur* at Wolfe's Cove, Quebec (Courtesy of Canadian Pacific).

rates to Toronto, but will be precluded from handling Quebec cargo because of the necessity of travelling back down the St. Lawrence River after discharge at Montreal. Because Canadian Pacific is able to be almost wholly self-sufficient, and does not rely on outside methods of transport, the company has not adopted the internationally recommended ISO sizes of container, and may shortly announce a standard size that does not in fact conform with the more accepted dimensions. This inward looking attitude of the company is perhaps typical of over-all strategy, and recently led to a threat of nationalization by the Government if co-operation with Government and other groups was not improved, and if a more adequate level of service was not offered to a larger number of cargo owners.

Manchester Liners has traditionally been a shipping company based in Manchester, and drawing on the northern and midland areas of the United Kingdom for its traffic. Cargo movements between Canada and the Continent, however, were increasing but Manchester Liners was unable to take advantage of the heavier flow. It was therefore decided to extend the activities of the line, and it was announced in March 1973 that a new container service between Europe and Canada was to start the following month. Vessels would load at Felixstowe and Rotterdam prior to sailing to Montreal, and it would then be possible to draw on the substantial tonnage of cargo generated by, and imported into, Continental countries, as well as extending United Kingdom cargo sources further south. The service out of Manchester was to be maintained, and Manchester Liners would still be based at Manchester. CP Ships had meanwhile been running services out of Liverpool, London, and the Continent, and it was evident, following Manchester Liners' extension, that the two lines would be directly competing for all their cargo. Neither line was a member of any consortia, and it was evident that some form of co-operation, while not necessarily benefiting the trade, would obviate the duplication of services. It was therefore announced in November 1973 that as from January 1974 Manchester Liners would abandon its Felixstowe and Rotterdam sailings, and that CP Ships would withdraw its Liverpool and Greenock services. Sailings would be rationalized, Manchester Liners once again being responsible for cargo in the northern and midland areas of the United Kingdom, while CP Ships were to maintain sailings out of London, Le Havre and Rotterdam. In order to operate Manchester Liners' additional sailings out of Felixstowe and Rotterdam, the fleet had been increased to six fully cellular vessels, but Manchester Liners was able to take advantage of the buoyant charter market for container vessels by time chartering two of its vessels to AECS, who as described earlier were at the time faced with a severe shortage of capacity.

The major source of competition for Manchester Liners and CP Ships comes from the very flexible system of operation presented by Cast Line. Cast has been running between Antwerp and Montreal since 1969, and has converted a number of former bulk carriers to ship some containers in addition to bulk cargoes. The service is non-conference, and uses the FAK tariff (see page 201) as a basis for assessing charges. All containers are 20 feet, only FCL cargo is shipped, and vessels confine their calls to Antwerp and Montreal. Inland terminals are not maintained, and the line has been able to keep operating costs on a comparatively low level. Cast was recently able to take advantage of the rising charter market for bulk freighters, and of the increasing flow of container cargo moving between Canada and the Continent, by releasing one of its vessels on charter to be used for conveying bulk commodities, while a fully cellular vessel, the first of its kind used by the company, was chartered to fill the gap. This type of option illustrates the flexibility of the Cast system which allows rapid movement into a potentially more lucrative area of shipping, while at the same time permitting return to the former area if conditions change.

The Nova Scotia part of Halifax relies heavily on the railways as a generator of containerized cargo. Built on federal property at a cost of $14 million, the container terminal began operations in November 1970, and largely because of the railway connections has been able to attract the deep sea containership companies. Halifax is situated away from the industrial regions of Canada and the United States, and was a declining port prior to containerization. But lying as it does further east than any other major Canadian port, the container lines were able to avoid unnecessary sailing times by calling at Halifax in preference to Quebec or Montreal. Through rates are quoted to Canadian and United

States points, using either the rail network, or such coastal container services as that between Halifax and Boston. The port also acts as the Atlantic transfer point for cargo moving over the trans-Canadian landbridge between Europe and Japan. Canadian National Railways are responsible for one of the two container berths, and the whole facility is run by Halifax International Containers Limited (Halicon). A further terminal is to be provided which will boost the present two-third share of general cargo which is moved in containers, and throughput at the roll-on roll-off facility, used principally by Atlantic Container Line, is also growing. The port authority's forward-looking and optimistic outlook coupled with the port's favorable geographical siting, may well enable development along the lines of a super ice-free deep sea terminal offering container, roll-on roll-off, and LASH facilities for cargo over a wide area of both Canada and the United States.

CP Rail are involved in developments not only at Quebec but also at Saint John in New Brunswick. In association with McLean Kennedy Limited of Montreal a company known as Brunterm Limited was formed to build up and administer the container facilities at Saint John. Following an initial investment of $4 million a container terminal was opened in August 1971 and CP Rail, in competition with Canadian National Railways at Halifax, are moving large numbers of containers between Saint John, and Montreal and Chicago. Saint John has proved to be especially attractive to lines who were formerly calling at Montreal using break-bulk vessels, such as NYK, but who have found that by using Saint John as a transfer point between their new container vessels and the railway system, the transit time between, for example, Japan and Montreal could be cut from 30 to 22 days. The 1971 container facility at the Rodney Container Terminal is being expanded at a cost of $14 million following a doubling of container cargo throughput during 1971/1972, and because of continued steady growth in tonnage handled, a second terminal is being built at a cost of $22.5 million on a 40-acre site. Competition between Halifax and Saint John is hotting up, and even though Halifax is 350 miles further east than Saint John, Canadian National Railways have equalized their charges from Halifax to inland points, with the rates quoted by CP Rail to identical points out of Saint John. The National Harbor Board is taking particular interest in the development of Saint John, and are undertaking a two-part study to determine requirements up to 1978 and in the longer term over a twenty-year period.

It has already been mentioned that Canada's west coast port at Vancouver has lost a considerable volume of containerized cargo to the nearby United States port of Seattle. The Ottawa-based National Harbors Board has been active in developing Canada's east coast ports, even though the port authority at Vancouver were in favor of placing less emphasis on the port's traditional role as a bulk handling port, and more on its role as a container handling port. It was once thought that Vancouver would act as the West Coast landbridge link with Halifax, but this too has not materialized, as Seattle has been successful in attracting the container vessels with landbridge containers travelling between Japan and Europe. Apart from lack of container facilities, a major cause for diversion of cargo to Seattle is the insistence of the longshoremen on unpacking and re-packing containers prior to release from the dock area. Instead of containers being conveyed direct to a Vancouver warehouse, they are being shipped through Seattle and are then taken overland to the warehouse at Vancouver for breaking down and re-delivery. Poor management of the port did not help matters, the chairman finding it necessary to resign in May 1973, but major plans are now underway to redress the balance toward container orientation. Only one container berth on a 15-acre site at Centennial Pier has so far been provided, and the one portainer used allows an approximate annual throughput of 36,000 boxes. Due to the preference given to Japanese vessels, United States flag containerships often had to wait before docking, and a further reason for diversion to Seattle arose. A new $21 million terminal is now under construction though, and the facilities to be provided over a 71-acre site will cater for container, LASH, and roll-on roll-off vessels. Completion is due in 1975, but meanwhile other even more extensive developments are being planned. A 76-acre terminal may be built near Lapointe Pier to include a $22 million high-rise container storage unit, and a predominantly bulk handling terminal incorporating three berths may be constructed at Lynnterm. Longer-term planning includes a vast 500-acre maritime complex at Roberts Bank Outerport, where over a 30-year period bulk and container handling facilities will be provided. The changing management outlook at Vancouver, which clearly sees the port in the future as one of the finest on the West Coast, is indicative of the slowing down of traffic diversions to Seattle, and endorses the decision of the National Harbors Board to channel nearly half of its budget for 1973 to the port.

Russia and the Trans-Siberian Railway

To see the landbridge concept in established use one must turn to Russia where considerable advances have been made in the carriage of containerized loads without the large-scale investment that the shipping consortia have become involved in.

In 1967 the possibility of utilizing the Trans-Siberian railway as a link in the through movement of cargo from Europe to Japan was explored, and trial container shipments were soon taking place. MAT Transport in association with CTI (Japan) was the first major operator on the route and they began moving boxes from northern Europe via Brest Litovsk near the Polish border, from where the Trans-Siberian railway carried the units to the port of Nakhodka on the Sea of Japan. The sea crossing to Yokohama in Japan was undertaken by a conventional vessel belonging to the Japan/Nakhodka Line. During the building up of the service the transit time from Europe to Japan varied from forty to as much as sixty days, but once the viability of running an overland service had become apparent, improvements were soon forthcoming. The main bottleneck was at Nakhodka where containers were often delayed while waiting for the vessel to Yokohama, but the introduction of a converted Russian vessel, the *Grodekovo*, helped to ease the situation and made possible the co-ordination of sailings to fit in with the arrival and depart-ure of trains. A further Russian vessel, the *Kavalerovo* allowed a regular sailing every five days to Yokohama.

Following these early movements it soon became apparent that the rail route across Russia could be developed into an alter-native method of shipping goods to the Far East, and the Soviet External Transportation Corporation (V/O Sojusvneshtrans) (the

Soviet forwarding agent) began a regular service between Europe and the Far East in 1971. Their United Kingdom agents, Anglo-Soviet Shipping Company, acting as loading brokers for the Baltic Steamship Company, marketed the service within the United Kingdom, and conventional vessels of the Baltic Steamship Company were initially used to ship containers between Tilbury and Leningrad. In June 1971 the all-container vessel *Ivan Chernykh*, capable of carrying up to 100 20-foot units was introduced, and sailed every eleven days from Tilbury. Three more vessels have since joined the *Ivan Chernykh*, and it is planned to introduce a fifth vessel by the end of 1974. Handling at Leningrad used to be by conventional cranes, but at the end of 1973 a container facility was opened to quicken transfers between vessels and rail wagons.

Containers are hauled from Leningrad over the Trans-Siberian Railway to Nakhodka or Vladivostok, from where they are shipped to Japan or Hong Kong. The railway of course has been established for very many years, and has been moving containers of varying sizes for some time. These early containers were not built to internationally recognized standards, and with the coming of the ISO size units moving on an intermodal basis the need arose to modify existing, and introduce new railway equipment. This modernization is currently in progress, and following improvements to track, signalling, and rail wagons, and the introduction of block-trains to speed up transits, a larger volume of traffic will be carried. At the Russian Pacific coast railhead the second largest port in the USSR at Nakhodka is used as the transfer point between rail wagon and ship. Two Japanese portainers have been erected at the container terminal which opened in October 1973, and railway generated containers are shipped over the terminal into vessels belonging to the Soviet Far Eastern Shipping Company for the crossing to Japan and Hong Kong. Although the link between Nakhodka and the Japanese port of Yokohama was maintained by vessels belonging to the Japan/Nakhodka Line during the early experimental period of using the Russian railway as a landbridge, the Russians have become reluctant to allow the Japanese to develop the link. The Japanese have only been allowed to operate conventional vessels, and to carry goods moving between Japan and the Russian mainland only, while containers using the Trans-Siberian Railway to and from Europe are all shipped by FESCO vessels. Although it was originally agreed that Russia and Japan would ship half the cargo each moving between their two countries, the agreement did not extend to through railway containers, and the three Japanese lines who formed the Japan/Nakhodka Line are now trying to obtain control of part of the through traffic. It is unlikely whether the Japanese will obtain the 30 per cent share they are asking for, but in view of FESCO using Japanese container terminals, and of the considerable help that Japan is giving Russia in the provision of terminals, their share should by rights be quite substantial. A further difficulty is presented by the different operating costs of the Russian and Japanese ships, which has prompted Japan into asking for a freight rate increase to cover her higher costs. The question of Russian subsidies will be discussed shortly.

Non-operating freight forwarders are not allowed to directly enter the Trans-Siberian Railway trade without first obtaining a licence from Sojusvneshtrans. Only a handful of forwarders are in possession of the necessary licence, and most of these have been involved in the trade for several years. With the growing volume of traffic, especially traveling from east to west, Japanese forwarders are particularly keen to gain entry, but by giving volume discounts, which effectively makes new entrants with initially small tonnage uncompetitive, Sojusvneshtrans has been able to largely control the trade. Although the railway has so far had little effect on the conference shipping lines serving the Far East, it is still a fact that through rail rates are up to 25 per cent cheaper than conference shipping rates on a door-to-door basis, while a smaller saving can be realized on port-to-port movements, and following the improvements at Nakhodka containers moving over the railway have rarely been delayed. Transit times between Tilbury and Japan of 35 days and between Tilbury and Hong Kong of 45 days are offered, and with the build up of containers in use over the railway, annual movements will grow substantially. As European cargo owners become more aware of the advantages of the route, cargo flows in each direction should become more equal, but at present five times as much traffic is being conveyed from the Far East to Europe than in the reverse direction. Possibly reports of damage to goods have been over-exaggerated, and

European shippers have been further discouraged by the possible effects of Siberian winter conditions on transit times, especially where deadlines for delivery against large contracts exist. But although the trend recently has been for sea transport costs to rise at an alarming rate, largely because of the increased price of bunkers, it could be that in the future rail transport costs will rise faster than sea transport costs, and the competitive relationship between the Trans-Siberian Railway route and the conference ships in the Far Eastern Trade might alter.

Although the Russians have been slow to develop deep sea containership services, they have shown considerable interest, and indeed have been using container methods over internal trade routes for a number of years. The merchant fleet of the Soviet Union has grown dramatically from 1960, but to help maintain this growth in the realm of general cargo shipping it is realized that methods of cargo handling and transportation must keep up with developments in the West. Badly needed foreign exchange will be obtained through operating vessels over established trade routes, and Russia will have an increasing say in the maintenance of these ocean highways. Russia is therefore also looking for cooperation with other maritime nations, and agreements are being formulated for example with the United States of America regulating entry to each other's ports, and governing proportions of cargo to be carried by each other's ships, and with Sweden regarding the growth of two-way container traffic.

The Council of Economic Mutual Assistance (Comecon) is coordinating the transport provisions contained in the 1971-1975 five year plans drawn up by its individual members, and Russian transport policy is therefore in harmony with the rest of the Comecon countries. It was announced in Moscow in September 1971 that Comecon members were to adopt a single container agreement, that they were to standardize containers, and that vessels and other carrying media were to be converted to accept containers. East European countries have been trying to cut labor costs for several years, and modernization coupled with harmonization in the transport sector would offer tremendous benefits. The 1971 agreement meant that a unified container carriage system would follow from the switch over to containers in both domestic and international trades, and that container depots could be constructed in East Germany, Czechoslovakia, Hungary, Bulgaria, Yugoslavia and Poland, as well as in Russia. Container train trials were undertaken in 1972, and established services have been developed by Czechoslovakia between Rostock in East Germany and Prague, and by East Germany from Berlin to Warsaw and Moscow. The opening of the railway between Belgrade and Bar in Yugoslavia has provided another outlet for goods from Hungary and Roumania, and current developments at Bar could well include facilities for containerized traffic. Although Comecon has long been reluctant to recognize the European Economic Community, and much suspicion and hostility has been in evidence, Western countries are playing a major role in transport developments through supplying technical assistance and capital equipment. East European countries still maintain a very tight control over their own freight movements, affiliation to a state owned trading corporation usually being a prerequisite to operating a service, but it is to be hoped that the current move toward some degree of co-operation between Comecon and the EEC might lead to more co-operation in the transport sector.

While most of the Comecon countries are concentrating more on the development of overland container services, Poland has been active in the containerization of many of her deep sea shipping links, as well as in railway improvements. The state controlled Polish Ocean Lines obtained its first two semi-containerships of 12,000 DWT each in 1973, and a service linking Gdynia to United States east coast ports was commenced shortly after. Conventional vessels belonging to Polish Ocean Lines have been in the North Atlantic for several years, and it is now planned to completely convert the trade to semi-containership operation. Four similar vessels are to be placed in the Far East trade by 1975 under conference membership, and six container/roll-on roll-off ships will be engaged in the Australian trade by 1976. In addition to dry general cargo containers which are being obtained from both East and West European countries, ninety 40-foot refrigerated containers were ordered in September 1973 by Polish Ocean Lines from the United Kingdom, and a total of 7,000 units of all kinds should have been built up by 1975. It is said that a fully cellular containership is on order locally. The port of Gdynia has been able to handle vessels with a part container capacity since early 1973, and the new £1,500 million Northern Port deep water harbor under construction at Gdansk may be provided with container facilities in addition to the extensive bulk handling facilities for coal exports and oil imports. Container terminals are also to be built at Lodz, Wroclaw, and Szczecin. Poland's railway system is under the control of the other state institution, the Polish State Railways, and from holding practically no containers in 1972, the stock is due to stand at about 2,000 units at the end of the current five-year plan in 1975. Polish State Railways became a member of Intercontainer in April 1974, and the extensive developments in deep sea shipping, as well as in international rail transport, should put Poland right up among the leaders in transportation among Comecon countries.

Non-standard small containers have been used, principally over the Soviet railway system, for several years, but recently the ISO 20-foot size container has been adopted as the unit best suited to form the basis of medium-term development. Specialized vessel types, such as tankers and one-commodity bulk carriers, have also been widely used by the Soviet merchant fleet, and development of purpose-built container and roll-on roll-off ships will be a natural extension to past policy. Prior to the building of the new vessels, experiments in shipping containers by conventional vessels were undertaken, and the lessening of damage to cargo was encouraging. The Latvian Steamship Company of Riga has been accepting containers on its service between Riga and Liverpool since July 1971, and contamination of Russian cotton and flax was notably absent on arrival at United Kingdom markets. The service operated between Leningrad and Tilbury has already been mentioned and experiments also took place in the trades between Russia and Cuba and the Persian Gulf, as well as overland to Bulgaria and East Germany. Under the current five-year plan (1971-1975) particular emphasis is being placed on the transportation of cargo, and it is said that in 1972 forty container and roll-on roll-off ships were on order for the Soviet merchant fleet. In order to realize an immediate container requirement of approximately 25,000 units, and to accommodate a future requirement of over 300,000 units, containers are being leased in large numbers until domestic production becomes well established. A contract was signed at the end of 1972 with Container Transport International Incorporated (CTI) for the three-year lease of 1,500 units to be used by FESCO in the Far East to North American trade, and this was soon followed at the beginning of 1973 by the signing of a contract with Sea Containers for the lease of 1,000 British built containers. CTI were later involved, in December 1973, in a long-term lease to supply 300 40-foot containers together with 70 chassis.

In addition to floating new tonnage, Russia is keen to buy secondhand vessels of all types including containerships, to allow almost complete conversion of her overseas general cargo trade to container and unit load methods. It is estimated that Russia may have built up a fleet of 31 containerships by 1978 and that entry into the major trading routes will be but a mere formality. FESCO is already operating cellular containerships between the Far East and North America, and the Russians have penetrated into the American Great Lakes, an area from where Western shipping companies have withdrawn due to high operating costs. A conventional service has been maintained on the North Atlantic since September 1973, linking Baltic ports with those on the United States east coast, and it is planned to containerize this potentially lucrative trade in late 1974. Containerships with a roll-on roll-off capability and able to ship over 1,000 containers each are to be introduced to the Europe to Far East trade, as well as to the Europe to Australia trade. As mentioned above initial container requirements are being satisfied through leasing arrangements, but technical knowledge on container manufacture is being brought in with a view to expanding domestic production. Containers have been bought from Hungary, Czechoslovakia and East Germany, and were being manufactured in Russia in 1972 under licence from the French. As well as satisfying home demand it is intended that an export trade be established, and the Comecon countries in particular are likely buyers.

Russia's principal port development is concentrated at Wrangle Bay, not far from Nakhodka, where a huge port complex is under construction. Japanese and Russian groups are developing Wrangle, and even though difficulties have been encountered due to shortages of materials and labor, it was possible to have the port operational on a limited scale in 1972. In addition to two container berths, which should be open by 1975, extensive facilities will be provided for the handling of wood chips, logs and coal. A total of 70 wharves should be in use during the 1980's and annual throughput of all types of cargo is estimated at about 30 million tons. Container terminals are also being provided at Nakhodka, Leningrad, Riga and Iljichevsk, and 450 container stations are to be constructed to facilitate rail movements.

Although shipping companies in the West are quick to accuse the Soviet Union of heavily subsidizing its merchant fleet and of cutting its freight rates to below cost, it is probable that the defense put forward by the Russians accurately contradicts the argument. Oil, whether of indigenous origin, or whether supplied in quantity by countries such as Iran with whom bilateral agreements may exist, is plentiful, and the Russians may not have faced the rising prices that some other countries have. Labor is relatively inexpensive, and there is no difficulty in manning the merchant fleet. Vessel operating costs will therefore be less than costs found in Western shipping groups, and will be further suppressed through the absence of the often inflationary policies of the conferences. It is unlikely anyway that a potential earner of valuable foreign exchange would be allowed to operate at anything other than a profit. Although the Russian FESCO does not take part in conference activities, the line is being pressed to join the relevant Far East to North American conferences, in order, as the conferences state, to prevent further instability in the trade. While FESCO could continue to operate without conference backing, the line would be assured of a regular cargo flow by being a conference member through the regular spacings of vessel sailings.

In spite of intense activity in the realm of maritime containerization, the majority of Russia's container movements take place over the railway system. During 1973 31 million tons of container cargo was carried by rail, and the part played by the Trans-Siberian Railway has been touched upon above. The railways are very reliable during extended periods of bad weather, but a drawback when conveying international trade, is the necessity of trans-shipping to other wagons at border terminals due to the wider than standard gauge of the Russian network. To simplify domestic rating, and as a way of avoiding the necessity of using sophisticated pricing systems, tariffs are based purely on distance and on the potential capacity of the container used, the type and weight of the goods being immaterial. While the Soviet railways are being expanded, road services too are developing, and the international Russian road haulage organization, Sovtransavto, is running directly to the United Kingdom, as well as to other European destinations. Partly in conjunction with the railway system, experiments have taken place in the transportation of containers using inland waterways. The waterways have long proved to be an ideal medium for moving very large tonnage of bulk commodities between wide ranging areas, and they will prove to be important links in the future where container cargo is involved. The principal waterway, the River Volga, is connected to other rivers by canal systems, which has resulted in the joining of the Baltic and Black Seas. Waterway transport costs in Russia are already half those of rail costs, and in view of the possibility of rail costs increasing quite sharply, waterway transit for certain categories of cargo will become even more attractive. Several container carriers are actively developing waterborne routes, and Russia may even prove to be an ideal area for the operation of LASH systems.

India

The problems of introducing container services to developing countries largely revolve around the necessity of altering a labor-intensive method of cargo handling to a capital-intensive system, and differences in trade flows into and out of the country. India is no exception and is perhaps typical of less developed countries where many potential projects have valid claims on a limited amount of finance. But where conversion of part of a labor-intensive industry into a capital-intensive one is contemplated, such action might have repercussions unacceptable to the country even in the short term. A very high social cost in the form of unemployment would follow the mechanization of port handling, and indeed it has been estimated that in Calcutta out of a total of approximately 150,000 workers, either directly employed in dock work or dependent on the docks for their livelihood, approximately 100,000 could lose their jobs if mechanization of bulk and general cargo handling was fully developed. The effect on their families, and in many cases dependents, would be additional. Apart from the social costs, private costs in a country continually having to choose between a number of development schemes awaiting fulfilment, would be considerable, and before embarking on a port development programme many factors would have to be considered. For example, the absence of a good road system would defeat the real object of containerization, insofar as containers could not in many cases be delivered through to final destination, or supplied to a shipper having cargo available for export. The problem of differences in trade flows stems from an under-industrialized economy being largely dependent on imported capital and consumer goods until domestic manufacturing becomes more established, while export revenue is predominantly provided by primary products. If container services were to be started a large proportion of the country's import trade would be suitable for carriage by container, but comparatively low-value exported bulk commodities would be more economically shipped by bulk vessels. An unacceptable number of empty containers would have to be moved out of the country, and freight charges would not be competitive with the established break-bulk operators.

It was with such problems in mind that the Indian Government decided to commission a symposium and various study groups in an effort to determine whether conversion or development at ports to allow container vessels to be handled would be a practicable proposition. Preliminary reports indicated that the ports of Bombay, Calcutta and Cochin would be most suited to any possible development, and limited container facilities are being installed at Bombay and Cochin. But prior to anything approaching full commitment to containerization, some of the lines in the trade are to develop palletization and other unit load systems in an effort to quicken cargo handling, and obviate the current state of congestion to be found in many of India's ports. American President Lines though decided to go ahead with trial shipments of containers by conventional vessels as early as 1971, and it was later agreed to inaugurate a regular container service between Singapore and Indian ports using either ships gantries or their own mobile shore cranes, until portainers became available. The service started toward the end of 1973 conveying approximately 200 containers by each sailing, but numbers may rise as demand increases and wider experience of the trade is obtained. The state-owned Shipping Corporation of India (SCI) together with Scindia Steam Navigation are also examining container methods of shipping, and SCI put its first semi-container vessel the m/v *Vishva Aditya*, capable of uplifting 366 20-foot containers, into service in November 1973. Five similar vessels are to follow. SCI is meanwhile to expand conventional sailings to North America (the Great Lakes and the east coast of Canada), Ethiopia and Manila.

It will be several years then before fully cellular vessels are able to operate in the Indian trades, and meanwhile the lines may indeed decide that LASH systems offer more scope for modernizing cargo handling methods. LASH vessels would be able to take in general cargo and bring out bulk commodities, and would render the construction of expensive container handling berths unnecessary. Containers could still be used on a limited scale, but as they would form a part of the barge cargo, they would be handled by comparatively slow-speed conventional cranes after the LASH ship had discharged and had collected already loaded export barges. Barges would also be able to make use of India's river system, therefore placing less dependence on long inland hauls by road or rail. Thirty LASH barges are already being used at Madras as a method of cargo handling within the port, and LASH vessels are to become a more frequent sight at India's ports. Waterman Steamship Corporation began a regular service between the United States, the Middle East and India in mid-1974 and three vessels will eventually be in service, calling at Kandla, Colombo, Madras, Calcutta and ports in Bangladesh. Central Gulf Lines also have plans to introduce LASH ships, and a service should commence in 1975 between United States Gulf ports, the Middle East and India, and the Far East.

But the major ports in India are continuing on a limited scale, to provide facilities capable of handling ISO containers brought in by the semi-container and conventional vessels, as well as the smaller containers widely in use over the country's railway system. Bombay is currently only handling a few hundred ISO containers per year, but facilities are to be provided at Indira Dock and at Nhava-Sheva. Nhava-Sheva, across the harbor from Bombay port, is to be the site of a new port complex where, in addition to bulk cargo handling equipment, a container berth capable of handling the small railway containers and ISO units, is to be built. Construction will take about four years and will involve an investment of about £35 million. At Cochin a general cargo berth is to be adapted to handle containers, and at Colombo in Sri Lanka (formerly Ceylon), where much of the tea exported to the United States is now palletized, a scheme to further mechanization is to take place through construction of a container berth. Mention should also be made of the new port under construction ten miles to the east of Karachi in Pakistan to be known as Mohammed Bin Qasim. Conventional, container, LASH and bulk facilities will be provided, completion being due about 1985, although completion of the first phase in 1975 will allow partial working.

The smaller containers widely used by the Indian railways on a domestic basis have capacities of 4.5 and 5.0 tons and about 700 are currently in use. Over 30,000 movements take place per year involving these railway containers, and to accommodate the expected growth in traffic 1,200 additional units have been ordered. ISO-type containers will be carried as they come into general use, and new rolling stock and road chassis now being manufactured at railway workshops in Bombay and Madras will allow the railways to considerably extend the excellent services being maintained at present.

The viability of streamlining India's shipping methods is largely regulated by the speed with which economic development proceeds. A fifth five-year plan started in April 1974 with the objective of establishing self-reliance and reducing foreign aid to zero by 1979, but higher prices and inflation were soon to threaten fulfillment of even the basic industrial sectors of the plan. Modifications had quickly to be made involving cuts in non-industrial areas, and the planned for 5½ per cent annual growth rate may not be attained. It is essential, however, that the 2 per cent growth rate of previous years is improved upon, as when offset against a population increase of just over 2 per cent, per capita income has been declining. It was recently announced though that Russia was to prop up India's latest plan through the granting of massive aid, which will be used to improve existing steel plants and develop the heavy engineering, mining, power, and oil exploration industries. Russia is perhaps over-active in the granting of aid, and political motives are in evidence in addition to economic and social considerations. Russian aid extends to the part-subsidization of India's merchant fleet, but other countries are also active in this area. The United Kingdom is financing some new vessel building, and interest-free loans repayable over a twenty-five year period have allowed the building in Britain of a £5.8 million bulk carrier, launched in November 1974, for India's merchant fleet. Through co-operation with Iran, the Arya National Shipping Line of Teheran and the Shipping Corporation of India have agreed to set up a joint line, the Irano-Hind Shipping Company, to initially trade between Arabian Sea Ports and Iran and India, and to help boost the two countries' foreign exchange earnings. Iran will hold a 51 per cent share and India a 49 per cent share, and credit will be provided by Iran to finance vessel building. Services should start during 1975 with an initial tonnage of 500,000, and will allow the movement of cargo generated by trade agreements between the two countries. Vessel types and trades where future growth of cargo would warrant entry by the new line have not been announced, but there is little doubt that the financial backing of Iran and the technical assistance of India, will allow the company to join the ranks of some of the other powerful national lines.

South America and the Caribbean

Problems of a similar nature to those prevailing in India are also evident in South America. Finance to develop ports and communications systems is scarce, and trade flows conflict, but the size of the continent would allow transportation cost savings, assuming that future economic development were to warrant the establishment of a cellular containership service from Europe. But it will take several years before OCL, or any other line or group of lines, is prepared to containerize the trade, especially in view of the falling off of meat imports from the Argentine, and the fact that meat in any case will generally travel better by the refrigerated conventional ship already in the trade.

But containers are being shipped from North America to ports in South America, as illustrated by the movement of car parts which are assembled in South America principally to satisfy the seemingly inexhaustible demand for motor cars. Moore-McCormak is enlarging some of its vessels in the South American trade to take advantage of the growing volume of general cargo moving between North and South America, and Netumar Line will be operating semi-containerships by 1975 between the east coasts of Canada and the United States, and Brazil. Netumar vessels will accept up to 250 20-foot containers as well as conventional cargo, and the three vessels involved will be fitted with 60-ton derricks to overcome the problem of the total lack of purpose-built container cranes in Brazilian ports.

But without fully cellular services, and the up-to-date port handling equipment that go with them to allow rapid turn-round, the future of even semi-containerships or conventional vessels carrying a limited number of containers, is far from assured because of the severe congestion to be found at the ports. Once again then, at least until general development is sufficiently far advanced to offer an attractive climate for containerization, emphasis is being placed on barge carrying vessels which allow discharge and loading at a river or estuary mooring, away from crowded quays, and where specialized shore handling equipment is not required. As mentioned in the section dealing with the United States of America, Delta Steamship Lines of New Orleans are introducing a very flexible type of LASH vessel into the trade between the United States Gulf and South America, capable of accepting barges and containers in any combination. During the early years of operation emphasis will undoubtedly be placed on the shipment of barge traffic, and only a very few containers will be carried, but as shippers and receivers become more ac-customed to dealing in container loads, the standard configura-tion of 288 containers and 74 barges should be reached. Delta's South American ships, currently the largest of their type afloat worldwide, have been equipped with a gantry crane for container handling in addition to the familiar barge hoisting gantry, and container growth should not therefore be held back because of poor port facilities. To supplement cargo tonnage, Delta are also to operate small feeder LASH vessels capable of shipping up to 24 barges each between the Caribbean and New Orleans, and will therefore be offering a LASH service between the Caribbean and South America.

Pessimism surrounding large-scale containership operations in South American waters is perhaps illustrated by Brazil's desire to construct her own barge carrying vessels, even though her export trade alone is likely to grow by at least 10 per cent per year over the next ten years. To achieve as much benefit as possible from an intermodal container system, inland communication must be good, but the building of such projects as the Transamazonia highway linking ports in the north-east to the Peruvian border, while aiding development of uninhabited regions, will be of little benefit in encouraging container traffic. Brazil's industrial regions are concentrated along her coastline near to the ports, and until long-term development programmes based on economic need are embarked upon, prestige projects will continue to absorb scarce resources in other areas. It is also doubtful whether maintaining state-owned shipyards principally to create employment, as found in the Argentine, is wise in view of claims by competing sectors of industry for finance, but it is expected that Argentine's merchant fleet will grow from the present 0.75 million tons to about 1.5 million tons by 1979. The Argentine and the USSR have recently agreed to share the majority of their mutual trade between their own national flag vessels.

Prior to containerization reaching South America, cellular vessels will be operating between Europe and the West Indies and Central America. A four-nation consortium have formed Caribbean Overseas Lines (CAROL), and it is intended to build up a fleet of six vessels, beginning in 1976, able to carry 1,200 20-foot containers. Harrison Line, Hapag-Lloyd, KNSM, and Compagnie Générale Transatlantique, have come together to share vessel space, and in a similar way to TRIO members will retain individual marketing functions. Although a large proportion of cargo in the trade is suitable for containerization, the lines will continue to operate conventional break-bulk tonnage as well.

Caribbean Overseas Lines will be helping the port at Kingston in Jamaica in its bid to be an important trans-shipment center in the Caribbean. Partly assisted by Japanese finance, it is planned to invest $45 million in a 174-acre development at Kingston to provide facilities where large deep sea containerships can transfer cargo to other deep sea container vessels serving worldwide destinations. The complex will be situated at the Newport West and Gordon Cay areas of the port, and the first phase is to include the provision of four portainers at purpose-built container berths. Jamaica is ideally situated for the construction of such a complex, as cargo on a north to south run between North and South America, and on an east to west run between Europe and the Far East via the Panama Canal, could well be transhipped at the terminal. The number of vessels covering each sector of the journey will be regulated according to the volume of cargo offered, but as frequencies will also be tightly controlled, and may well vary between trades, total transit times might be longer when compared with the voyage time of vessels undertaking the entire journey themselves. As about 20% of all general cargo passing through the port of Kingston is already containerized, the port should be well able technically to cope with much larger throughputs following the establishment of additional container services. It is also anticipated that raw and semi-finished products will be shipped to Jamaica, where processing prior to re-exportation by container vessel will take place, and that bulk commodity shipments will be broken down into smaller parcels for re-distribution to overseas destinations. Developments in the Caribbean will be further boosted if plans to construct a double track railway in Mexico between Salina Cruz and Coatzocoalcos materialize. The 175 mile long link would ease congestion in the Panama Canal, as well as offering a considerably faster transit time for containerized cargo, but the estimated cost of $1,000 million, in spite of interest being shown by the United States of America, Japan and France, might well prevent the railway's construction.

South Africa

The trade between Europe and South Africa will be the next major area for containerization, and decisions have already been taken by the conference committing some of its members to operating cellular containerships by 1977. Studies have been undertaken on behalf of the South African Government, and it was indicated as far back as 1971 that container services should be developed. Similar studies were carried out by the conference, but the South African Government had to be convinced that real cost savings would follow from conversion to container systems, before it was prepared to sanction the change. Some of the studies indicated that dual-purpose roll-on roll-off containerships would be better able to handle the varying trade flows than pure cellular vessels, and the lines in the trade were divided between the different systems. A lot of wheeled agricultural machinery and other mobile equipment is imported by South Africa, while such seasonal produce as deciduous and citrus fruit is exported, and a strong case was presented by some lines for the operation of more flexible tonnage. It was also proposed that containerships incorporating a horizontal system of on-board container movement over conveyor belts might ideally be suited to the trade because of the poor South African port facilities, but this method of the future, which will be discussed later, was eventually discarded.

Although the conference lines were eager to go ahead with some form of unitization, they were still unable to definitely decide on the ideal method, as it was not clear what the South African Government was going to do about the poor state of the ports and the overland rail links. Some form of updating of the trade was already overdue, and indeed had unitization been introduced earlier, capital expenditure would have been less than the estimates that were then being put forward. But in March 1974 the conference lines were given the go-ahead by the South African Government for full containerization of the trade, and the lines were offered a fifteen-year contract, valid from 1977, regulating the return on capital invested. The actual return has not been disclosed, but it is thought that the lines would require from 15 to 18 per cent per annum before committing themselves to operation of a large number of fully cellular vessels. Full containerization of the trade will cost in the region of £500 million and provision will be made for a number of multi-purpose back-up vessels capable of shipping unusual and awkward loads. About 100 conventional ships currently in the trade will be replaced by fourteen cellular vessels, five multi-purpose vessels, and four specialized lumber carriers. Ten of the cellular vessels will be in service between North European ports (including the United Kingdom) and South Africa, while the remaining four will cater for Mediterranean/South African cargo. The five multi-purpose ships will carry containers and other unit loads and the four specialized lumber carriers will predominantly ship lumber and associated products southbound for Scandinavian countries, and fruit northbound. A 5½-day frequency will be maintained, and it has been estimated that the total annual fuel consumption of the new ships will be half that of the consumption of today's conventional vessels. Eighty- to ninety-thousand containers will eventually be needed, and orders have been placed for the supply of 60,000 for delivery by 1977, by which time initial vessels should be in service. These ships will be of about 50,000 GRT and will be capable of carrying up to 2,450 containers each. Although freight rates will continue to rise throughout the changeover period, and new building costs have been inflated partly due to the scarcity of credit, it is estimated that very shortly after introduction of the cellular service, freight rates will be at a level below where they would have been had conventional break-bulk ships continued to serve the trade.

The participating lines will be running a joint service operation similar to AECS, and each line will be able to ship containers by her partners' vessels through a slot sharing scheme. South African Lines has been absorbed by the other South African flag carrier, South African Marine Corporation Limited (Safmarine), and Safmarine, together with Springbok Shipping Company will control 40 per cent of the trade. Safmarine has integrated its ship management functions with those of British and Commonwealth Shipping (Clan Line and Union Castle) and Cayzer Irvine, to form International Liner Services who will act as United Kingdom loading brokers. British and Commonwealth together with Ellerman Lines and Harrison Line though will be responsible for contributing a total of at least three vessels, unless OCL meanwhile decides to operate containerships herself in the South African trade. As British and Commonwealth is a member of OCL, such a decision must be made by OCL which may also involve adjusting British and Commonwealth's shareholding in the consortium. Continental and Scandinavian lines will be responsible for three or four ships, while Lloyd Trestino and Safmarine will each provide two vessels for use in the Mediterranean.

Prior to the decision of the South African Railways and Harbors to heavily invest in new equipment, the lines were faced with either running semi-containerships and roll-on roll-off tonnage, or with providing much of the port handling facilities themselves. The state run authority is now committed, however, to the updating of port facilities by 1977/8, and to the speeding-up of overland container movements over the railway system. £150 million is to be spent at Cape Town, Durban and Port Elizabeth, and Paceco portainers are to be manufactured under licence in South Africa. Cape Town and Durban, where container quays are in and await to be equipped, will be major container ports, and a container berth will also be provided at Port Elizabeth on reclaimed land. East London has little room for expansion, and will be served on a feeder vessel basis, while Lourenco Marques and Beira could in time develop into deep sea terminals rivaling Cape Town and Durban. Lourenco Marques is especially well suited to act as a major terminal, serving as it does much of the industrial region of the Transvaal. In view of the severe state of congestion to be found at South African ports, containerization cannot happen quickly enough in the opinion of a number of groups if only to alleviate the necessity for congestion surcharges which currently stand at 20 per cent of the freight.

While it is known which South African ports will be called at by the new containerships, the picture is less clear with regard to the United Kingdom. The twenty-two conference lines have had discussions with a number of United Kingdom port authorities, and although it is generally regarded that Southampton will eventually obtain the trade, especially in view of the uncertainty surrounding the building of a containerport complex at Maplin in the Thames estuary, this is by no means certain. Southampton badly wants to extend its container terminal, and is hoping for National Ports Council and Government approval to embark on a £5-10 million expansion programme that would provide extra berths to accommodate the South African vessels by 1977. But the lines may decide to base their United Kingdom operations at one of the other large ports able to handle all the trade—for example, Liverpool or London—or they may feel that the traffic should be divided between a southern and a northern port. If the latter attitude were to be adopted, a large number of smaller port authorities, unable to accommodate all the trade but well able to handle half of it, would be in the running, and would be able to quote very competitively.

While preparations have been going ahead regarding the full-scale conversion of the Europe/South Africa trade to carriage by container, a few lines have been active in actually shipping containerized cargo in the trade. Compagnie Maritime Belge are able to accept up to 50 containers on some of their conventional sailings out of north European ports, and Enterprise Container Lines (ECL) of Johannesburg has been operating a regular container service out of Rotterdam since the beginning of 1973. ECL was formed in June 1972 as a non-vessel operator, but through associations with a shipping company was able to offer space. The company has its own network of agents in Europe and South Africa generating traffic which is conveyed within Europe by feeder vessels to and from Rotterdam, and at present confines movements to full container loads only. Tonnage employed varies from multi-purpose, self-sustaining general cargo bottoms, with limited container securing, to 40,000 DWT bulk carriers with under-deck container capacity southbound, and limited deck space for containers northbound. In 1974 it was decided to take long-term lease equipment into the system, and containers are now offered to shippers free of rental. ECL has been successful in shipping some bulk commodities northbound by container, and is now able to offer a fortnightly sailing in each direction. ECL's success can be put down to the normal advantages to be found in a containerized system, and can be regarded as a gauge indicating the future success of full conversion of the trade to containers.

Before even ECL became aware of the urgent need to provide cargo owners with a container service in South Africa, a coastal shipping company, Unicorn Shipping, had on charter from Sea Containers Incorporated the m/v *Voorloper* which was able to carry up to 150 containers between South African ports. The vessel has a stern ramp to facilitate container handling at ports

without container cranes, and the fleet may be expanded to provide a regular feeder service tying in with the deep sea containerships of the future.

It is perhaps surprising that the Japanese had no plans to enter
the South African trade as at January 1974, but later on in the
year it was announced that involvement might begin through a
tie-up between Mitsui OSK and NYK, and Safmarine. Services
between South Africa and the Far East could start as soon as
South African port facilities allow, and the indications are that
such a service will commence shortly after the European service
becomes established. Safmarine has meanwhile placed orders
worth £120 million with French shipyards for the building of
four 2,450 container capacity cellular vessels having a service
speed of 21 knots and due for delivery commencing 1977. Seventy
per cent credit for these vessels, which will be placed in the
Europe to South Africa trade, has been granted by France with
a seven-year period from date of delivery for repayment, while
the remaining thirty per cent will be raised in the money markets.
Safmarine have also ordered a smaller vessel from an Italian yard
for use in the Mediterranean to South Africa trade, and it is
expected that the group's Mediterranean partners—Lloyd Trestino
—will shortly be ordering two similar vessels.

It will be several years before all handling of South African
cargo is fully mechanized, and the often poor state of the roads
away from the industrial regions will act as a further potential
source of damage to containers, as well as to cargoes. In an
attempt at reducing damage to equipment, all steel containers
will generally be in use in the trade, and the extra strength possessed by such units should obviate constant repairing and replacement. Another peculiarity is the difference in trade flows,
and the necessity of using some refrigerated containers northbound to accommodate the deciduous and citrus fruit movements. Primary products such as ore, wool and maize are major
contributors to South African exports, and have traditionally
been shipped by bulk freighter. Experiments are taking place
though with a view to shipment of such products by container,
and the indications are that in the absence of alternative methods
such as LASH, some regular container shipments of primary products will occur. The problem of trade differences would then

largely be solved, but the long-term feasibility of such movements must be wholly dependent on the costs involved.

East Africa

In the East African countries political unrest has led to general
lack of confidence and to a decrease in the volume of overseas
trade. Although Uganda has suffered most, both Kenya and
Tanzania have had their share of instability, and such measures
as currency revaluation and stricter control on imports have
dampened still further the area's import trade. Common services
such as transport and harbor administration are controlled by
the East African Community by corporations made up of representatives from the countries involved, but where the ports are
concerned, intense rivalry has developed between Mombasa (Kil-
indini) in Kenya and Dar es Salaam in Tanzania. The Dar es
Salaam-based East African Harbor Corporation, which has Social-
ist leanings, is unable to agree with the more Capitalist-inclined
port of Mombasa, and Mombasa has been withholding revenue
payments to the administration at Dar es Salaam. These payments are in settlement of purchases undertaken at Dar es Salaam
on behalf of the port of Mombasa, and by withholding them the
more efficient and larger port at Mombasa is trying to obtain a
degree of independence. Malpractices are also reported to be
widespread among top management controlling the ports, and in
view of the East African Community's dependence on the ports
as a gateway to overseas markets, drastic measures must be put
in hand to remedy the situation.

The most obvious manifestation of inefficient management is
the severe state of congestion to be found, particularly at Dar
es Salaam, and to a lesser extent at Mombasa. Antiquated working methods and lack of proper equipment in the ports must
largely be blamed for slow working of vessels, and for a four-
week waiting period for a berth at Dar es Salaam, and one week
at Mombasa. Congestion began to build up toward the end of
1973, and although the conference was able to withhold imposing surcharges for a few months, it soon became necessary to levy
surcharges of up to 30 per cent. (Eastern Africa National Ship-

ping Line—state-owned by the governments of Tanzania, Zambia, Kenya and Uganda—decided to subsidize all extra costs caused by congestion.) With congestion on this sort of scale, new rail links like that between Zambia and Dar es Salaam lose their attractiveness as a speedy and efficient method of moving the country's copper exports, and point to the urgent necessity of updating the ports. But existing rail links must also be improved, and new rolling stock is being obtained to keep cargoes flowing. Mombasa is to be provided with two new conventional berths by 1975, and a new port may be constructed on the Kenya coast.

There are no plans to containerize the Europe to East Africa trade, and conventional break-bulk ships together with bulk freighters will continue to serve the area for some considerable time. Port and transport investment will continue to be apportioned to "patching up" operations, as illustrated by the improvements to be undertaken at the Afars and Issas port of Djibouti at the entrance to the Red Sea. Following the re-opening of the Suez Canal, Djibouti will regain her former importance, and with the building of a road link to Addis Ababa in Ethiopia, the port will draw cargo away from Assab. Further road construction may provide a link between Lagos in Nigeria, and Mombasa, and passing as it would through the EEC associate member countries of Uganda, Congo, Central African Republic and Cameroon, would act as a channel for goods to and from the EEC countries in Europe. Many of the African developing states want to retain an association with the EEC with a view to the granting of tariff concessions on imports into the EEC without reciprocal agreements in Africa, and to the guaranteeing of stable prices within the EEC for African primary products. Such measures, if successful, will considerably boost export trade, but will not be instrumental in increasing the inward flow of semi-manufactured and consumer goods, which might warrant the establishment of a container service.

It remains to be seen whether the East African Harbors Corporation will have to be taken in hand in a similar way to the East African Railways Corporation, which has had to succumb to outside management following collapse of the former administration. Poor management and bad accounting practices led to

the calling in of a group of management consultants already employed by the Canadian National Railways, and extensive reorganization is expected. It is said that railway manpower exceeds
actual requirements by as much as 25 per cent, but it is doubtful
whether the Community will agree to labor cuts in a sector
where employment has traditionally been brisk. But without
such cuts, and without a more stable system of management, in
the ports as well as the railway system, the medium-term future
of both sectors in a climate of general modernization elsewhere,
is bleak indeed.

West Africa

West Africa is an area where general cargo shipment possibilities are expanding fast, while at the same time they remain a
small part of total trade. Trade flow differences are much in evidence as exemplified by 80 per cent of export cargo being bulk
commodities, and about 25 per cent of imports being suitable
for containerization. Import traffic will continue to increase,
and although volume purchases are often made up of heavy
capital equipment such as oil prospecting machinery, goods ideally
suited to carriage by container will become more prevalent, and
will allow an expansion of existing container services.

West Africa is therefore not an area where the type of trade
is ideally suited to containerization, and other factors must have
been in evidence to help promote the concept to its present
stage of development. The most important of these is the fact
that prior to containers being used by the shipping companies,
it was not unusual for up to 20 per cent of conventional cargo
to vanish after it had been landed at Lagos/Apapa. Containerization appeared to offer the best remedy to prevent such losses,
and insurance underwriters, who had not previously been keen
to accept cargo risks, were encouraged by losses almost dropping
to nil where container cargo was concerned. Pilferage is particularly insignificant when containers are transferred direct to the
operator's own shed for unloading when necessary, but where
the customs authorities are insisting on cargo checks on the
berth involving unloading and re-packing, losses will often be

substantial. The other bane of the West African trade, and a contributory factor to pilferage, is congestion. Movement of cargo through the ports is often too slow due to out of date handling methods, and attempts to keep up with recent import tonnage increases have not been successful. Lagos/Apapa in particular is experiencing difficulties, and long queues of lorries are to be seen in the port area. Lagos/Apapa handle about 80 per cent of Nigeria's overseas trade, and perhaps congestion could be eased if some of this trade were to be handled at alternative ports, and if individual vessels were to uplift cargo destined for a far smaller range of ports than is currently the practice. It would then be possible for some vessels to omit Lagos/Apapa from their sailing schedules, and for others to carry predominantly Lagos/Apapa cargo.

West African trade interests, in addition to being much concerned with reducing pilferage and easing congestion, are also keen to achieve economies in shipment and handling of cargo. Slings, pallets, units and containers all have a contribution to make, and as the containership consortia have shown little interest in the area, containerization does not necessarily mean commitment to the ISO sizes of container. What is important is to achieve cost savings, often utilizing existing ship and port handling methods, and small size containers have shown themselves to be better suited to the trade than 40-foot units. Some operators have great faith in the 318 cubic foot capacity container, which is about a quarter the size of a standard 20-foot long unit, while others widely use 10-foot long containers. Fully cellular ships will therefore be unsuited to the trade because of the nonstandard container sizes in use, while semi-containerships will be able to cope better. Another factor against complete specialization is the tendency for containers to be under-utilized, and of the necessity for cellular containerships to be large and have access to a constant flow of containerized cargo. As road conditions often make internal transit of containers slow, and as the percentage of container cargo to cargo in general is quite small, equipment will not be used intensely enough, and in order to offer regular cellular containership sailings, vessels would have to be too small to be economic. Elder Dempster Lines were experimenting with the carriage of containers and other unit loads

FIGURE 19 Roll-on roll-off vessel engaged in the West African trade loading at Le Havre (Courtesy of Le Havre Port Authority).

several years ago, and as their contribution to the United King-dom/West Africa Lines Joint Service (UKWAL), a group of six established shipping lines serving 35 ports in the area, they are operating semi-converted conventional tonnage capable of ship-ping pallets and other unit loads, conventional cargo, and 20-foot ISO containers on deck. It was at one time thought that Elder Dempster would introduce side loading pallet ships to the trade, but it was eventually decided that a combination of containers and unit loads would be more suitable. More recently the line has been introducing semi-containerships of 12,000 DWT each in the Nigerian trade, and three such vessels representing a total investment of £8.5 million and able to carry up to 410 20-foot containers each, in addition to palletized and loose cargo, will soon be in service. Fork lift trucks have free access in the holds, and 36-ton on-board derricks allow the handling of containers at ports where facilities are poor.

In 1964 three of the present members of the UKWAL, Palm Line, the Nigerian National Shipping Line, and Elder Dempster Lines, formed African Container Express (ACE), with a view to operating a regular container service, initially using conventional vessels, between United Kingdom ports, and Lagos/Apapa and Port Harcourt. The group started by shipping full container loads on a door-to-door basis, with the main intention of reducing the then high levels of pilferage, especially at Lagos/Apapa. The majority of containers travel empty northbound, and southbound freight rates have had to reflect the fact. Efforts have been made though to ship cocoa beans and groundnuts out of Nigeria using the type "318" small container of non-metal construction, and these plywood and synthetic material units have been instru-mental in reducing sweat damage. A groupage service was started in October 1974, and it is reported that cellular vessels are to be introduced later. A gradual swing to greater container and unit load utilization is therefore underway in the West African trade, and the current re-investment plans will inevitably lead to a higher level of freight rates. Continental lines are moving with the swing, and container services are maintained out of Rotterdam and Hamburg to Abidjan and Lagos/Apapa, using vessels able to convey up to 180 20-foot containers. The move to containeriza-tion though will be a controlled one, and indeed the West African conferences are more in favor of developing and improving palletized methods of shipment than of wholesale container development. In view of the independent study undertaken by the Economist Intelligence Unit on behalf of the Unit Load Council which indicated that container methods of shipment in the United Kingdom to Nigeria trade could offer a 15 per cent saving in transport costs over break-bulk methods, while unit load shipments would offer as much as a 25 per cent saving, the preference for palletized methods is understandable. It should be pointed out though that the study was based on the use of standard size pallets mechanically handled, and that the container costs were calculated using conventional berths and cranes.

The other principal mover of container cargo between the United Kingdom and ports in Nigeria is the Africa Container Line (AFCL), a private British company that began its service as a non-vessel operator using space on non-conference ships. AFCL clearly saw the need to reduce the 20 per cent pilferage rate, and container shipments have been so successful in this respect that full Lloyd's warehouse to warehouse insurance cover is now granted. Lagos/Apapa and Port Harcourt are called at, and over 300 containers ranging in length from 10 up to 40 feet are owned. Whereas Africa Container Express has only recently introduced an LCL service, Africa Container Line have been offering both LCL and FCL facilities since inception. There has been a definite demand for LCL groupage facilities, and as much as 30 per cent of southbound traffic moves on this basis. Although little cargo is carried northbound by container, AFCL is hoping for regular two-way traffic, and has been partially successful in shipping bulk commodities. Timber, veneers and rubber are products that it has been possible to convey by container. In March 1974 AFCL introduced its first vessel into the trade by chartering the containership *Anja*, which was shortly followed by a second chartered ship, the cellular vessel *Weser Exporter*. Ship's gear is used, and through avoiding delays during discharge, congestion surcharges are not levied by the line.

Although the lines have been successful in running their container services to Nigeria, their task has not been eased by the state of development at the ports. Three conventional berths are maintained at the Lagos customs quay on Lagos Island opposite the Apapa complex, but conditions are cramped and the facilities are old. At Apapa fourteen berths are available, one of which predominantly handles container cargo, but again the facilities are old, and often as many as 50 per cent of the cranes are not functional. In an effort to overcome the severe congestion at Lagos/Apapa where vessels currently have to wait at anchor outside the harbor for up to a month for a berth, and where shippers have to finance a 30 per cent congestion surcharge levied on basic freight rates, the Nigerian port authorities are to install specialized equipment at purpose-built berths. It is hoped to have a container berth functional by August 1976, and three additional berths for handling unitized and break-bulk cargo are also to be built.

Nigeria has been able to increase her wealth largely following exploration of oil, and this new found affluence has led to an increasing demand for capital and consumer goods. The level of trade is growing, particularly with the United Kingdom, and national fleets such as the Black Star Line and the Nigerian National Shipping Line will earn substantial amounts of foreign exchange for the Nigerian economy. The Nigerian National Shipping Line which was founded in 1958 to extend state participation in private industry already owns fourteen vessels. A ten-year road development scheme within Nigeria began in 1970, and through linking up with such developments as the proposed road link across Africa between Lagos and Mombasa, a substantial amount of container cargo could be drawn to the container berths at Lagos/Apapa in the future.

Among bulk handling ports in West Africa mention should be made of the interest the Chinese are showing in the construction of a port at Nouakshott in Mauritania 280 miles north of Dakar in Senegal. It is not planned to install container berths, and the port will be built primarily to handle the large tonnages of iron ore and copper exported by the former French state. The most prosperous of the former West African French colonies is the Ivory Coast and the port at San Pedro is to be expanded at a cost of over £17 million to ease the strain on the busy port at Abidjan. The partly Government-financed scheme will provide extensive timber and conventional general cargo berths, and bulk systems for iron ore and foodstuffs will be extended. Container berths may also be provided. Perhaps the Ivory Coast is forging ahead too quickly with new building, some of which can only be regarded as prestige projects, and high rise blocks are surrounded by wide tracts of unused land. The Government announcement that the San Pedro scheme had been extended to include a city for 100,000 people was premature, and already 20,000 are squatting in the vicinity.

Zaire (formerly the Democratic Republic of Congo) has plans for a new deepwater port at Banana to predominately handle the country's export trade of copper, cobalt, manganese and zinc, but until the port is built a lot of Zaire's trade will continue to pass through Lobito after being conveyed by rail over the Benguela Railway. The railway runs for 838 miles through Angola from Lobito on the coast to Dilolo on the Zaire frontier, from where it connects with other railway systems serving areas as far apart as Lake Tanganyika, Zambia, and South Africa. Since Mr. Ian Smith closed the Rhodesia/Zambia border in January 1973 the privately owned Benguela Railway Company has seen its annual tonnage of freight, particularly of copper, grow considerably, but the additional load placed on the port facilities at Lobito has led to serious congestion. A general deterioration in working conditions at Lobito has worsened the situation still further, and round-the-clock working has been disbanded. Vessels are having to wait for up to 50 days for a berth, and a congestion surcharge of 70 per cent has been imposed by the conference lines. There are no plans for container facilities at Lobito, but two more wharves involving a total cost of $7 million are to be built. Meanwhile Angola's other port at Luanda is being expanded to overcome the current shortage of facilities, and plans include the installation of an alongside wharf to handle pallets and containers. Angola Provides port and transport facilities for a large area of Central Africa, and 15 per cent of the country's investment during the period 1968-1973 was devoted to transport. More money is to be invested in road and harbor schemes, and it is hoped that the present political instability will not prevent the systems from becoming economically of value.

The Mediterranean

In some parts of the Mediterranean, as in several other areas of the world today, revenue accruing from oil is having a marked impact on wealth and on patterns of trade. The desire for higher living standards leads to an increased demand for goods, and this is particularly so in North Africa and the eastern Mediterranean. Since 1970 there has been a sharp increase in the number of container and roll-on roll-off terminals either completed or in the course of construction, and shipping companies not previously connected with the area have started services. The diversion of cargo to north European ports during the period of over-tonnaging on the North Atlantic practically ceased when the North Atlantic lines found they could fill their container vessels to capacity without having to subsidize the overland movement of cargo from southern Europe, and most of their traffic now moves over Mediterranean ports either to be fed to a deep sea vessel, or for direct shipment. The Mediterranean trade indeed is far better organized than some other trades where containerships have been in service for a longer period, and over-tonnaging and inter-line disputes have not occurred. Increased affluence from oil revenues though is leading to economic nationalism in some countries, and the desire now is to operate national fleets.

Because of the varied nature of cargo types, and of the large number of ports warranting some form of shipping service in the Mediterranean, roll-on roll-off methods of shipment have grown at a faster rate than container methods. At tidal ports where enclosed docks do not exist, problems in aligning cargo decks of roll-on roll-off vessels to the quay arise, especially where tidal differences are marked, but as such variations in the Mediterranean are slight, operation of roll-on roll-off vessels has again been boosted. Container services are confined to those ports having a regular two-way throughput of cargo, while ports dealing in predominantly seasonal produce, or where inward and outward cargo types differ markedly, are better served by the more flexible roll-on roll-off type of vessel. Ports in the Mediterranean anyway are too numerous to allow expensive purpose-built container terminals to be economic, in view of the comparatively small annual cargo tonnages passing through them individually. The smaller ports have therefore largely remained poorly equipped, and container handling is undertaken either by ship's derricks or by mobile shore cranes. Nearly all ports able to handle containerships and roll-on roll-off vessels have been converted to their present state of development, instead of being purpose-built, and while co-operation between Mediterranean ports has been rare in the past, several western ports are now exchanging ideas and opinions with a view to working closer together. Containers will often be shipped by roll-on roll-off or conventional vessels between the smaller ports, and a container terminal elsewhere for transhipment to a deep sea cellular containership, and a stern loading ramp will make container handling possible when port facilities are nil. Some of those lines who have already containerized their short sea services between north European ports and the Mediterranean may have been a little quick in committing themselves to such an inflexible system, and several other lines are now holding back to see if roll-on roll-off can develop into the principal system. Deep sea containership companies serving such trades as the North Atlantic, Pacific, and Far East, however, will be better placed to operate cellular vessels as they will limit their ports of call in the Mediterranean and rely on the large number of feeder vessels to collect and distribute their boxes. Whether one such port will develop into a large terminal in the future, through which the majority of Mediterranean deep sea containers will pass, will be examined shortly.

Prior to the closure of the Suez Canal in 1967, large volumes of cargo were transhipped at Mediterranean ports, notably Port Said, but this entrepot trade has now practically ceased. With the prospect of the canal opening in 1975 or 1976 Port Said will regain its importance both as an entrepot, and bunkering port, and vessels will be able to cut out the long voyage round the Cape of Good Hope. While the canal will be particularly of benefit to general cargo vessels sailing for example between London and Bombay, enabling them to save up to two weeks by using the canal, fast containerships connecting the United Kingdom and Australia would only be able to save one day by similarly using the canal. Although such a gain would appear to be negligible, it becomes quite significant when it is realized that the round voyage time of the large containerships, inclusive of port calls, is considerably less than that of conventional cargo ships. Usage of containerships is very intense, and what is really important is the number of round trips undertaken each year, and not sailing time. The greater the number of round trips, the fewer will be the number of vessels required, and both fixed and variable costs will be comparatively less. The canal will not be viable though if political instability forces up rates of insurance to such a level that any savings from a freight rate reduction are immediately absorbed.

In North Africa large-scale port development is to take place at Tripoli and Benghazi, as well as at Port Said where container and roll-on roll-off berths are to be constructed. Libya is to invest some of her vast wealth at her two main ports, and it is planned to spend a total of £100 million at Tripoli alone. In 1973 three million tons of cargo were imported through Tripoli, and to accommodate an estimated seven million tons per annum by 1980 purpose-built container berths are to be provided. A major harbor project is also planned for Benghazi where 16 new berths are to be built. Four of these will be for roll-on roll-off vessels, while one will be a deep water container berth.

Up-to-date container facilities have been available at Israel's main ports for several years, and direct container services connect the state with the United Kingdom and elsewhere. It is expected that during 1974/75 container traffic will increase by about 65 per cent, and the Israeli Ports Authority is currently in the middle of a I£250 million scheme to principally provide and extend facilities at Ashdod and Haifa to allow the majority of overseas trade to be containerized by 1976. This development is part of a much larger undertaking aimed at drawing up coordinated plans for the future expansion of all Israel's merchant marine, as well as the ports. The Israeli Railways are co-operating, and fast container trains made up of flat container wagons are already linking Ashdod and Haifa with inland points. While Israeli trade with the United Kingdom is generally in balance, a lot of the state's exports consist of seasonal produce such as fruit, and congestion is a problem at the ports for part of the year. During the fruit season delays to vessels of from 6 to 8 weeks are common, but it is hoped that the more efficient container methods of handling will considerably ease the strain even during the peak periods. But congestion is also partly caused by the recurring wars in the area and the ever-present political instability, and shippers and importers may find that the inland terminal being built near Tel-Aviv is only able to move the state of congestion away from the ports.

Both Ashdod and Haifa are well equipped and would be able to offer up-to-date facilities to vessels using the Suez Canal. Ashdod was first to install container berths, but both ports now have a 45-ton container crane serving two container berths, and good back-up handling equipment. Three more portainers are to be constructed at Ashdod and one more at Haifa, and as all future equipment, including transtainers, is to be of the MACH type, automation will be possible later on. Container throughput at Haifa doubled during 1973 to half a million tons, and in addition to expansion of the port itself, a new container terminal is under construction nearby at Tel Hanan where emphasis will be placed on the handling of LCL traffic.

Israel's national shipping line, the Zim Israel Navigation Company, showed an early interest in containerization by initially buying 8,000 containers from the USA at a cost of I£12.5 million and arranging for additional units to be manufactured locally. The Zim Container Line was established to maintain a non-conference service to the Far East outside the Med Club, and many of Zim's other services have already been, or are in the process of being converted to container or roll-on roll-off operation. As a large proportion of traffic carried by Zim is seasonal, the line has adopted a policy of chartering much of its tonnage, which allows almost complete flexibility of operation.

Increased trade in the eastern Mediterranean coupled with the diversion of some Middle East traffic following the closure of the Suez Canal, has led to severe congestion at ports in the Lebanon and in Syria. Beirut is poorly managed, the port is too small, the facilities available are very old, and the labor force is prone to erratic working. The road haulage industry is badly organized, and because of the frequent closure of the Lebanon/Syria border, cargo movements out of Beirut overland are slowed down. Purpose-built container handling facilities do not exist, but the United Kingdom management consultancy firm of Peat Marwick Mitchell has been appointed to re-organize and extend the port at Beirut. In the meantime shippers of cargo to and from the Middle East will continue to review the state of congestion at Beirut and the Syrian port of Lattakia, and route their goods through whichever port is able to offer the quickest transit at a particular time.

Famagusta, the principal port of Cyprus, has already been modernized at a cost of £2 million, but port handling is still slow. A 35-ton container crane is under construction though, and the port could now develop into a free trade zone in view of its close proximity to Nicosia. In May 1970 work began at Limassol on the construction of an artificial harbor and port involving an investment of over £8 million, and even though container berths were not included in the original plans, a 35-ton container crane, similar to that at Famagusta has since been provided.

Possibly because of the lack of any central control over the ports in Greece, port modernization has not proceeded as it should have. Because of a mountainous interior, an intricate coastline, and a large number of islands, the Greeks have always heavily relied on shipping to transport their goods, and have developed into a maritime nation. But in spite of their history, they are heavily dependent today on other countries' merchant fleets to ship container traffic, and have continued to develop break-bulk conventional methods of shipment. Seventy per cent of the country's trade passes through the port at Piraeus, but due to the lack of modern facilities the majority of this cannot be containerized. Those containers that do pass over the quays at Piraeus have to be handled by mobile or floating cranes, but a 40-ton gantry crane for containers is now in the process of erection. A roll-on roll-off berth has already been provided, and LASH vessels belonging to Prudential-Grace Lines have been calling at the port for a number of years. Five LASH ships are used, to connect the United States with the Mediterranean, and after discharge some barges are towed to the second Greek port of Thessaloniki where they are moored alongside conventional quays to have their cargo handled by conventional cranes. Thessaloniki has even worse facilities than Piraeus, and vessels have to either utilize their own derricks, or, if a heavy lift is involved, a floating crane is available. Because of its comparative nearness to the Suez Canal, it is possible that Piraeus may develop into a large transhipment center for both break-bulk and unitized cargo, but facilities would first have to be vastly improved. Turkey is similarly placed to Greece as far as port handling equipment is concerned, and also as in Greece her ports are having to face increasing competition from international road hauliers carrying cargo between north Europe and the Mediterranean area. The harbor facilities at Izmir are to be expanded though, and new quays for both conventional and container vessels are to be built.

Malta, situated in the middle of the Mediterranean, has been connected with the United Kingdom by direct containership sailings for a number of years, and before these by a container service by road or rail, and roll-on roll-off vessel or containership, over the French port of Marseilles. The Maltese dock labor force have always opposed the construction of modern cargo berths and container cranes on the grounds of diminished job opportunities, and containers have had to be handled in the port at the Grand Harbor area of Valletta by more conventional systems. But a container terminal is now under construction and with the addition of two roll-on roll-off berths as well, the present poor facilities at Valletta will be converted into an up-to-date cargo handling center. An inland container depot and new roads are also planned which should considerably quicken the handling of the Tl million tons of cargo that pass through Valletta annually.

Development then of roll-on roll-off, and to a lesser extent container berths and ancillary equipment, is to continue in the Mediterranean and port authorities have generally adapted to the changing situation. Even the port of Cagliari in Sardinia is connected to Italy by a roll-on roll-off vessel, and it is even being considered that part of the island could be used as the site of a huge container terminal where the really large vessels of the future could tranship units to the growing number of feeder vessels operating in the Mediterranean that are able to call at the many smaller and not so well equipped ports.

Italy and Sicily

Italy's traditionally strained economy has been the cause of slow development in the shipping and cargo handling sectors, and finance has frequently been diverted to areas considered to be more in need of support. Lloyd Trestino was to have been the first Italian shipping company to put a containership into service, but due to various delays a consortium of three lines were able to commence cellular operations before Lloyd Trestino in 1971. A partnership had earlier been announced between Fassio Line of Italy and Hansa Line of Germany to operate cellular tonnage between the Mediterranean and ports along the eastern seaboards of Canada and the United States. The joint service, that was to be based at Genoa, was to be known as the Atlantica Line, and orders were placed for two new containerships. The link was inaugurated though by using two vessels previously belonging to Hansa, and a policy of chartering principally from Hansa has periodically continued. Both lines had previously been operating their own container service in the trade, either by running cellular or conventional tonnage, and a third line who were operating a similar service, Fabre Line of France, increased Atlantica's membership to three. By the end of 1973 a total of $46 million had been invested by the group, and today four either purpose-built or adapted cellular vessels are in use. Following the lengthening of three of the vessels by adding new center sections though, the charter on the fourth vessel will be relinquished. Atlantica Line have been successful in bringing back to Genoa much of the North Atlantic container traffic that used to be hauled overland for shipment through north Continental ports, and this trend has indeed spread into the realm of short sea shipments between north European and Mediterranean ports, as cargo owners have found that sea freight costs are often more stable than overland freight charges. Lloyd Trestino's first cellular containership was the *Lloydiana* which joined the Australia to Europe Container Service early in 1973, and through their participation in the Mediterranean–Far East Container Service, (the "Med Club"), the line's containership fleet was expanded in October 1973 by the *Nipponia* entering the Far East trade, and in March 1974 by the *Mediterranea* entering the same trade.

Because of the Italian government's policy of encouraging growth in the road and railway sectors, it has often been difficult for the ports to raise sufficient capital to finance their development schemes. This was particularly the case up until the end of 1971, but since then it has gradually been realized by the administration that without extensive port modernization and new building the growing number of containership, and especially of roll-on roll-off, operators would look to other countries to handle their Mediterranean traffic. More recently development has accelerated, and in addition to the ports and shipping companies, a whole range of associated industries have either materialized, or in turn have expanded to keep pace with the larger traffic flows. Unfortunately though regulation of the dock labor force has been difficult, and some of the Italian ports today are grossly overmanned. Genoa, for example, is finding it difficult to remain competitive with double the manpower it needs, and Palermo in Sicily has three times the number of dockers it requires. Coupled with this is the fact that the volume of Italy's foreign trade is insufficient to maintain all the country's ports, and port authorities are having to rely more and more on transhipment cargo. Although the Italian State Railways have been more favorably placed with regard to Government finance, expansion has not been rapid enough to cope with the upsurge in container traffic, and many boxes have had to be diverted to the roads. Additional railway container terminals are, however, being built, and the numbers of flat wagons are being increased.

Italy's principal port at Genoa is hindered from developing on a large scale because of the mountainous coastal strip running immediately behind the port. Congestion is severe and packing and unpacking of LCL containers is generally undertaken at an inland collection and distribution center 70 km to the north at Rivalta Scrivia. Container handling at Genoa began on a limited scale in 1969, and is today centered at the Ponte Libia and Ponte Ronco terminals. Three portainers are in use, and if Government approval is granted a further two will be provided at a new container terminal planned at Colata Bettolo. Although Genoa has lost some container cargo because of high port charges, traffic between both the Far East and Australia and Italy would be boosted if the Suez Canal were to be opened. While some of this cargo would be generated by the Italian market, there could be a considerable flow to and from Northern Europe, and if Genoa were able to cope the medium-term future of the port would be assured. Already both the USSR and Japan have indicated that they intend using Genoa for Italian traffic and for transhipment cargo.

The Rivalta Scrivia complex was planned during the 1960's by a private consortium of shipping, banking and forwarding interests, and was intended to ease the congestion at Genoa by funnelling LCL cargo to the center for packing into and unpacking from maritime containers. It was opened in 1968, and after an initial increase in throughput of over 500 per unit during 1969-71, growth has fallen away markedly. While forwarding agents, loading brokers, and banks established offices or branches to provide cargo owners with a comprehensive service, a lot of the hoped for Genoa traffic did not materialize, and although operators such as Atlantica Line and the members of AECS are using the complex, a large proportion of space remains unutilized. The terminal is ideally situated halfway between Genoa and Milan, is customs controlled and has its own railway connection, but possibly due to the lack of sufficient handling equipment it has not been successful in attracting cargo generated by the industrial northern part of Italy. New plans are being drawn up for future operation, and if the containership companies serving the Mediterranean area, and Intercontainer, can agree the complex may function as a rail terminal building block trains of containers shipped through Mediterranean ports.

La Spezia principally handles short sea containers at Garibaldi Pier where use is made of a 30-ton and a 28-ton container crane. Some traffic has been gained because of the high charges at nearby Genoa, but a more serious rival to Genoa is Leghorn. The purpose-built Sintermar Container Terminal at Leghorn opened in 1972 is possibly the most up-to-date facility in the Mediterranean, and is capable of handling over 50,000 units per year. Containers are also handled at Carrara Wharf, and at a number of other general cargo berths.

A container terminal is planned for Venice in the Adriatic, and one is already in use at Trieste's Pier No. 7. Roll-on, roll-off and container traffic is handled at Venice, and like at many other Mediterranean ports container cargo could grow dramatically when the Suez Canal re-opens through the handling of units moving, for example, between Central Europe and the Far East.

Ports in the southern part of Italy and in Sicily are concentrating on developing their facilities to offer principally transhipment services to avoid reliance on industries that are not diverse enough to maintain an assured traffic flow into the future. While the area around Naples does generate quite a lot of cargo suitable for containerization such as tinned tomatoes, the port will not be provided with a purpose-built container berth until the late 1970's. It is planned though to use Naples as a transit point in the movement of containers between Europe and North Africa via Sicily. Intercontainer would rail units through Europe to Naples from where they would be shipped by roll-on roll-off vessel to Sicily for transhipment to North African ports. Naples already handles a large volume of rail traffic for the rest of Europe, and utilizes a 35-ton transtainer at the rail transfer terminal.

The Sicilian port of Palermo is developing into one of the principal container handling centers in the Mediterranean. Six roll-on roll-off berths are already in use, and the container terminal being constructed at Puntone quay was provided with a 35-ton portainer in 1973. Although £73 million worth of damage was caused to the port during the storm and high seas of October 1973, the container terminal was luckily undamaged, and the expansion programme which included the provision of a second portainer was able to proceed relatively unaffected. Palermo is used extensively by short sea operators from north European ports, the majority of the current container throughput being generated by the Fiat car factory on the island, but North Atlantic containerships also call at the port. Fruit is exported in containers but the reason behind the large-scale port development at Palermo is a desire to boost the Sicilian economy, Employment both in the dock area and in associated or connected industries will be buoyant through the provision of a number of services to vessels and to cargo owners, and receipts from dues on ships and cargo will steadily increase, particularly as transhipment tonnage grows. It is intended to use Palermo as a large Mediterranean transhipment center when the Suez Canal re-opens for Far Eastern and Australian container traffic, in a similar way that some Atlantic container operators use the port today. As already mentioned several other Mediterranean ports also see their future as a "clearing station" for worldwide container traffic when Suez opens, but it is ports such as Palermo, that are today pushing ahead with ambitious terminal construction projects, who will be able to offer to the containership companies of tomorrow exactly the type of facility needed at the time it is needed.

Spain and Portugal

Until quite recently Spain was for many years economically backward. A mountainous terrain hindered the free movement of people and goods, and navigable rivers were few in number. Parochial communities developed, and much of the domestic trade that took place was shipped between the two hundred odd ports that were established over the years. Today though, Spain has one of the highest sustained growth rates in the world, and development of the transport sectors is given high priority. Port investment and planning is well co-ordinated, with finance coming from the government in Madrid, and duplication of facilities has been largely avoided. There is no centralized shipping ministry though in Spain, and shipowners have to negotiate with a multitude of different government departments. In spite of this the shipping industry has been able to progress quite rapidly, and vessels are modern. A relaxation of state restrictions in the future should act as a stimulus for even further development, and owners will be allowed to order tonnage abroad, and will be given more financial help.

The first container service between the United Kingdom and Spain was inaugurated by MacAndrews-Swedish Lloyd in April 1967, and since then many other operators have changed to unit load systems. Others will follow, and it is estimated that as much as 80 per cent of cargo passing between Spain and the United Kingdom will soon be containerized. During the early years of the current road and railway development plans, a lot of southbound traffic consisted of transport equipment, as well as of capital goods and iron and steel, but as the Spanish economy expands trade flows are becoming more balanced. The state owned railway company, Red Nacional de Ferrocarriles Espanoles

(RENFE), is vying with private road hauliers for both domestic and maritime generated traffic, and fast container trains (TECO) connect the ports with Madrid and other inland points. Although the TECO trains were developed to initially convey domestic traffic, rail terminals are being constructed at Bilbao, Valencia, Vigo and Cadiz with a view to considerably increasing maritime tonnage. The extensive motorway construction projects being undertaken in Spain, however, are having the effect of raising the percentage share of traffic conveyed by road, as compared with rail, but in future as oil becomes even more expensive, some of this traffic must surely return to the railways. The road transport industry, consisting as it does of numerous small firms with no central directive, is anyway less well organized than the railway system, and has been slower than the railways in adopting container carrying equipment.

The only customs controlled inland terminal in Spain is at Madrid, and the ports are therefore having to cope with the majority of cargo clearances. In spite of this the ports have managed to remain comparatively efficient, and having realized that the majority of their deep sea container trade will in all probability pass through one Mediterranean port complex in future, are actively competing with French and Italian ports to attract the large containerships of the future. Spain is geographically well suited to handle Mediterranean/North Atlantic transhipment traffic, but is less well situated to accommodate Far Eastern and Australian traffic, assuming that the Suez Canal reopens.

The northern Spanish port of Bilbao has developed into a roll-on roll-off and container center handling short sea and feeder vessels from north Europe, and distributing cargo over a wide area of Spain. Bilbao is the second largest Spanish container port, and is being provided with a new terminal with an annual potential throughput of two million tons of containerized traffic. The port area has developed into a center for maritime services, shipbuilding and container manufacture predominating, and has the largest throughput of bulk solids in Spain. A lot of Bilbao cargo is railed to the Barcelona area, and as traffic also travels in the reverse direction for shipment over Bilbao's quays, Barcelona has lost a considerable volume of cargo to the more northern port.

It was such diversionery activities, but this time through north European ports, that prompted Barcelona to form an alliance with Marseilles, Genoa, and Leghorn, to co-ordinate marketing policies. Barcelona's container terminal opened in July 1972, and two 50-ton portainers are in use. In an effort to develop the port into one of the largest container complexes in the Mediterranean, a new container berth is due to open in 1976, and it is hoped that the number of deep sea operators using the port will rapidly increase.

Whether the Barcelona port administration is able to realize its ambitions though will largely depend on progress made by the more southerly port of Valencia. Valencia is situated in a rapidly growing manufacturing area (Ford are to build a $350 million plant there), and is nearer to Madrid than Barcelona. Short sea roll-on roll-off traffic is already well established, and an initial investment programme of $13 million has allowed the construction of the Turia container terminal, as well as of four roll-on roll-off berths. Rail and road connections to Bilbao, Madrid, and other prominent areas are good. It is anticipated that deep sea container throughput will quickly grow, and the port has the potential to be the largest container center in Spain. Although Cadiz, near the entrance to the Straits of Gibraltar, is unlikely to develop into a large transhipment port, approximately half of her future trade will be accounted for by feeder vessels. Cadiz is at present the first and last call for some United States/Mediterranean services, and some of this cargo is fed to North Africa and other Mediterranean ports. Two container berths are under construction, and the port is well connected by road and rail.

Development of container facilities in Portugal has been even slower than in Spain. Political unrest and very rigid customs regulations have combined to discourage intermodal movement of boxes, and as industry in any case is clustered around Lisbon and Oporto there is little incentive to develop long inland hauls. While few deep sea containerships call at Portuguese ports, short sea operators have containerized, but General Steam Navigation Company is not alone in maintaining a conventional break-bulk short sea service. In spite of the rarity of inland container movements, Portuguese Railways (CP) are developing container carrying systems, and SPC Containers, a company formed by banking, finance, and shipping interests, has shown confidence in the future by establishing a container terminal at Matinha on the Tagus estuary, and an inland terminal near Lisbon. SPC now plan to open additional inland terminals.

Portugal's principal port at Lisbon attracts much of the available container traffic, and throughput has grown from 86,000 tons in 1970 to approximately 350,000 during 1973. Two container berths have already been provided at the Santa Apolonia terminal, and containers are also handled at the Poco do Bispo and Matinha areas. A roll-on roll-off berth completes the facilities, and as part of Lisbon's plan to be a future transhipment center, for example, for containers travelling between North America and central Europe, a £3 million expansion programme is in progress. Seven miles outside Lisbon at the mouth of the River Tagus is a new port being built largely on reclaimed land. A capacity of up to 300,000 containers per year is envisaged, and through joint management with Lisbon and Setubal it is hoped that the very large deep sea containerships carrying Mediterranean cargo will be attracted when the complex opens toward the end of the 1970's.

At Oporto a 30-ton container crane now supplements the original semi-portable crane for container handling at the Via Nova de Gaia wharf, while at the nearby new artificial port at Leixoes, currently without container facilities, it is planned to build a new container terminal. Leixoes is easily accessible to large vessels and could in time develop into a terminal larger than Oporto and even into one to rival Lisbon. Mention should also be made of another new port planned at Sines, south of Lisbon, which will incorporate an industrial area and a whole new town. While the port will principally cater for oil tankers at three large berths, a general cargo terminal handling conventional and container vessels will be included, and a study is being undertaken into the feasibility of an ore terminal. Stage one at Sines will cover harbor works costing £48.5 million, and the new port should be partially operational by 1976. Total investment is estimated at £230 million.

France

Generally the ports of France, until quite recently, have left much to be desired. The Communist-led French dock labor force has a worse strike record than its British counterpart, and in spite of subsidization of the main ports much overseas trade has had to be routed through Antwerp, Rotterdam and Genoa. Although the French docker is just as militant today, and indeed in view of current modernization of port working methods is probably more so, the position of the French ports vis-à-vis those in other EEC countries is changing dramatically.

It was decided by the French government in 1965 to allow six of the country's ports to be self-governing, and autonomous port authorities were accordingly set up under the control of the local Chamber of Commerce. There was therefore little central planning, and a spirit of competition between the ports began to emerge. This competition, however, has been largely confined to construction of harbors and berths, and to the provision of land for industrial development, while efforts at attracting the shipping companies have taken second place. Advantage has therefore been taken over a relatively short period of time of EEC development funds which have been concentrated at the six ports, and it is widely thought that France will soon be in favor of ending port subsidies within the EEC as her own modernization programme will be completed. Perhaps development has been too rapid though, and even with the increase in community trade many of France's port facilities might soon be underutilized.

Trade between France and the United Kingdom is expected to grow at a faster rate than with the remainder of France's EEC partners, and links are already being established between trading and manufacturing interests in the two countries. While the majority of cargo between France and other Continental countries will naturally go by road, rail or canal, links with the United Kingdom using roll-on roll-off ferries have been established to convey road trailers and containers. But due to cargo types widely varying there has been ample scope for the development of other forms of transport, and the lift-on lift-off containership and pallet-ship have also become established as cross channel movers of cargo. Although the French merchant marine has been slower than some other countries in adopting more modern methods of sea carriage, and their present container fleet is small, moves are now under way to remedy the situation. A new holding company formed to protect France's position in international shipping, and to be known as Compagnie Générale Maritime, was established in January 1974, and will co-ordinate the activities of Companie Générale Transatlantique and Messageries Maritimes.

France's largest port complex is being constructed at Fos/Marseilles on the Mediterranean. The old port at Marseilles had developed into the third busiest port in the EEC, but because of the surrounding hills further expansion was not possible. Plans were therefore submitted for the construction of a new port and industrial zone around the Gulf of Fos thirty miles to the west of Marseilles, and approval was given in 1962. Development began in 1968, and today the natural deep water harbor formed by the gulf allows very large tankers and bulk carriers to use the port in addition to containerships, roll-on roll-off vessels, and conventional vessels. The industrial development, said to be the largest maritime development of its kind in the world, includes a steel-works which alone cost £1.159 million and which is fed direct by ore carriers. The port and industrial area covers an area approximately the size of Paris. Following the establishment of provisional container handling facilities at No.1 Dock, a total of three portainers and a mobile container crane will operate at the new No.2 Dock, and it will be possible to turn round the largest containerships afloat or currently planned. Fos/Marseilles is having to actively compete for container trade with other major French ports such as Le Havre, and in addition to labor problems stemming from the militancy of the local dockers, is also having to contend with problems arising from the closure of the Suez Canal. After showing initial concern over the closure, the Port of Marseilles Authority was confident that shipowners would be keen to use the port as a southern gateway to France and the rest of Europe, but in the event a surplus of capacity exists with owners often giving preference to North European ports. Although about 90 per cent of throughput is accounted for by oil, the importance of the container is not being overlooked, and considerable efforts are being made on a world-wide basis to raise the current annual container throughput of approximately 50,000 units. The indications are though that container traffic will not increase dramatically until transhipment cargo is forthcoming following the re-opening of the Canal.

Currently the fastest growing port in Europe, and one to rival both Fos/Marseilles and possibly Rotterdam, is Le Havre, situated at the mouth of the River Seine. Le Havre is France's second largest port, and like Fos/Marseilles relies heavily on oil for its revenue. An outer harbor capable of handling tankers of 500,000 tons is planned, and nine roll-on roll-off berths and two container terminals incorporating eight portainers have been provided for general cargo movements. The original container terminal was at the Quay de l'Atlantique while a newer facility has been provided at the Quay de l'Europe, and plans are now being submitted for the construction of a third terminal. A new £3 million roll-on roll-off terminal is also under construction, and combined container and roll-on roll-off throughput amounts to nearly 50% of total general cargo throughput. Le Havre is particularly well situated to attract large container vessels as well as dry bulk carriers and oil tankers, not only because it is the first major port in the English Channel for eastbound vessels (and the last for westbound), but also because it is well clear of the shallow and congested Straits of Dover.

After their almost total destruction during the Second World War, Dunkirk and Calais both embarked on re-construction projects that were eventually to lead to closer ties. Dunkirk today is the most heavily subsidized of the French ports, receiving during 1974 126 million francs, while Fos was granted only 70 million francs. Possibly the subsidy was in anticipation of the building of a Channel tunnel, which may have drawn deep sea containerships to the area to off-load cargo for distribution to the United Kingdom as well as to Europe. Whether or not the tunnel materializes though the future of the two ports would appear to be secure through the establishment of a large industrial zone. The area has been declared a center for industrial expansion, and port facilities together with adjacent industry will stretch along the coast. Development of the port complex alone will take about twenty years, and will eventually rival even

FIGURE 20 Deep sea and feeder vessels at Quay de l'Europe, Le Havre
(Courtesy of Le Havre Port Authority).

Rotterdam. A new outer harbor under construction at Dunkirk will allow the handling of 300,000-ton oil tankers, and following the link up with Calais facilities will exist for tankers and dry bulk carriers of up to 500,000 tons. Increasing emphasis is also being placed on unit load facilities for container and roll-on roll-off vessels, and two container berths and a roll-on roll-off ramp have been provided at Quay Freycinet XIII in No.VI Dock at Dunkirk. A new container and roll-on roll-off terminal is to be built at a new west basin at Dunkirk.

France's fifth largest port is Rouen situated on the River Seine seventy miles inland and about midway between Le Havre and Paris. Rouen is the second largest dry cargo port in France, and has traditionally been a center for inland waterway traffic. Although this traffic is still important today, the port sees its future as another port/industrial area, and as a transhipment center for European and deep sea cargo. The Seine is a natural area for industrialization, and development of industry at Rouen is progressing hand in hand with port development. Both French and British firms are being attracted, and dredging of the river has allowed access to vessels of up to 30,000 tons, while further dredging will allow 60,000-ton vessels to dock. Expansion is therefore taking place along similar lines to that at Fos, and also as at Fos transhipment cargo is being encouraged. Cargo from the United Kingdom is already being transhipped at Rouen to deep sea vessels operating services that are not available from southern British ports, and it is hoped that this traffic will expand, together with transhipment cargo for Paris and further inland. Partly because of a general state of overcapacity at French ports though, traffic has not increased as quickly as was hoped, and although through freight rates to French inland points from the United Kingdom are lower than rates when using one of the Channel ports, through transit times are longer. Recent subsidies under the port's Sixth Special plan have allowed the construction of a container berth at Quevilly wharf served by two 25-ton container cranes, and supplementary to two former berths, and of a roll-on roll-off gangway at Petit Couronne.

Although the Channel port of Dieppe has plenty of room to expand, development has been comparatively slow because of the lack of suitable ports in England, other than the British Rail port of Newhaven, to join up with. Dieppe's fortunes have large-ly been built on the banana trade, but following containerization of the trade, and because of the lack of suitable facilities, this mainstay could well be lost to nearby Le Havre. A lot of EEC trade with Britain does however pass over Dieppe's four roll-on roll-off berths, and although a 35-ton crane capable of handling containers has been provided, it is expected that two-thirds of the port's throughput will soon be roll-on roll-off traffic. The present harbor is confined though, and future prospects really depend on whether a subsidy is granted that would give the go-ahead to a proposed £20 million development project at Neuville les Dieppe. An outer harbor would provide, among other facili-ties, four or five new roll-on roll-off berths, and would help to fulfill the port's ambition of being the largest roll-on roll-off port in the Channel. Although the granting by the French government of the necessary subsidy has for some time appeared unlikely, a different attitude may be taken by the government in the light of a further cancellation of a Channel tunnel, but construction could not begin anyway before 1978.

One of the smaller Channel ports, and one that has tradition-ally relied on passenger traffic, is Cherbourg. Until the comple-tion of roll-on roll-off facilities, cargo throughput had not been very significant and was largely confined to traffic generated by Townsend-Thoresen Ferries. Throughput increased though when Truckline Ferries began their roll-on roll-off link with Poole in June 1973 following dredging at Cherbourg, and was further boosted when British Rail started a similar service out of Wey-mouth in 1974. The port is thus developing its roll-on roll-off capability, and containers are confined to those mounted on road vehicles. Boulogne is evolving along similar lines to Cher-bourg, and has provided three roll-on roll-off berths. Boulogne is unconcerned at the prospect of a Channel tunnel, and is to pro-vide additional roll-on roll-off capacity on reclaimed land at the Terminal Four development. Both Boulogne and Cherbourg have maintained better than average labor relations, and are conse-quently able to offer a good service to actual and potential users. A port new to cross-Channel traffic is Roscoff in the western part of Brittany. Brittany Ferries have been operating a roll-on roll-off service between Roscoff and Plymouth since 1973, establishing the link to principally carry the vegetable produce that was expected to flow into Britain when she joined the EEC, and to return with manufactured goods such as farm machinery originating in the Midlands, Wales and the west of England. A £1 million terminal was constructed at Roscoff, but due to the vegetable throughput being smaller than anticipated, the line is now shipping a wide variety of traffic.

Further south in the Bay of Biscay, Bordeaux is contending with problems brought about largely by her geographical position. Although situated on the River Garonne, the immediate hinterland does not support any large-scale industry, and general cargo volumes through the port are not very significant. North Atlantic containerships are not keen to call following a decision to equalize freight rates to a wider range of ports, and while a container service does operate to Felixstowe the majority of general cargo is break-bulk. Bordeaux has traditionally been a wine exporting port, but even much of this trade has now been lost to more northern ports as methods of shipment have changed, and as communications have not kept pace with the needs of intermodal movements. A roll-on roll-off berth has been provided though, and two other berths are capable of handling containers. Whether the adjacent Ford plant is able to stimulate trade remains to be seen, but in anticipation of a general increase in traffic, a container berth serviced by two portainers is to open at the Verdon oil terminal at the mouth of the River Gironde in 1976.

It will be evident that France has every intention of catching up on her formerly backward state of port development, but it will also be evident that a large proportion of the subsidized expenditure will have helped to establish a situation of over-capacity, and maybe of unnecessary duplication of facilities. A project largely taking place in France though, and one of less doubtful economic advantage, is the construction of a canal/river system that will eventually link the Mediterranean with the North Sea, and make access to France's agricultural and industrial regions much easier. The River Rhone is to be joined to the Rhine, using the River Saone and a 125-mile long system of canals and locks, and barges will be used to carry mainly bulk commodities to and from France and other EEC countries, and between LASH and BACAT terminals for shipment abroad and distribution throughout Europe. While work is due to be completed by 1981, progress in the French sector is said to be behind schedule, and legal difficulties are adding to the problems. It is desirable that freedom of navigation be established throughout the waterway, but until a common policy can be established regarding the link between the Saone and Rhine that would replace the multitude of local and national policies, further delays are likely. A similar scheme also scheduled for completion in 1981, but taking place in West Germany, will join Regensburg on the River Danube to Bamberg on the River Main to form a link between the Danube and Rhine.

West Germany

The ports of West Germany have been far quicker to adapt to the container than have the French ports, and even though the majority of container movements take place over only two port complexes in Germany, tonnage has been significantly greater than in France. This is all the more surprising when it is realized that over half West Germany's foreign trade is with Continental Europe, but port throughput is to an increasing extent being supplemented by transhipment traffic particularly from Eastern European countries. Following the division of Germany after the Second World War, and the establishment of Eastern Germany, the port of Hamburg lost its pre-eminent position as the main gateway for the overseas trade of the industrial hinterland, and West Germany found itself with a comparatively short coastline. This combination of a large volume of inland foreign trade, and an almost landlocked country, has led to two significant developments. While the two port complexes have built up their container handling facilities to a very high level, increasing importance is being given to the extension of overland communications, but the West German merchant marine has not been able to develop nearly as quickly as have the fleets of most of the other Western maritime countries.

Overland rail links are provided by the German Federal railways (Deutsche Bundesbahn). It has already been mentioned that the DB have been able to establish reliable services, especially for cargo owners with full container loads, through the widespread use of manufacturers' own private sidings. The majority of full containers moving between Hamburg and Bremen, and inland points, are rail-borne, while the road hauliers carry containers over shorter distances, and to areas where the railways do not consider that the volume of traffic deserves a regular service. Fifty container handling depots provide facilities for grouping cargo into full container loads and for their carriage to and from the ports, but partly due to the very widespread cover given the railway system remains somewhat underutilized. As part of the current phase to update overland communications in West Germany, the entire transport system is to be modernized during 1976-85 at a cost of DM1,200 million. An integrated system is to be developed embracing rail, road and waterway traffic, which is to be established alongside the shipping industry, but as port modernization is well advanced and as the railways are already utilizing modern rolling stock, the principal beneficiary will be the road transport industry followed by the waterways then the railways. Examples of current and future projects are the West German sector of a waterway linking Portugal and Scandinavia, a canal extension leading from the River Elbe, and the Rhine/Main/Danube canal.

The second consequence of West Germany's large volume of overland foreign trade, and of her almost landlocked state, is the relative size of her merchant fleet in comparison with other advanced Western nations. Growth of the shipping industry has been restricted, and today accounts for only 3 per cent of total world tonnage, which in turn has meant that earnings against the country's "invisible" account (shipping, insurance, banking, etc.) have been small. West Germany's three major shipping lines however are heavily committed to the container principle, and to LASH methods, and they completed their initial build-up of new tonnage in 1973. Hapag-Lloyd is active in the North Atlantic container trade as well as being a member of the TRIO Far Eastern consortium, while Hamburg-Sud through a subsidiary—Columbia Line—maintains a container link between New Zealand and North America. DDG Hansa is a member of Atlantica Line operating container vessels between Mediterranean ports and

North America.

West Germany's principal port is Hamburg where over DM2,000 million has been invested since 1950. Eighty per cent of the port was destroyed during the Second World War, but continuous substantial investment has led to the completion of initial development of container handling facilities. Container complexes spread over an area of 148 acres, and include 12 container berths serviced by 13 container cranes, as well as 6 roll-on roll-off berths, and wider development possibilities using an additional 130 acres are being examined. A variety of industry has been attracted to Hamburg, and bulk commodity vessels find access through the wide River Elbe estuary comparatively easy, although dredging to 13.5 meters at medium tide will allow larger bulk vessels to dock as well as the largest containerships currently in service. Container throughput has grown quickly, and during 1974 over 300,000 units were handled in comparison with 15,000 units during 1967 when the early North Atlantic containerships were using the port as their container terminal.

Hapag-Lloyd's terminal at Kaiser-Wilhelm harbor, completed in June 1971 at a cost of DM25.5 million can accommodate fully cellular container vessels, semi-container vessels and pallet ships, and is perhaps typical of developments that have taken place at Hamburg which have involved emphasis being placed on flexibility as compared with full committal to one system only. The port's largest terminal though is the Burchardkai Terminal in Waltershoffer Hafen operated by Hamburger Hafen-und-Lagerhaus AG, or HHLA as it is usually called. The terminal has taken nearly nine years to construct and has involved an investment of DM220 million. Seven container berths and a roll-on roll-off center with two ramps have been provided, and room exists for a further four berths on land remaining to be developed. A larger than average proportion of containerized traffic passes over the quays at Burchardkai, 70 per cent of the port's total container flow being handled, and this figure may be higher still if the terminal is successful in securing the South African trade which is due to start in 1977. Additional container facilities have been provided at the Europa-Quay Terminal and the Tollerot Terminal. Hamburg's transhipment cargo is principally handled in the freeport zone where there are no customs restrictions or customs charges, and where goods may be stored, sampled, and even processed. In addition to container, roll-on roll-off, pallet, and conventional berths, Hamburg has also provided facilities for LASH vessels, and the construction of a deep water port at Cuxhaven at the entrance to the River Elbe estuary will allow handling of bulk commodity cargo vessels bringing in the raw materials that will be required with the build-up of industry around the Elbe. This diversification of services available to shipowners and charterers will mean that Hamburg will rival major terminals such as Fos-Marseilles and Rotterdam-Europoort.

Bremen and Bremerhaven are jointly managed by Bremer Lagerhaus-Gesellschaft and together are the second largest port complex in West Germany. Bremen is the most southerly of Germany's ports, offering shorter overland hauls, and is located in the city area 40 miles away from Bremerhaven. Containers were being handled as far back as 1966 (Sea-Land), and before the much larger build-up of container facilities at Bremerhaven, Bremen was the dominant container center. A roll-on roll-off terminal was opened in December 1972 at Europhafen on reclaimed land. The North Sea coast deep-water port of Bremerhaven can handle the largest containerships afloat, and following deepening of the entrance channel to 14 meters will be able to accommodate bulk commodity vessels exceeding 100,000 tons. Being on the coast, vessels using the port are able to save 8 hours' steaming time as compared with calling at Bremen, and a very fast turnround is offered. Very few conventional cargo handling facilities exist at Bremerhaven, and container handling is concentrated at the Containerkreuz Terminal (Container Crossroads Bremerhaven) eventually completed in 1972 at a cost of DM300 million. Redevelopment at Bremerhaven has not taken place without incident, a tender that was accepted for the building of facilities for the Stromkaje terminal later being found to drastically underestimate the cost of the project, and it was necessary to replace the original contractors. Three container berths and a roll-on roll-off facility are now operational at Stromkaje, and adjacent land will allow further expansion as required. At Nordhafen where North Atlantic containerships, and LASH and Seabee vessels are principally catered for, four container berths and another roll-on roll-off facility have been provided. Throughput at Bremerhaven is expected to grow significantly in future, and during 1975 a further DM42.2 million is to be invested. A joint undertaking with Hamburg will provide an electronic data processing system to quicken paper work flows and to speed up container movements.

Belgium

In spite of the unstable nature of Belgium's system of government, the Kingdom today is economically sounder than in previous years, and is continuing her policy of encouraging foreign investment in both manufacturing and the service areas. Belgium is a small country with few natural resources and is highly dependent on trade both to supply raw materials, and as a source of employment in the port and other maritime fields. About 25 per cent of this trade is entrepot traffic which Belgian ports are particularly suited to handling because of the country's ideal geographical location at the middle of the EEC and on the North Sea coast. The flexible nature of customs control is also a distinct advantage, and allows the sorting, storing and processing of goods prior to any payment of duty, and without the formality of a bond undertaking. But Belgium, like her neighbor West Germany, is not well enough represented in the ship operating field for her to exercise much influence in the industry, and her principal shipping line, Compagne Maritime Belge, mainly operates as a carrier of break-bulk cargo. Compagne Maritime Belge is however expanding its area of activity, and in addition to having an interest in containerization through a one-third share in Dart Containerline, has expanded, in common with many other shipping companies, into other sectors of the transport business.

But what Belgium lacks in vessel tonnage, she has more than compensated for in port productivity, road and rail networks, and river/canal systems. Consistently good dock labor relations, round the clock working, and a high degree of flexibility between vessels, have combined to give Belgium's ports the highest productivity rating in Europe, and have allowed Antwerp to become the largest general cargo handling port in Europe. In the road haulage industry restrictions are few, preference though being given to established operators, and very fast growth has meant that about half the available freight is conveyed by road. Modernization of the railways is continuing, and currently about 30 per cent of cargo carried is generated by the terminal operators at Antwerp. The River Scheldt has long been a highway for barge traffic to and from Antwerp, and is connected at Ghent northward to both Zeebrugge and Ostend by canal. The importance of the River Maas which rises in France and passes through Belgium and Holland before flowing into the left arm of the Rhine (the River Waal), will grow following the widening and deepening of the Albert Canal which forms a link with the Scheldt between Liège and Antwerp, and barge traffic will then be able to move from Antwerp to the River Rhine.

On the southern edge of the vast delta formed by the Scheldt, Meuse and Rhine rivers lies Antwerp, Belgium's largest port and the biggest general cargo port in Europe. Being at the center of the trade routes covering the EEC, Antwerp is well sited to act both as an entry/exit point for EEC countries, and to handle a lot of the transhipment traffic moving between Europe and overseas countries. But Antwerp's geographical position in the middle of a large river and canal system, while generating waterborne cargo (nearly 50 per cent of cargo moves by waterway to and from the port) also acts as a limitation on the size of vessels able to enter the port because of the canal and lock system. A further drawback is the difficulty of navigation in the River Scheldt which means that large containerships can only enter or leave the port during certain states of the tide, which has resulted in many containers being diverted from Antwerp's quays to other nearby ports where some lines prefer to call. This problem though has only become really serious following the introduction of large containerships carrying cargo that would formerly have been shipped by smaller break-bulk vessels, and to enable Antwerp to continue handling this trade it is planned to widen and straighten the Scheldt estuary, and to dredge to allow entry to vessels of up to 125,000 tons at all states of the tide.

In spite of these problems Antwerp has built up a reputation of ultra-efficiency principally in the handling of general cargo, and has immediately at hand an enormous potential volume of container traffic in the form of some general cargo currently being shipped by break-bulk vessel. Already about 12 per cent of the port's general cargo throughput is containerized, and it is forecast that up until 1980 container traffic will increase by about 13 per cent each year. It is also expected that a larger number of containership companies serving many different parts of the world will include Antwerp in their sailing schedules, and that North Atlantic trade, which presently accounts for over half total container throughput, will be less dominant. Present-day competitiveness is based on very good labor relations and resultant high productivity, which meant that additional dockers had to be recruited in 1974 to cope with the growing cargo volume. Very few strikes have occurred, and round-the-clock working including holidays is considered as normal. The port authority's willingness to adapt to new methods, coupled with the co-operative spirit of the labor force, has resulted in a comprehensive system of cargo handling berths which have been adapted where necessary to accommodate container vessels. An expansion programme in the realm of construction of general cargo berths began as far back as 1956—to date over £88 million having been invested—and development is to continue. Along similar lines to other ports looking firmly to the future, Antwerp is planning an industrial development at Kallo on the River Scheldt which will include a petrochemical complex, and which will be provided with a new dock and lock system giving access from the open sea to the inland waterways.

Antwerp's terminals are financed by private enterprise, usually in the form of prominent stevedoring companies, while the Port Authority is responsible only for the provision of such amenities as land, quay walls, and basic services. Facilities are made available to forwarding agents, ship's chandlers, and other parties, and in addition to the direct loading and discharge of vessels in the port, consolidated cargo is packed into and unpacked from containers passing over other nearby ports. While competing with each other, the various terminals will often co-operate, and it is not unusual for container cranes to move along a quay from one terminal to another. The principal operators are all to be found in the Churchill Dock in the sixth and seventh Harbordock where a total of eight gantry cranes are in service. The largest terminal is run by Stevedoring Company Gylsen SA, in which Compagne Maritime Belge has a controlling interest, and as Maritime also owns one third of Dart Containerline, Dart's North Atlantic container vessels are frequent visitors at the terminal. Apart from handling nearly half of Antwerp's container traffic, Gylsen handle a very substantial tonnage of iron and steel, as well as much of the conventional trade with East and West Africa. Two portainers, a variety of conventional cranes, and a number of straddle carriers are used for cargo handling. On the southern side of the Churchill Dock, Noord Natie C.S., another privately owned independent stevedoring company offers facilities to both deep sea and short sea lines. Two container vessels can be handled simultaneously using the two portainers, and back-up equipment includes five straddle carriers. Noord Natie specialize in the handling of perishable cargoes, but in addition a wide variety of other cargo types pass over the quays including roll-on roll-off traffic. A container freight station is attached to the terminal, which is also used as a transfer point for container cargo originating at or destined to other nearby ports. LASH and Seabee barge traffic is concentrated at the Hessenatie-Neptunus SA terminal which also handles the container/roll-on roll-off ships of Atlantic Container Line and the container/bulk vessels of Cast Line, while Sea-Land maintains its terminal at Antwerp's Havenbedrijf Pays NV facility.

Belgium's second largest port is Zeebrugge, the outer port of Bruges, which had to be almost entirely rebuilt following the Second World War. Zeebrugge was formerly a short sea port catering for roll-on roll-off and container vessels running between Belgium and the United Kingdom, but following the opening in 1971 of Ocean Containerterminal Zeebrugge (OCZ) deep sea traffic has become increasingly significant. The first users of OCZ were the member lines of AECS who were previously using the excellent facilities provided by Antwerp, but who decided to move to Zeebrugge and Flushing to be nearer the main European wool markets at Lille and Bruges. It is only recently that wool shipments have been containerized, but in future the Australian Wool Corporation will be moving much larger quantities by AECS boxes to Zeebrugge, from where sorting and distribution will also take place. Indeed Zeebrugge will very soon be challenging Flushing in Holland for the position of Europe's largest wool port, and expansion to accommodate the increased tonnage is planned, which will provide sufficient capacity to handle the South African wool trade as well. As warehousing charges are generally cheaper in Europe than in Australia, extensive stockpiling will occur, which will also allow immediate access to the markets in accordance with price fluctuations. The Short-Sea Container-terminal opened in 1968, which in common with OCZ is operated by Société Belgo-Anglaise des Ferry-Boats, has been provided with four roll-on roll-off berths and is used by, among others, British Rail and Comar Containerline. While total container throughput at Zeebrugge has during recent years remained comparatively static (about 100,000 boxes annually), roll-on roll-off traffic is growing very fast. Massive port development should allow considerable further growth of both types of cargo.

Both Ostend on the North Sea coast and Ghent on the River Scheldt have been provided with roll-on roll-off facilities. Ostend currently deals in a high proportion of roll-on roll-off traffic at its three specialized berths, but a new deep-water berth now under construction will allow the handling of large containerships. The land-locked harbor at Ghent which is connected to both Ostend and Zeebrugge by canal, as well as to Antwerp by river, was provided with a new lock entrance in 1968 to allow access to vessels of up to 60,000 tons. Cargo volume grew five times during the following 5½ years, helped in part by traffic passing over the recently built roll-on roll-off berth.

Holland

The Dutch ports of Rotterdam, Amsterdam and Flushing are situated at the heart of Europe's wealthiest area. Holland lies on the delta formed by the rivers Rhine, Meuse and Scheldt, and the three ports additionally draw on the Ruhr and Rhine areas of north-west Germany, Belgium, the northern industrial area of France, and the United Kingdom for their cargo throughput. A comparatively small industrial contribution to the country's gross national product has been boosted by a significant contribution through trade, and over the years a vast interest in nearly all forms of freight transportation has been built up. Today Dutch interests control over 40 per cent of all EEC road haulage, and half inland Rhine shipping, while the Dutch merchant marine has slowly but steadily increased its stake in both deep sea and short sea container and roll-on roll-off methods of shipping.

Traditionally about half the Dutch merchant fleet has been engaged in the carriage of general, as distinct from bulk cargoes, and in order to remain competitive with other maritime nations conversion to container and roll-on roll-off systems was a necessary move, but in some quarters an unwelcome one. Holland America Line was the first Dutch line to participate in the new methods, first through involvement in Atlantic Container Line, and later in the LASH system adopted by Combi Line. Holland America have benefited little through the new systems, ACL only just becoming profitable while Combi continues to lose money, and a pessimistic view is held of the immediate future. Koninklijke Nedlloyd, the liner division of the Nederlandse Scheepvaart Unie group, are operating two container vessels within the Scan Dutch consortium serving the trade between Europe and the Far East, while Holland's third major shipping group Koninklijke Nederlande Stoomboot Maatschappij (KNSM) entered unitized shipping more recently through participation initially in short sea routes. KNSM have a 25 per cent share in the roll-on roll-off Tor Line, and joined up with Harrison Line and Hapag Lloyd in 1973 to operate containerships between Europe and the Caribbean. The company also operates Rhine vessels, and controls Amsterdam's largest container terminal.

Until quite recently Holland had long been faced with a labor shortage, and while some other countries were having the utmost difficulty in pacifying their dock labor force during the introduction of modern systems of cargo handling, Dutch ports were able to bring in the new methods peacefully. Progress, particularly at Rotterdam, was rapid and efforts are now being made in association with ports in Belgium to establish a common maritime and port policy to co-ordinate future planning and methods of operation. There would be no flag discrimination, operating at below cost by utilizing government subsidies would end, handling charges would be equalized between ports, and a competitive spirit especially with regard to service would be encouraged. Other associated effects such as pollution by industry especially in the Belgian port zones, would be better controlled. While such a move would make the adoption of an EEC ports policy that much easier, intermediate co-operation between ports in Holland and Belgium is not welcomed in some parts of the EEC, and it is pointed out that such co-operation would bring even more unitized traffic to Rotterdam and Antwerp at the expense of ports in France and Germany. Conversely though, port development in Holland and Belgium is slowing down, while development in France, especially in the provision of huge outer harbors to accommodate the largest oil tankers afloat, is proceeding rapidly.

The River Rhine has for long been the principal artery for a large part of European trade, and Rotterdam situated at the mouth of the river was ideally placed to transfer cargo between river craft and ocean vessels. This ease of access led to development of Rotterdam and its seaward approaches on a vast scale, and today the area is the largest port complex in the world handling a total of 300 million tons of all types of cargo annually. While half of this is made up of oil imports, Rotterdam is still the largest European container port with most of the deep sea containerships serving the European trades calling at one of the three terminals. This in turn has led to many other lines coming in to Rotterdam to operate either short sea feeder vessels, or to uplift deep sea transhipment cargo, and annual container throughput grew from 235,000 units in 1970 to over 653,000 units in 1973. Ore, oil, grain and timber also figure prominently as transshipment cargo, and the port is a growing distribution center for foreign manufactured goods, and a base for industrial development. Although Rotterdam is still very dependent on the waterways as generators of cargo, 60 per cent of container traffic arrives at or leaves the port by road, while the railways are steadily increasing their share of container movements.

The port is administered by the Municipality of Rotterdam, who provide and look after the basic infrastructure, while the private terminal operators are responsible for the berths and equipment. Being in an already highly industrialized area, the port does not qualify for substantial government and local subsidies for new construction, and projects are not approved until there is a real necessity for them, and unless they are capable of being operated competitively at a profit. The new terminals that have been built are sited down river away from the older docks in the city area, and many of these older docks have had to close. Very good labor relations are maintained, and 24-hour manning spread over three shifts seven days a week allows continuous vessel working. A massive container throughput is obtained without congestion building up by labor adopting flexible working methods which allow uninterrupted movement between vessels, and ready acceptance of mechanical handling. At some terminals labor will switch from one job to another, and such movement between for example container cranes, fork lift trucks, and straddle carriers, offers variety of work and consequently less likelihood of boredom. In return the employers keep their labor force, only 60 per cent of whom are union members, well informed of current progress and of future developments.

Fifteen miles down river from the city center on the southern side of the approach channel into the River Maas (Meuse), Rotterdam has extended its confines by building the petrochemical and bulk handling complex generally known as Europoort. Oil refinery is dominant among industrial processes carried out at Europoort, and it was planned to extend industrial development partly by allowing access to tankers of 500,000 tons and over. The approach channel was to be dredged, but in 1973 it was decided to postpone further work in the light of more recent thinking regarding the feasibility of very large tankers calling at North Sea ports at all. It was argued that the considerable outer port development planned at French ports such as Le Havre would be favored by tanker owners and charterers as navigation of the narrow Straits of Dover would then be avoided. It was also argued that 500,000-ton tankers should not be allowed anyway to discharge in an industrial and built up area such as Europoort because of spillage and subsequent pollution. The present approach channel depth of 65 feet will be maintained, and will allow entry to tankers of up to 260,000 tons, as well as to the largest containerships planned.

A little further inland Bell Line are operating their own terminal facilities at Rozenburg for their short sea container services to the United Kingdom and the Republic of Ireland, while Sea-Land has its own private berth within the confines of the Europe

Container Terminus (ECT), Rotterdam's largest terminal. A joint venture involving five large stevedoring companies and the Dutch Railways, ECT has so far cost over £17 million to develop but has hardly become profitable. It was the first major container terminal at Rotterdam, and began to handle boxes in 1967. The following year saw a throughput of 65,000 units, while in 1974 a total in excess of 500,000 units passed over the terminal's berths. The present annual capacity is 600,000 containers, while development of an adjacent area of 50 acres would allow the handling of 1,000,000 per year. Eleven portainers (four of which are used by Sea-Land) have been provided together with a large variety of other handling devices, and container control is partly automated using a punch card system. Users other than Sea-Land include the member lines of AECS, Atlantic Container Line, Hapag Lloyd, and United States Lines.

Rotterdam's second largest terminal is the now fully computerized Unitcentre facility at the former bulk handling center at Waalhaven Pier 7. Established in 1967, and part of the very diversified SHV group, Unitcentre is capable of handling 250,000 containers per year using six converted ore cranes and five transtainers. The present terminal facilities are considered to be adequate for requirements up to 1979, and while the ECT may eventually move to a new development on the Meuse Plains, Unitcentre has no such plans in spite of the surrounding roads being at times very congested. Present users include the TRIO consortium, Columbus Line, Zim, New England Express, and European Unit Routes, and it is hoped that part of the South African container trade will also be obtained.

Pakhoed Holding NV control Rotterdam's third major terminal at Waalhaven Pier 2, a newly built multi-purpose facility costing Guilder 8 million to construct. The Pakhoed terminal was opened in 1973, and being multi-purpose, and able to handle many types of unit loads as well as containers, has greater flexibility than Rotterdam's other terminals. Six converted conventional cranes utilizing spreader attachments for container handling are used, and during 1974 about 16,000 containers passed over the terminal's berths. Pakhoed has a potential capacity of about 30,000 units per year, and through connections with the USSR merchant marine which will entail handling a large amount of Russia's growing container trade, could soon be in a position to reach this capacity. Containers travelling over the Trans-Siberian railway are already being handled, as well as traffic for East German and Chinese shipping lines.

It was realized several years ago that Rotterdam's terminals would at some time be unable to handle in an efficient manner the growing volume of container traffic being generated by the shipping companies, and that additional facilities would have to be provided if some of these companies were to be prevented from using alternative European ports. Plans were accordingly drawn up for yet another container terminal, to be sited at Rijnpoort on the northern side of the River Meuse (Maas) near the town of Maassluis. Due to the port's unwillingness to provide handling capacity until it is really required, and to the existence of spare capacity at the present three terminals, the Rijnpoort project was not due to become operational until at least 1980. It was envisaged that predominantly container and roll-on roll-off short sea traffic would be handled, and berths would be provided for unit load carrying hovercraft and for barges. At the beginning of 1974 however it had to be announced that Rijnpoort had been rejected as being too expensive, but it is also likely that objections on environmental grounds by the local farming community were sympathetically looked at. As an alternative to Rijnpoort, approval was given in March 1974 for the construction of a massive container port and oil terminal on the Meuse Plains opposite the Hook of Holland to be known as Maasvlakte. Land reclamation would avoid the use of existing residential or farming land, and it was agreed that in order to become even more competitive in the handling of containers, a terminal nearer the open sea should be built which would allow easy access to even larger containerships and, of particular importance in the short sea trades, would reduce steaming distances. Phase 1 involving an investment of Guilder 68 million will create a container capacity of about 300,000 units per year, and following further extensive building it is envisaged that the Europe Container Terminus will eventually transfer to the new facility. Industrial development will include a steel mill, and dredging of the approach channel to a depth of 68 feet will give access to oil tankers of up to 400,000 DWT. Although Maasvlakte will potentially be the largest oil terminal in Europe, it is doubtful whether the larger tankers will call considering the state of congestion in the Straits of Dover, and in view of the excellent facilities provided at Le Havre.

It will be evident that Rotterdam has no intention of slowing down her rate of growth for very long, but a port expanding at such a pace is vulnerable to the detrimental effects of rapid change, just as it will benefit from the more favorable effects. For example, Rotterdam was the first European port to be used by the LASH barge carrying vessels, but due to congestion these vessels switched to Antwerp. Similarly, previously good dock labor relations became strained following a spate of redundancy, and unrest is gradually building up. While the congestion problem can be solved by extending and mechanizing berths, an increase in container traffic will not improve the employment situation.

Any port only 38 miles from the largest maritime cargo handling center in the world is bound to feel a little overshadowed, and this is just how Amsterdam feels in relation to Rotterdam. While Amsterdam is well connected by road, rail and waterway to the hinterland, the port's location at the inland end of the fifteen kilometers long North Sea Canal is not conducive to attracting today's containerships, which are constantly looking for faster turnround possibilities. Amsterdam was formerly a thriving general cargo and bulk handling port, but principally due to the limitation placed on the size of vessels entering the lock at the seaward end of the canal at Ijmuiden, much of this trade has been lost, and has not been replaced by significant volumes of containerized traffic. The lock is unable to accept vessels exceeding 90,000 DWT, and shipowners are opting to call at Rotterdam or other north European ports in increasing numbers. The resulting state of depression at Amsterdam has precipitated much of the dock labor force being laid off, and vessels diverted for any reason from Rotterdam usually avoid the port and go instead to Antwerp. While Amsterdam is in favor of a link up with Rotterdam, Rotterdam is content to go its own way, and the Dutch Government show no signs of intervening. Amsterdam's only hope is approval by the Government, and incidentally also by the Municipality of Rotterdam, of a scheme to build an outer port at Ijmuiden that would provide facilities for vessels of up to 180,000 DWT, and it is expected that the Government will subsidize about two-thirds of the £50 million cost. Whereas Rotterdam's Maasvlakte project is not connected by either road or rail, Ijmuiden already has good connections, and a decision to go ahead and build the outer port was expected to be taken by the end of 1974, that would have meant that the complex could have been operational by 1979. Some sort of delay, however, has held up the decision, and as well as Amsterdam being unable to plan ahead with confidence in the knowledge that an outer port will or will not be built, both Rotterdam and Antwerp are being affected in a similar manner. It is cases like these that show the urgent need for a common ports policy in Holland and Belgium, and indeed throughout the EEC.

The present container facility at Amsterdam is wholly controlled by one of Holland's three largest shipping groups, KNSM (see page 283), and is situated in the new western harbor. It is known as Container Terminal Amsterdam (CTA), was the first purpose-built container terminal in Europe, and was financed by a number of stevedoring companies and by KNSM. Following the *en masse* move by the containership companies though to Rotterdam, all the original backers other than KNSM withdrew their support, and the terminal is now wholly controlled by KNSM. Four container cranes service the three container berths, and these, together with the roll-on roll-off berths are generally underutilized. Plenty of room is available for expansion, and a new roll-on roll-off berth is planned, together with improvements to the rail connections. American Export Lines returned to CTA after a brief absence, and the tide-free berths which obviate adjustments to loading ramps, have helped to attract large volumes of Japanese motor car business from Rotterdam. It is expected that the growing Russian merchant fleet will also make regular calls, but the long-term future of Amsterdam operating as it is today in isolation is far from secure.

Although much of Amsterdam's former and potential traffic is passing through Rotterdam, Europe's largest wool port at Flushing, where plenty of room is available for further development, has also benefited. A deep sea container terminal costing Guilders 11 million was opened in June 1971 at the Sloe-haven, where two portainers service two container berths, and where

FIGURE 21 The Container Terminal Amsterdam (CTA) at Amsterdam
(Courtesy of Combined Terminals Amsterdam B.V.).

roll-on roll-off vessels are also handled. Flushing is attempting to attract some of Rotterdam's surplus container traffic, arguing that the proposed Rijnpoort development is unnecessary, but has been more successful in obtaining a proportion of the Japanese motor car imports from Antwerp. The port authority estimates that about 30 per cent of its future throughput will be container-ized, and already the vessels of AECS members are prominent at the container terminal. In accordance with the port's intention of also attracting roll-on roll-off ships, the Scandinavian line Scan Austral is loading at Flushing, and a short sea feeder link is maintained with Ramsgate in the United Kingdom.

Scandinavia

Merchant vessels operating in Scandinavian waters have to cope with different trade flows leaving and entering the area. Timber and forest products have for long been important earners of foreign exchange, while sea-borne imports have largely consist-ed of finished and semi-finished goods. It is therefore necessary for any new methods of shipment and cargo handling to be flex-ible in operation, and when the container principle crossed the Atlantic from the United States of America it was generally thought among Scandinavian shipowners that this particular method did not allow the required degree of flexibility for hand-ling their own overseas trade. Prior to the 1950's timber had been either banded or shipped loose in conventional holds, but with the growth of the roll-on roll-off concept it was found more con-venient to ship in standard-sized units on pallets or flats. It was usually impracticable to produce sawn timber to suit the 20-, 30- or 40-foot container lengths, and while timber could not be shipped by container vessels, roll-on roll-off vessels could ship a number of different units, including containers, if the trade demanded it.

In accordance with Scandinavia's ability to innovate, Wallenius Lines of Sweden introduced the first roll-on roll-off vessel on the North Atlantic in the early 1950's, which was used to ship cars from the United States to Europe. Experience gained at the time later led Wallenius to suggest that a regular roll-on roll-off service

FIGURE 22 Prepared roll-on roll-off units at Helsingborg's Skane Terminal (Courtesy of Port of Helsingborg).

be established on the Atlantic to compete with the growing number of fully cellular vessels in the trade. The outcome was the setting up of Atlantic Container Line and the decision to operate principally roll-on roll-off vessels, but with a limited built-in container capacity as well. Meanwhile roll-on roll-off had become the dominant method of moving cargo over the North Sea short sea routes between Scandinavian countries and Europe, as well as between Scandinavian countries themselves, while lift-on lift-off container shipments were largely restricted to deep-sea trades where partial containerships were in service, and to the feeder routes linking Scandinavian ports with the large container ports on the Continent. Typical of the roll-on roll-off lines operating over the deep-sea routes is Scan Austral, a consortium of Danish, Swedish and Norwegian owners, who link Scandinavia and European ports with Australia via the Panama Canal. Five 22,000-ton vessels are in service carrying a combination of palletized and other unitized cargo, as well as containers and break-bulk traffic.

In contrast with Scan Austral, Johnson Line decided as far back as the late 1960's that cellular vessels could be successfully operated from Scandinavia provided that cargo types in the trade were correct, and vessels with a capacity of 744 20-foot units were put into service between Gothenburg and the Pacific coast of North America. Meanwhile the East Asiatic Company of Copenhagen had linked up with Blue Star Line to form Scan Star Line, and in 1972 Scan Star were joined by Johnson to form Johnson Scan Star. Johnson Scan Star are now running nine fully cellular vessels between Scandinavia and Europe, and the west coast of the United States, and are able to remain competitive in spite of the significant tonnage of semi-bulk products in the trade. Another consortium committed to fully cellular vessels is Scan Dutch, the major rival to the TRIO group in the Europe to Far East trade. Scan Dutch evolved through the joining together of the Scandinavian Scanservice consortium with the Dutch operator Nedlloyd in 1972. Six vessels each able to carry 2,000 20-foot containers were in service by 1973, and in the same year the group was joined by the French line Messageries Maritimes.

A major Scandinavian line that for long was a firm advocate of palletized systems is Maersk Line of Denmark. Part of the

A.P. Moller group, Maersk finally came round to the container system in 1973, and is currently investing over $300 million on nine cellular vessels. Although Scandinavian lines were slow to wholeheartedly adopt containerized systems, and the Oslo-based Unit Load Council continues to convincingly argue that unit load methods of shipment will bring cost savings, they are today among the largest container fleet operators in the world. Against the advice of the Unit Load Council then, the lines have at last followed the lead of the United States of America, and have provided cellular capacity, in some cases against their better judgement, either by converting one or more holds of an existing vessel, or by investing in new purpose-built cellular tonnage or in partial containerships. The movement of 40-foot units is growing in popularity, and the wider use of containers in general, most of which are railed between the ports and inland points, was not preceded by large-scale investment in handling equipment. Timber was already being handled at the railheads by gantry cranes, and it was possible to utilize the same cranes with the addition of spreaders for container handling. As the Scandinavian countries diversify their export trade, and become less reliant on forest products, a larger proportion of traffic will be able to be shipped by container, and more reliance, especially in the deep-sea trades, will be placed on multi-purpose and cellular vessels.

The Scandinavian's dependence on merchant vessel operation is very significant and is very old established. As well as being active in short and deep sea trades involving their own countries, a very high proportion of the total fleet operates on cross routes not involving the Scandinavian countries. The modern vessels are manned by small crews, which keeps running costs down and allows frequent replacement by even more up-to-date ships. Scandinavian shipping companies indeed are often fairing better than companies of other countries serving the same route, as shown by the expansion of the Swedish Tor Line while the British EWL (part of Ellerman Lines) cuts back.

In Norway many small but efficient ports have become established, most of which depend on trade with other Scandinavian countries, and because of the limited availability of handling equipment side-loading and roll-on roll-off vessels predominate. The operation of side-loading vessels is dominated by the Norwegian Fred Olsen Line, who did not find it necessary to raise large amounts of capital to initiate their service as containers and container cranes were not required. The pallet and the fork lift truck form the basis of Fred Olsen's operation, and it was found more economical to convey palletized, as compared with containerized cargo, in a mountainous country where conditions are not suited to the haulage of larger units. Fred Olsen though is one of the few national lines to be found operating in home waters, the majority of Norway's merchant fleet (the fourth largest in the world) running over one or other of the cross-trades. Norway is nevertheless highly dependent on exports for the maintenance of a healthy gross domestic product, and her traditional trade in timber, fish and ores is becoming more diversified through the addition of capital and consumer goods, as well as oil and gas from the North Sea.

Development at Oslo has been concentrated on unit load handling systems, and the extensive Fred Olsen terminal is one example. But roll-on roll-off using bow or stern ramps predominates, and roll-on roll-off berths are scattered throughout the harbor. Lift-on containers can also be handled using Norway's first container crane, a 30-ton portainer, but a large proportion of containers for Oslo pass over Gothenburg's berths. If container traffic were to grow, however, Oslo would be willing to extend its container facilities, and a terminal would almost certainly be constructed on reclaimed land at the Ormsund-Kai. Meanwhile additional roll-on roll-off berths are being provided.

Drammen on the mouth of the River Hallingdals in Oslofjord principally caters for roll-on roll-off vessels, and has plans for expansion in the Holmen and the Lierstranda areas, while Bergen on Norway's west coast has recently completed its Jeteviken container terminal. Bergen was formerly a purely roll-on roll-off port, catering for the Bergen Line, who preferred to remain uninvolved in containerization, but today with its variety of berths it is growing in importance as a gateway for Norway's overseas trade.

The Swedish Tor Line has been able to develop a multitude of roll-on roll-off services between the United Kingdom, Scandinavia, and north European ports, and bases its operations at Immingham in the United Kingdom and Gothenburg in Sweden. Services began in 1966 with the intention of shipping pallets and flats, but the more modern vessels in the fleet of six are each able to accept up to 90 12-meter trailers, and over 200 20-foot containers. Tor operates its own terminals, as well as its own vessels, and both the sea and shore staff in the United Kingdom and Sweden work 24 hours a day six days a week on a shift system. The excellent labor relations allow the line to keep closely to its advertized sailing schedules.

Gothenburg in Sweden is Scandinavia's major container port, and handles the majority of the area's container traffic either through direct access to deep sea container (and semi-container) vessels, or through the many feeder vessels that come in from north European ports. Container activities are centered on the Skandia Harbor terminal which opened in 1966, and which is now equipped with four portainers, seven deep sea berths, and seven roll-on roll-off berths. The £30 million terminal situated on the River Gota estuary is partially on reclaimed land, and has been so successful that there has been no real need to build similar terminals elsewhere in Scandinavia. It has therefore been possible to avoid wasteful and costly duplication of facilities, but some potential container ports have in consequence found it difficult to build up regular container traffic. Other berths with modern handling equipment are located in the river estuary, but most of the older city berths in Gothenburg are now obsolete. To the west of the Skandia terminal a new harbor, a few berths of which are already functioning, is under construction largely on reclaimed land. This new center known as the Alvsborg Harbor is to be used for handling both unit load traffic and bulk products, and is due to be completed by 1979. Oil tankers exceeding 200,000 tons handled at the Torshamnen oil jetty mean that 75% of throughput at Gothenburg is already accounted for by oil, and the new Alvsborg terminal will help to boost this figure considerably.

Malmo, almost at the southernmost tip of Sweden, handles containers, roll-on roll-off, and bulk cargoes. The container terminal, situated within the free port zone, is supported by a large back-up area, and vessels are handled at four container berths using two 40-ton portainers. Ten roll-on roll-off berths have also been provided. Malmo is almost wholly constructed on reclaimed land, and as reclamation continues more industrial development is being drawn to the port area, which in turn will help to promote the principal activity of working oil and other bulk cargo vessels.

About 25 miles north of Malmo lies Helsingborg, Sweden's second largest port for unitized cargo. Both container and roll-on roll-off facilities are centered at the Skane Terminal, and a 45-ton capacity portainer has been installed at the container berth to handle the short sea and feeder cellular vessels that regularly call there. Although lift-on lift-off container traffic is growing quite fast, about half of Helsingborg's total cargo throughput is accounted for by roll-on roll-off traffic, and a new roll-on roll-off terminal, the Sound Terminal, will shortly be fully operational. This development includes provision for an extension to the Skane Terminal involving land reclamation.

The commercial center of Sweden, Stockholm, is situated away from the industrial regions in the south of the country, but close to sources of timber. But while the timber figures prominently in the port's export statistics, provision has been made for container traffic at Lindarangen in the free port zone where roll-on roll-off traffic is also handled. Additional roll-on roll-off ramps have been provided at the Varta Harbor.

Among other ports in Sweden where unit load vessels can call are Norrkoping, which handles containers by using two 25-ton conventional cranes and where roll-on roll-off vessels with their own ramps can dock, Gavle where two container berths in the Fredriksskans area have been provided, Oselosunds Hamn where the container terminal also acts as a roll-on roll-off berth, and the privately owned roll-on roll-off port of Wallhamn where containers are also handled by utilizing a 24-ton crane.

In Finland development of the roll-on roll-off concept has been particularly strong because of the dominance of forest products among the country's exports. Roll-on roll-off traffic has grown very fast, especially in the southern part of the country, and trade with other Scandinavian countries is almost wholly maintained using pallets and flats, and roll-on roll-off vessels. The individual vessel size of Finland's merchant fleet, which makes only a small contribution to gross national product, is restricted because of the limited depth of water along the coastline, and

FIGURE 23 Short-sea vessels at the Skane Terminal, Helsingborg (Courtesy of Port of Helsingborg).

container vessels have in some cases been phased out in favor of roll-on roll-off tonnage. For example, the joint container and conventional service maintained by the Finland Steamship Company, the United Baltic Corporation and Oy Finnlines, between the United Kingdom and Finland changed to using roll-on roll-off ships, and became known as Oy Finanglia Line in June 1973. It was found more convenient to ship timber and lumber products on flats and pallets than in containers, but as a growing proportion of Finland's trade is made up of items able to be containerized, such as capital and consumer goods, provision has been made for the shipment of containers on deck which are secured by slotting into deck fixtures instead of by lowering into cells. Containers are handled by deck gantry cranes, and the carriage of TIR trailers as well allows a very flexible service to be maintained.

Lift-on lift-off containers are still handled at Helsinki, in spite of Oy Finanglia's preference for roll-on roll-off, and the new Saukonlaituri container terminal in the West Harbor is equipped with a 40-ton portainer. Roll-on roll-off facilities have been provided in the South Harbor and at Sompassari. At Hamina, to the east of Helsinki in the Gulf of Finland, a roll-on roll-off and pallet terminal has been built, which will improve even further the existing highly mechanized facilities, and at Kotka the Hietanen roll-on roll-off terminal has just been completed.

In the short sea trades between Denmark and the United Kingdom the Esbjerg-based roll-on roll-off DFDS line is the most prominent, and carries about 80 per cent of the available traffic. £16.7 million was initially invested in six roll-on roll-off vessels which replaced thirty conventional vessels, and over £4 million was spent in building a unit load terminal at Esbjerg. To counteract growing competition in the trade a further two roll-on roll-off vessels were ordered at the end of 1973, and provision will be made with this more recent tonnage to carry up to 400 20-foot containers or trailer space equivalent. During the phasing in of the original six new vessels cargo tonnage shipped by DFDS rose by approximately 80 per cent, helped in part by traffic railed between Esbjerg and Copenhagen by the Danish State Railways.

Denmark's principal **port** at Copenhagen is well served by container, roll-on roll-off, and pallet ships sailing to the United Kingdom, and the port also acts as a collection and delivery base for containers conveyed by feeder vessels between Denmark and the deep sea terminals on the Continent. Copenhagen though has been comparatively slow to adapt to the container, in spite of the fact that a lot of former break-bulk traffic is now being shipped by container through the port, but since the introduction of modern methods of shipment total annual cargo throughput has fallen. But Copenhagen's ability to change, albeit slowly, is shown by the eventual completion in 1974 after several years' building of the Levant Quay container terminal in the free port zone. The former break-bulk facilities have become largely obsolete as Levant Quay, where plenty of room is available for expansion, is coping with the help of two portainers, with both deep sea and short sea vessels, as well as with the feeders from Continental ports. Additional facilities for unitized traffic are available at the Ferry Port North roll-on roll-off and container terminal, and to remedy the general shortage of cargo at Copenhagen the port is trying hard to attract business from Russia.

Copenhagen's lack of sufficient cargo is in no small way due to the geographical position of Esbjerg, and to the excellent rail and road links between the two ports. Esbjerg is much closer in terms of steaming-times to the United Kingdom than the other Danish east coast ports are, which include Copenhagen, and the daily container train between Copenhagen and Esbjerg funnels traffic to the east coast port. Esbjerg originally developed as a butter and bacon exporting port, the first container terminal opening in 1967 to handle the bacon exports of the forward-looking Danish Bacon Board. A unit load terminal was opened shortly afterwards to handle the flats, pallets and containers shipped on the roll-on roll-off vessels belonging to DFDS. Containerships are also handled in Denmark at Aarhus where a portainer has been installed at the container quay, and roll-on roll-off vessels make use of the three roll-on roll-off berths.

Chapter 9
The Future

The Rochdale Report

During the 1960's it became evident that other countries were expanding their merchant fleets at a faster rate than the United Kingdom. Adverse effects, particularly on the United Kingdom's invisible trade accounts followed from placing greater reliance on foreign tonnage to carry the country's export and import trade, and in an attempt to determine the reasons for the decaying nature of the industry, the United Kingdom government established a committee—the Committee of Inquiry into the Shipping Industry—in 1966 under Lord Rochdale to investigate. When the Committee reported its findings in May 1970 the industry emerged comparatively unscathed, and indeed a bright future was forecast if the prevailing spirit of enterprize were to continue, but Rochdale made it clear that the industry should not regard itself as different from other competitive enterprizes, even though several problems peculiar to itself did exist.

The Committee maintained that too many comparatively small firms were in existence trying to compete with the larger operators, and that more merging of such companies would be beneficial to the whole industry. With regard to shipbuilding in the United Kingdom it was recommended that the system of investment grants, whereby credit was granted by the shipyards, should be replaced by investment allowances granted by the Government. This would have left the industry in the same tax situation, which was conducive to new building, but the then Government rejected the proposal and withdrew all financial assistance

301

except for a depreciation allowance. Government policy is today still aimed at raising the competitive level of the industry through merely backing bank loans secured in the finance markets by the shipowner, but due to continual poor productivity in comparison to overseas yards, it now appears certain that the shipbuilding industry will be nationalized.

Rochdale further recommended the setting up of an industrial training board to make recruitment into the Merchant Navy more attractive, the formation of a shipping research and development institute to merge the many bodies engaged in R & D, and indicated that the shipping industry should be allowed to develop at a natural pace in line with the increase in international trade, and that it should be free from undue government interference that tended to either speed up or slow down the process. With regard to the problem of shipping conferences the report recommended that a code of conduct be established, possibly on a world-wide basis, but recognized the need for maintaining a closed conference system in order to stabilize freight rates. As will be seen presently an efficient conference should be able to maintain regular sailings, should help to stabilize basic freight rates, and will encourage consultation with shippers' councils and other interested parties when rate adjustments are proposed. But the conferences have been criticized for many years due to their inherent threat of monopolistic power, and because of the veil of secrecy surrounding their activities, and their position was further weakened by actions taken by some shipping companies, especially in the North Atlantic trade, that were aimed at attracting custom by subsidizing ocean freight rates and granting unofficial rebates. As mentioned earlier shipping companies in a number of trades introduced self-policing systems in an effort to overcome such "unhealthy" competition. Merchants generally agree that cut rates will not be conducive to a satisfactory service being rendered, and that such rates will anyway subsequently rise. Stability must exist in each trade to further the aims of both shippers and shipowners, and it is here that the Rochdale report comes out strongly in favor of the continuance of the conference system, provided that the services offered are fully rationalized, and that conference methods are more open to public examination and debate. It was hoped that a check would then be placed on the falling profits of many of the British lines, and that the future would begin to look a little brighter for the shipping industry.

A Move Into Profitability

Following the establishment of any highly capital intensive industry, losses are almost bound to be recorded, but during the early operational years of some of the "pioneer" containership services, such as in the North Atlantic trade, the activities of a number of the participating lines considerably worsened the situation. American Export Industries (owners of American Export Lines) made an operational loss of some $3 million during 1972, while the Seatrain group (shipbuilding and chartering interests as well as containership operation) reported a net loss of $23 million for the fiscal year ending June 1973. While part of the reason for these losses was undoubtedly due to very heavy capital debt repayments, rising fuel costs, the dollar devaluation, and overdue rate increases, it should not be forgotten that an equally important reason, and one that was wholly self-generated, was the desire of a number of lines to increase to a disproportionate level their share of the available cargo through dishonest means. Conversely, some other lines, especially in Britain, still maintained the view that providing a service was more important than making profits, but it was now becoming clearer that rate stability and low levels of freight charges would have to be sacrificed if the lines were to move away from their feeling of despondency. Accordingly, during 1972, world-wide liner freight rates began to move upwards at an alarming pace, and in the United Kingdom the combined effect of a large modern fleet and higher freight revenues led to increasing contributions by the shipping industry to the invisible trade accounts. For example, the 1972 contribution of £441 million increased to £616 million in 1973, and the United Kingdom Chamber of Shipping was at pains to point out the true significance of the figures to a complacent shipping industry.

The tide though was now turning, and following OCL's losses during the period 1969-71, and the small profit of 1972, the long

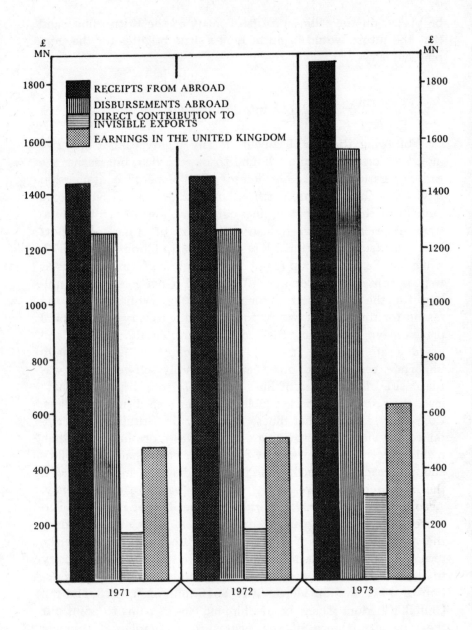

FIGURE 24 Earnings of the United Kingdom shipping industry in overseas trade 1971-1973 (Courtesy of Chamber of Shipping of the United Kingdom).

awaited breakthrough eventually came in 1973 when OCL reported a profit of £17.75 million and a return on capital employed of 13 per cent. OCL's profit in turn boosted its member lines' returns, P & O for example reporting a profit of £34 million for the fiscal year 1972-73, and Furness Withy making £12.8 million in 1973. During this period a boom in international trade was well under way and shipping company receipts were rising not only because of higher freight charges, but also because vessel capacities were consistently fully utilized. Although OCL is continuing to invest heavily in new routes, and has begun to replace outdated equipment, the consortium is forecasting that the 1975 results will be down on 1974, largely due to a considerable slackening off in international trade.

Subsequent Growth

Toward the end of 1973 containerships were operating in most of the world's major trade routes, and container growth was slowing down. Only less heavily tonnaged routes such as the Europe to South Africa and South America trades now remain to be containerized, and future growth will be more closely aligned to increases in the level of world trade, and to supplying the replacement market in vessels and equipment. In the container manufacturing field a slump that put many firms out of business followed the boom years of 1969-70, and although a partial recovery occurred in 1974 precipitated by the replacement market and by large orders from the leasing companies, the level of production has settled well below its former artificially high level. At the beginning of 1974, out of a world total general cargo ship tonnage exceeding 70 million, over 6 million tons were accounted for by fully cellular containerships, and individual containership sizes were growing. Toward the middle of 1974 the average deadweight of container vessels on order was 17,860 tons, many individual vessels exceeding 25,000 tons, and service speeds were generally to exceed 25 knots. Capacities were frequently to be above 2,000 units per vessel, and it was forecast that by 1975 about 200 containerships would be in service in the principal trading routes taking the place of about 750 conventional vessels.

TABLE 1

SIZE AND AGE OF FULLY CELLULAR CONTAINERSHIPS

WORLD TOTALS

DIVISIONS OF TONNAGE	0-4 Years		5-9 Years		10-14 Years		15-19 Years		20-24 Years		25-29 Years		30 Years & Over		TOTAL	
	No.	Tons Gross	No.	Tons Gross	No.	Tons Gross	No.	Tons Gross	No.	Tons Gross	No.	Tons Gross	No.	Tons Gross	No.	Tons Gross
100 — 499	4	1,994	6	2,883	...	...	1	436	...	...	...	...	...	...	11	5,313
500 — 999	8	7,162	8	5,405	...	...	5	7,065	...	...	...	...	...	...	16	12,567
1,000 — 1,999	38	57,849	10	14,885	3	4,203	...	...	...	...	1	1,019	...	...	57	84,821
2,000 — 3,999	21	65,581	6	16,582	1	2,186	3	10,553	...	...	...	...	...	...	31	94,902
4,000 — 5,999	21	98,721	3	13,647	2	10,742	...	...	...	...	...	...	...	...	26	123,110
6,000 — 6,999	3	19,434	...	...	...	...	1	6,233	...	...	...	...	...	...	4	25,667
7,000 — 7,999	3	21,869	1	7,105	...	...	...	...	...	...	4	30,028	6	45,563	14	104,565
8,000 — 9,999	3	26,348	2	18,533	...	...	...	...	...	...	...	...	11	98,731	16	143,612
10,000 — 14,999	15	185,562	9	113,865	1	14,952	3	38,928	1	14,469	15	182,183	10	112,464	54	662,423
15,000 — 19,999	20	356,390	24	420,080	3	49,554	1	15,024	8	126,828	8	142,113	7	118,874	71	1,228,863
20,000 — 29,999	51	1,228,848	10	256,639	...	...	...	...	...	...	...	...	...	...	61	1,485,487
30,000 — 39,999	17	576,366	...	...	...	...	...	...	...	...	...	...	...	...	17	576,366
40,000 — 49,999	12	512,031	...	...	...	...	...	...	...	...	...	...	...	...	12	512,031
50,000 — 59,999	22	1,234,842	...	...	...	...	...	...	...	...	...	...	...	...	22	1,234,842
60,000 — 69,999	...	...	...	...	...	...	...	...	...	...	...	...	...	...	...	...
70,000 and above	...	...	...	...	...	...	...	...	...	...	...	...	...	...	...	...
TOTAL	238	4,392,997	79	869,424	10	81,637	14	78,239	9	141,297	28	355,343	34	375,632	412	6,294,569

DIVISIONS OF AGE

NOTE:: This table includes 103 ships which were not purpose-built but have been converted to fully cellular containerships subsequently.

Source: Lloyd's Register of Shipping Statistical Tables 1974.

The trend therefore among the major shipping companies is to modernize fleets whenever possible by discarding outdated vessels and by ordering new tonnage, and to look again at methods of operation with a view to rationalizing services. In the United Kingdom alone about £3,000 million was committed to new vessel building during the period 1965-75, and during this period the fleet increased in size by over 50 per cent. Even though the industry is moving into a period of over-capacity, the United Kingdom Chamber of Shipping is urging that a still larger fleet be provided to help counteract a loss of revenue that followed on from the country's adverse terms of trade and continual industrial troubles. But a larger more efficient fleet must be properly utilized to ensure an adequate contribution to the invisible trade accounts, and the only way of achieving this might well be to introduce policies aimed at protectionism and isolationism. The Chamber is right to condemn such actions, but should also point out the necessity for having new building programmes based on reasonable expectations of future market forces. It should be borne in mind that while a 1,500 unit containership cost about £5 million to build in 1969, the cost for a 2,000 unit vessel in 1974 stood at around £25 million. One way of avoiding wasteful duplication of services would be to extend the principle of grouping lines into consortia, which would also ease the cost burden of building new vessels, and to encourage discussion among the consortia when building schedules are being prepared. It should be emphasized that this type of co-operation would not take the place of active competition once services are under way, as it would be confined to avoiding trade routes becoming over-tonnaged. Competition between the consortia will partly offset the monopoly threat of greater amalgamation, and this type of competition already exists in the Europe to Far East and Europe to Australia trades.

Little can be done about the cyclical forces that the shipping industry is subjected to following changes in market forces and the volume of world trade, but where future growth is restricted because of government policies, these policies should be reviewed. Container shipping will become more secure when management is better able to maximize individual container usage, which should lead to more stable basic freight rates through elimination of excessive spare capacity, and an increase of leasing of containers may promote such usage. For each container slot on a typical deep sea vessel five containers are required to ensure that each slot is filled with a cargo-carrying container. With each 20-foot unit costing about £1,300, and with 2,000-3,000 slots to fill, it will be seen that leasing will allow a considerable saving in capital investment costs over outright purchase. Leasing also of vessels and other equipment will continue to grow. Future growth of container shipping is also partly dependent on the successful introduction of a form of combined transport document acceptable to all interested parties.

While discussing future growth though one should never lose sight of the fact that a growing proportion of world trade will in future be shipped over the established trade routes by shipping companies and organizations who were previously not involved in these trade routes. For example, the USSR is building up a modern fleet of containerships for service in the North Atlantic outside conference jurisdiction, and the low level of rates that will be offered could well precipitate another North Atlantic rate "war". The Russian involvement in the trans-Siberian Railway has already led to rates being quoted for through movements between Europe and the Far East up to 50 per cent below the rate level of TRIO and of the other members of the Far Eastern Freight Conference. The shipping industries of the established liner maritime countries have frequently had to overcome operating difficulties to remain competitive, but competition apparently unrelated to costs (but denied by the USSR) may be unsurmountable. As the container shipping industry has grown stability has therefore been lost, and practices detrimental to all those engaged in moving goods internationally, such as rate cutting, have at times flourished, and have led to the withdrawal of several shipping companies who were trying to operate legitimately. A need arose to establish a central body consisting of representatives from groups of shippers, shipping companies, banks, marine insurance underwriters, railway authorities, and road haulage operators, to promote discussion over a wide sphere with the intention of possibly contributing to greater stability, and in March 1975 a start was made by setting up the General Council of British Shipping. Although the Council will be representing United

TABLE 2

Merchant tonnage at 1.7.74 by type and country of registration
in millions of gross tons (steamships and motorships of 100 tons gross and upward)

	Oil Tankers		General Cargo		Container (fully cellular)		Barge Carriers	
	No.	grt	No.	grt	No.	grt	No.	grt
Liberia	877	33.750	553	3.403	19	0.209	–	–
Japan	1537	16.012	2864	5.443	42	1.026	–	–
UK	581	15.203	1109	5.025	90	1.352	–	–
Norway	297	12.203	895	1.969	1	0.052	2	0.074
Greece	389	7.560	1490	6.361	4	0.037	–	–
USSR	477	3.658	1674	6.854	9	0.048	–	–
USA	314	4.883	554	3.918	110	1.871	19	0.517
Panama	248	4.682	1172	3.712	3	0.018	–	–
Italy	322	3.670	512	1.148	6	0.097	–	–
France	125	5.509	279	1.319	7	0.139	–	–
West Germany	133	2.141	1345	2.652	46	0.626	1	0.037
Sweden	117	2.145	323	1.061	7	0.154	–	–
Netherlands	109	2.514	657	1.877	13	0.153	1	0.037
Spain	108	2.260	571	0.998	11	0.021	–	–
Denmark	70	2.198	743	1.145	5	0.179	1	0.001

Source: Lloyd's Register of Shipping Statistical Tables 1974.

Kingdom shipping interests only, it is hoped that discussion with similar bodies abroad will be fruitful, and may eventually lead to the setting up of an international body.

The container shipping industry will benefit more on a regional basis than on an international basis following a reopening of the 99 mile long Suez Canal. The canal was closed following the Arab Israeli war of 1967, and while vessels were soon able to adapt to re-routing via the Cape of Good Hope, ports in the Mediterranean suffered a setback to their planned growth schedules at a time when container traffic was needed most. These same Mediterranean ports, Genoa being a typical example, together with manufacturing and trading concerns in southern Europe, will also be the principal beneficiaries following a reopening. Containerships sailing between Europe and Japan will also benefit through saving over 3,000 miles by using the canal, but vessels in the Europe to Australia trade would save only 880 miles on a trip between London and Sydney. It is the lines capable of reducing steaming distances only marginally who may well find that the new scale of canal charges are so high that any fuel and time savings are more than outweighed by canal tolls, and these lines will continue to sail via the Cape. Plans to deepen the canal navigation channels to allow access to tankers of up to 100,000 DWT had to be shelved following the closure, and today's largest containerships (over 40,000 DWT) are already too big to enter with their draught of 40 feet. A 73,000 DWT tanker steaming south in ballast however will only draw about 24 feet and could therefore proceed to the Persian Gulf via the canal, and a 29,000 DWT containership drawing 35 feet could also use the canal. Following a reopening it is now planned to dredge during a three-year period to allow entry to vessels of up to 150,000 tons, and after a further three years to vessels of up to 250,000 tons. The clearance of mines and wrecks is almost complete, but it remains to be seen whether the expected reopening during mid-1975 will now take place in view of increased tension in the area.

Nationalism

For the past hundred years, following the repeal of the Navigation Acts, Britain has had a very free attitude to shipping, and has been firmly opposed to restrictive legislation. Prior to the repeal of the Acts though, Britain had adopted a very nationalistic outlook, and had placed severe restrictions on foreign vessels entering British ports. Early competition with the United States merchant marine in the North Atlantic trade soon flagged following America's preoccupation with river shipping, and with opening up east-west domestic trade routes, and Britain was soon to own about half the world's merchant fleet. A handful of other countries have likewise been able to become strong maritime powers, enjoying the benefits of substantial contributions to their invisible trade accounts, but at the same time providing reliable shipping services from their own countries, and between third-country nations. In the United States though, efforts have been made for several years to recoup some of their merchant fleet capacity through the imposition of discriminatory government measures aimed at channeling American cargo into American vessels, and similar nationalistic tendencies are spreading, especially among the less developed countries of the world. Freedom of shipping is being eroded by the unilateral action of individual countries, and by bilateral actions of countries forming trade agreements, and the position of the established maritime powers as the principal conveyors of international liner traffic is seriously being challenged.

Measures that would increase government interference in the freedom of liner shipping, possibly to an unacceptable level, were proposed at the United Nations Conference on Trade and Development (UNCTAD) Conference held in Geneva in November 1973, which was called to draft a convention for a code of conduct for liner conferences. Attempts were made to obtain far greater bargaining strength for cargo owners, to restrict the rate-fixing power of those shipping companies who have formed themselves into conferences, and to control the activities of non-conference shipping companies in the cross-trade routes, i.e. trade routes between two or more foreign countries. The less developed countries have often found it difficult to obtain membership in the conferences for their national fleets, and have therefore been obliged to utilize foreign flag vessels to carry a large proportion of their liner cargo. It was accordingly recommended at the UNCTAD conference that the two countries involved in conference controlled trades should each be allowed to ship 40 per cent of the available cargo in their own flag vessels, while the remaining 20 per cent would be open to the cross trades. Each participating country, irrespective of the size of its merchant fleet, was allowed one vote, and as the less developed nations as a body could muster about 90 votes out of a total of about 130 the outcome of this particular resolution was a foregone conclusion. If the resolution is later ratified, the liner conferences will have no choice but to adopt bilateral cargo agreements that will have the effect of radically readjusting cargo volumes being carried by their present members, and some of these members will be forced to leave the conferences and even cease trading. The countries most opposed to the UNCTAD resolution are Britain, Greece, and the Scandinavians, while the USSR and some other countries who have only recently built up a large merchant fleet, often active in the cross-trades, apparently contrary to their own policy voted in favor of the resolution. The USSR would undoubtedly have been better off if the resolution had been rejected, but they have no wish to offend the less developed countries. Greece and Norway, the two major free flag merchant fleets in the world, have to rely on cargo generated by the cross-trades, as trade between their own countries and overseas is small, but the effect on Greece would be cushioned as she is more active in the tramp market than in the scheduled conference liner trades. Although the USA maintains that she is not in favor of bilateral cargo agreements (appearing to favor unilateral arrangements instead), she is already a party to bilateral agreements with Russia, Brazil and Venezuela. In apparently defending the freedom of shipping, the USA Federal Maritime Commission points out that the UNCTAD cargo sharing resolution is a threat to the established conference system, and is purely a method of boosting the merchant fleets of the less developed countries. Coordinating bodies opposed to the resolution include the United Kingdom Chamber of Shipping and the Committee of European National Shipowners Associations (CENSA). CENSA incidentally had already approved an earlier code of conduct for her liner conferences in 1971 drawn up on a commercial basis and formulated by shippers councils and shipowning interests. The European Economic Community has so far expressly excluded shipping from its policy making, and is opposed to bilateral cargo agreements, but if a Common Market shipping policy were to evolve it would almost certainly be along parochial lines if only to counteract United States flag discrimination. Nationalism and its attendant distortionary effects would then be here to stay on a worldwide basis.

Although the less developed countries as a whole are insisting on carrying their own liner cargo in their own vessels, it is difficult to see how several of these countries will be able to manage as their merchant fleets are either nonexistent or are in a very rudimentary stage of development. In cases such as these it is likely that the established maritime nations will enter into management contracts with the less developed countries concerned, and will ship all or a proportion of cargo in the trade. The formation of management contracts though will not solve the problem of falling cargo volumes during the long term, but will merely allow the less developed countries time to build up their fleets, while at the same time maintaining trade flows. More permanent solutions would be for the established shipping companies to leave the conferences and operate independently outside the jurisdiction of the UNCTAD resolution, or to form their own selective group that would exclude the high cost inefficient lines run by the less developed countries. Conference rates are largely aligned to the operating costs of the least efficient member, and if these less efficient members are prevented from joining the new groups, rates charged by the group will be less than the former conference rates which could well lead to the eventual downfall of the UNCTAD groupings and a return to free and competitive shipping.

Probably a better reason for condoning bilateral cargo agreements is to point to their restraining effect on the rapidly growing merchant fleets of a few comparatively small but rich countries who were previously largely unconnected with shipping. Oil revenue has allowed some Middle East countries to develop quite large fleets, as in the case of the Arya National Shipping

TABLE 3

Merchant tonnage in millions of gross tons by country of
registration (steamships and motorships of 100 tons gross and
upward)

	1914	1924	1934	1944*	1954	1964	1974
Liberia	–	–	–	–	2.4	14.5	55.3
Japan	1.7	3.8	4.1	–	3.6	10.8	38.7
UK	18.9	18.9	17.6	–	19.0	21.5	31.6
Norway	2.0	2.4	4.0	–	6.8	14.5	24.8
Greece	0.8	0.8	1.5	–	1.2	6.9	21.8
USSR	0.8	0.3	0.9	–	2.4	7.0	18.2
USA	4.3	14.7	12.3	–	27.3	22.4	14.4
Panama	–	–	0.3	–	4.1	4.3	11.0
Italy	1.4	2.7	2.9	–	3.8	5.7	9.3
France	1.9	3.3	3.3	–	3.8	5.1	8.8
W.Germany	5.1	2.9	3.7	–	2.2	5.2	8.0
Sweden	1.0	1.2	1.6	–	2.7	4.3	6.2
Netherlands	1.5	2.5	2.6	–	3.4	5.1	5.5
Spain	0.9	1.2	1.2	–	1.3	2.0	4.9
Denmark	0.8	1.0	1.1	–	1.6	2.4	4.5

*Not compiled.

Source: Lloyd's Register of Shipping Statistical Tables 1974.

Lines of Iran, and the Kuwait Shipping Company of Kuwait. Both these lines found conference entry difficult, and when they were accepted they both expected cargo volume shares higher than they were entitled to. Venezuela is also building up a national fleet with the assistance of oil revenue, and is further involved in the setting up of a seventeen-nation Caribbean shipping group to include Mexico, Colombia and the Central American states. Although national shipping interests in the Caribbean have for long maintained that existing conference rates are too high, it is doubtful whether they would be able to reduce costs by running their own services. Puerto Rico is also trying to establish its own merchant fleet by nationalizing the lines at present connecting it with the USA. While some countries such as Japan have experienced similar rapid growth of their merchant fleets, but based on commercial profitability usually within the conference systems, over-rapid growth of some national fleets, which can often only be sustained for example by insisting that goods connected with Government contracts are carried by the national line, should be curbed until these lines are able to operate competitively without prolonged subsidization. If this unnatural growth is not curtailed, several national fleets will shortly be able to follow the lead of the USSR and enter the cross-trades, where they will not only severely disrupt the services maintained by the established maritime nations operating without subsidies, but also the UNCTAD groupings.

Government interference then in shipping is rife and is having a harmful effect on the established fleets of the maritime nations by removing their traditional air of freedom. Low freight rates covering the export trade of less developed countries will eventually be reflected in higher rates for the exports of the developed nations, and legislation such as that found in the United Kingdom Merchant Shipping (Miscellaneous Provisions) Bill of 1973 is indicative that the established maritime nations are beginning to formulate their own counter protectionist policies. This particular bill, which introduces into the United Kingdom for the first time this century measures aimed at countering overseas flag discrimination, can only add to the turmoil of rate manipulation and unilateral cargo carrying arrangements, and will strengthen still further the nationalistic movement. A liberal policy is surely preferable to one of discrimination, and maybe more discussion and co-operation among governments, coupled with the opening up of conferences to outsiders, would make it unnecessary to introduce policies that can only have a long-term harmful effect on the efficiency of moving goods by sea.

Computers and Automatic Terminals

Mention has already been made of ACL's "Datafreight Receipt", which replaces the traditional bill of lading by a non-negotiable receipt to allow computerized transmission of shipment details and title to the goods from the port of loading to the port of discharge. The use of computers by shipping companies and port authorities will grow, and time sharing schemes will allow the smaller operator to benefit from more efficient data collection and assimilation, and from better location and control of containers. ACT are to use space satellites to link their computer network, and marketing information will be conveyed from their Australian offices, for example, to assess container demand. US Lines have installed a computer at their New York office that can locate the exact position of any one of their 30,000 containers, whether on land or on board one of their five vessels, and container losses have been cut dramatically. Port authorities and terminal operators will also make more use of computerized systems, both for container handling and location, and a computerized container stacking complex manufactured in Japan is being used in Hong Kong by the Kowloon Container Warehouse Company. A computerized container control system has also been installed at Liverpool's Seaforth container terminal, capable of determining the position, contents, and destination of any of the 12,000 containers that may be in the marshalling area at any one time.

Mention has also been made of the Modular Automated Container Handling System (MACH), developed by Paceco and designed to give maximum berth throughput during loading and unloading using computer controlled portainers, in conjunction with an automated back-up and storage area for containers. This type of system will be adapted for use at the automated transit terminals of the future, where large deep sea containerships will load and discharge containers already generated by, or to be on-carried by, smaller feeder vessels between the terminal and the ports. Such terminals are already planned in the Mediterranean, and as containerships increasingly tend to restrict their number of calls, similar terminals may be developed to serve other large regional areas. One such terminal was proposed for Falmouth in England by a consortium of companies collectively known as Falmouth Container Terminal Limited (FACT), but the rather premature nature of the scheme led to its rejection in 1971 by the United Kingdom Government on the grounds that England already had a sufficient number of deep sea container terminals. The consortium envisaged that approximately 90 per cent of the terminal's throughput would have been fed to small container-ships for on-carriage to other United Kingdom and Continental ports, while the remaining 10 per cent would have been absorbed by the domestic rail and road systems. While these "push button" complexes will initially have to be equipped with batteries of automatic portainers, container handling systems may eventually have to change to accommodate an entirely new breed of con-tainerships incorporating new methods of on-board container handling and stowage.

New Vessel Types

Although it will appear that very large containerships should be able to convey cargo across the oceans at a cheaper rate per ton than smaller vessels, several factors exist to prevent such economies of scale being realized. Principal among these are design and constructional problems of large containerships, costs of proceeding via one of the Cape routes compared with transit through the Suez or Panama canal, and the desirability of more frequent sailings using smaller vessels. Containership size will therefore increase at a far slower rate than growth of oil tankers and other types of bulk carrier, as these bulk vessels are trading in commodities having a relatively constant demand where fre-quency of sailings is less important than regularity, and where vessel size is large enough to reduce freight costs per ton via one of the Cape routes by a greater amount than any savings that may have accrued through using smaller vessels and proceeding via Suez or Panama. Until it becomes feasible to build very large containerships, vessel size into the medium-term future will not be significantly greater than the size of today's TRIO vessels, with their length of 900 feet, breadth of 95 feet, and a gross tonnage of between 50,000 and 58,000. This specification is related to the 97-foot width of the Panama Canal locks, and the length and draught of the TRIO vessels are already too large in relation to the breadth of the ships. But even without canal lock restrictions, larger vessels will not be built if it is found that a smaller containership, with a capacity of about 2,000 containers, sailing faster than a larger vessel capable of shipping about 3,000 containers, can move the same tonnage of cargo as the larger vessel during a specific period.

Constructional problems relate to reduced vessel strength of large containerships, and in turn lead to restrictions on entry to many ports because of increased draughts. As containerships that have containers loaded and discharged vertically into open cells become bigger, hatch openings at deck level will become larger, and weaknesses will appear. While a double hull and a double bottom will help to overcome a weakened structure, very substantial hatch openings associated with large containerships will require extra strengthening at deck level. This strengthening will cause the center of gravity to rise which in turn will have to be compensated by extra ballast. Vessel draughts will then increase, but few of today's ports have container quays capable of accommodating very deep draught vessels. While transition from early converted vessels, where space was wasted because holds were not squared off, to modern purpose-built containerships such as Sea-Land's fleet of SL7's, has been rapid, it is now becoming apparent that further developments regarding containership design will be necessary if vessels are to become larger, and if today's ports are to continue to handle deep sea containerships.

Probably the most interesting design is that proposed at a conference in Rotterdam in 1971 by P. Meeusen which allows a closed deck construction. Containers would be loaded and discharged not into vertical cells, but horizontally through two stern openings at different levels using a system of on-board conveyor belts. Containers would be stowed along horizontal lanes, and movement between lanes on different levels would be by elevator. Such vessels would overcome the longer loading/discharge cycles that large vertical cell containerships would require, but would have to be backed up by new terminal techniques probably along the lines of those envisaged for the automated transit terminals of the future, to allow efficient handling of massive throughputs. Conventional portainers would not be required, as an on-board gantry, for long out of favor because its use is restricted to time spent in port, would be utilized for transfer of containers between shore and ship, and ports without the necessary handling equipment could then be called at. The first of a series of horizontal loading containerships that will have space for 1,000 20-foot containers (or their equivalent in other sizes), or 2,000 cars on four decks is already under construction in the Ukraine. The vessel will be powered by gas turbines at a service speed of 25 knots, and will have a 35,000-ton displacement.

Although construction of fully cellular containerships will continue, and indeed 70 per cent of container carrying vessels (including partial containerships, roll-on roll-off vessels, and barge carrying vessels, etc.) to be built up to 1977 will be of the fully cellular type, there is a growing demand for more flexible vessels able to carry a variety of cargo types. Fully cellular ships are only able to ship cargo that can be put into a container, while roll-on roll-off and LASH vessels are capable of shipping a wide variety of other traffic, including bulk commodities and large wheeled items, as well as containers. This more flexible type of vessel will become more popular in specific trades where cargo flows are mixed, or in the case of LASH barge carrying vessels where at least 50 per cent of the barge movement is along an inland waterway. There will also be a need for comparatively small but fast containerships, having a part cellular and part roll-on roll-off construction. An example of a truly multi-purpose vessel is the 9,000 DWT *Ponape Maru* operated by the Japanese Daiwa Navigation Company from Japan to Taiwan and Guam. The ship is able to carry up to 284 containers in cells and on deck, 460 cars on the car deck, and general break-bulk cargo in a separate hold. A 30-ton on-board container gantry crane has been provided. The extent to which the roll-on roll-off concept can be taken is illustrated by Transamerican Trailer Transport's 24,000-ton vessel the *Fortaleza*, engaged in the Baltimore to San Juan (Puerto Rico) trade. This 700-foot long vessel, the longest roll-on roll-off ship in the world, can accept 240 40-foot trailers and 400 assorted road vehicles (cars, buses, lorries, etc.). Loading/ discharge takes place over three land-based steel ramps positioned at intervals along the vessel's starboard side, and virtually any cargo type mounted on wheels can be accepted for shipment.

Looking further into the future, the sectional ship, and vessels either totally or partially submerged may well become commonplace, and may offer an alternative to today's containerships if they are able to maintain handling and operating costs at an even lower level than the containership can. The sectional ship would be based around bow and stern sections that would separate from cargo carrying center sections. These center sections would be large floating holds that could be towed, rather like LASH barges, to a wharf for cargo handling, while another set of already loaded center sections would be "clipped" on to the waiting bow and stern sections. Cargo handling would be even further removed from the area of vessel operation, and turnaround time would be very rapid indeed. The potential advantages of submersible vessels stem from their ability to navigate areas impenetrable to conventional shipping, and to their lower resistance to water. A totally submerged cargo ship would be able to shorten voyage distances by navigating beneath the Arctic Ocean, and would be able to maintain consistently fast speed levels because of less water resistance. The water resistance factor is paramount in arguments in favor of the semi-submerged vessel, which would have twin hulls placed one on top of the other connected by vertical members. The lower hull would be totally submerged, and would either be permanently in ballast, or partially in ballast and have a partial cargo carrying capacity. The upper hull, which would be well above the water line, would be used for carrying containers or roll-on roll-off traffic, and principal resistance to the water would be confined to the supporting struts only. This type of vessel would be capable of travelling at about 35 knots, which is faster than the fastest containerships of today. When container vessels, or for that matter any other types of surface vessel, are driven too fast into heavy seas structural damage can occur, especially to hull plates, and with present day designs containerships have already reached their maximum safe operating speeds. If such lines as Sea-Land and Seatrain wish to continue in their rather fruitless bids to be "fastest in the North Atlantic" they may well have to look at some of these alternative designs.

Vessel propulsion systems are based on steam turbines, diesel engines, gas turbines, or nuclear powered plants. The steam turbine is by far the most widely used power plant with its comparatively low consumption of fuel, while the gas turbine is sometimes preferred for installation in containerships because of its greater power output (but higher fuel consumption), the small amount of space it requires, and its ability to be removed for servicing or complete replacement within 24 hours. Nuclear-powered merchant vessels have not yet entered into the regular trade routes for a combination of reasons. Principal among these are that until quite recently operating costs have always been too high in relation to the former cheapness of oil, and that countries would forbid entry of nuclear powered vessels to their ports because of the risk of contamination. But renewed interest is now being shown in nuclear power largely because of the rising cost of oil, and it may well become competitive by the mid-1980's. It is widely held that vessels requiring power plants generating upward of 80,000 shp could be more economically run using nuclear power, but before the commercial construction of purpose-built ships, vessels such as Sea Land's 41,000 GRT SL7's generating 120,000 shp may well be converted to nuclear power. Conversions such as these might be of particular benefit to vessels carrying high-value containerized cargo that have to consistently maintain speeds in excess of 30 knots, but purpose-built nuclear ships carrying more conventional cargo would probably have to be very large before they became competitive. It has indeed been suggested in the USA that vessels would have to be of at least 400,000 DWT to be run economically, therefore restricting nuclear power to oil tankers.

The principal difficulty of developing and running a nuclear-powered vessel does not relate to sources of uranium, but is how to construct the reactor—the nuclear steam supply system—on a

FIGURE 25 Sea-Land cellular containership *Sea-Land Finance* in the North Atlantic (Courtesy of Sea-Land Containerships Limited).

production line basis, while at the same time maintaining exceptionally high standards of workmanship. Over one third of the
vessel's cost would be accounted for by the reactor, and since
the first nuclear-powered vessel, the *Savannah* was built, it has
become possible to progressively construct much smaller reactors
than the *Savannah* was fitted with. But the risk of contamination
is ever present, and until safety requirements are universally accepted, problems of port entry will remain. It may be possible
to help overcome such problems by initially constructing a standard type of vessel, and port authorities would not then have to
examine different specifications before giving clearance for entry.
Additional difficulties will arise with regard to insurance of hulls
and cargo, and to adequate safety of the crew while at sea.

Construction of nuclear-powered ships has so far been confined to the provision of research vessels. The first of these, the
USA-built *Savannah* is now laid up, but two other vessels are
currently in use. West Germany's *Otto Hahn* has been used by
the country's nuclear research body since 1968, and in future
may be utilized as a crew training and testing vessel by Hapag-
Lloyd in anticipation of the introduction of nuclear merchant
ships to liner trades, and the Japanese have been carrying out
nuclear trials since the end of 1973 with their vessel the *Mutsu*.
Several countries now have plans to construct commercially viable
nuclear-powered vessels, but because of the cost and technologi-
cal expertise involved most of these projects are on a joint basis
with other countries. West Germany and Japan have been co-
operating since 1972, and West Germany's Hapag-Lloyd may be
ordering up to five 80,000-ton nuclear-powered containerships
from Japan by the end of 1975. The West German and United
Kingdom atomic energy authorities have been having detailed discussions since 1973, that might later be extended to include
Japan and the USA, and it is possible that six large nuclear containerships (50-60,000 tons each) costing a total of £300 million,
and capable of travelling at between 30 and 35 knots, will be
built for operation in the Europe to Far East trade. In the USA
opinion is divided over the optimum size of nuclear vessels, and
over whether or not government subsidies should be granted for
their construction. Subsidies covering the difference in cost between nuclear and conventional vessels are expected to be granted

though for three cargo ships to be designed by Babcock & Wilcox, while other United States interests may be involved in the construction of a nuclear oil tanker of about 400,000 tons.

While resources devoted to the development of a nuclear power plant that can be built at a reasonable cost are fully justified, not only because of rising oil prices, but also because quite soon there will be a serious world oil shortage, resources devoted to some other recent projects are more difficult to justify. There must be a very real social or economic need for a project before development commences, and technology for technology's sake, as in the case of the programme to construct a tracked hovercraft system in the United Kingdom, should be avoided. As far as more conventional hovercraft are concerned, it should be remembered that a disproportionate amount of energy expenditure is required in lifting in comparison to that required for horizontal propulsion, and that a 5,000-ton craft would need so much fuel for its adapted aero engines that very little room would be left for cargo. It is uncertain whether cargo carrying airships could be operated satisfactorily, but development is meanwhile progressing quite slowly largely because the record of previous disasters lingers on. In place of the traditional hydrogen formerly used to obtain lift, today's airships use the inert and safe helium gas, and fire risk is therefore considerably reduced. Airships for operation between the United Kingdom and the Continent having a 30-ton payload, a range of 1,600 miles, and a speed of 80 knots have been proposed, and it is estimated that each unit would cost about £1 million. Moving up the scale one comes to the so-called "transporters" with a 500-ton payload, that would remain airborne while a number of smaller feeder airships would attend to the loading and discharge of containerized cargo. International airship conferences are already being held, and it is being pointed out that while it is not intended that the airship should take the place of the containership or the aeroplane, it could act as an alternative to both. It is estimated that the approximate per ton cost of moving cargo between London and Hong Kong by airship would be £100 and the transit time would be about five days, whereas a comparison by air freight would be £400 and two days, and by containership £50 and thirty days. Cargo carrying flying saucers are also being mooted, and it is said that a prototype could be built before 1980. Lift of the 700-foot diameter and 208-foot high craft, to be called *Skyship*, would again be by helium gas, but permanently sealed in, and it is said that ten turbo-prop engines would provide horizontal movement. The £10 million saucers would be able to land and take off both at sea and on land with a 400-ton payload of bulk and/or container cargo. The immediate future though of carrying containerized cargo by air would appear to be more confined to the use of specially adapted "jumbo"-type aircraft, and already jumbo jets are being used to air freight containers across the North Atlantic.

Further Notes
on the
Conference System

Evolution

Following the industrial revolutions in Britain and on the Continent, international trade went through a boom period that only began to slacken off in the 1860's. Shipping companies serving the recognized trading routes had expanded their fleets, and newcomers had entered these trades in an endeavor to obtain for themselves part of the continually growing cargo flows. But the partial recession was to continue up until the 1890's, and by this time shortage of cargo meant that many companies had had to cease trading. Services were too often duplicated, and it was clear that some form of co-operation among the lines would be needed if rate stability and regularity of sailings in the various trades were to be restored. But rationalization was to come to the canals and railways where excessive competition was creating instability, before it was to come to the merchant shipping industry, and a general merging together of the many railway companies and canal barge companies in the United Kingdom made for a much better service for the cargo owner at rates acceptable to the operators. The changes at sea took a little longer, as although trade in capital and consumer goods was growing fast in specific areas, the majority of seaborne trade was still bulk traffic shipped in tramp vessels. But with the continual raising of living standards, demand was increasing for frequent and fast services to carry larger volumes of general cargo. Frequency of sailings and stability of freight rates were becoming more import-ant than low rates, and the liner companies therefore began to form themselves into international groups or "conferences", to enable them to provide the required services. Conference member-ship has traditionally been made up of the established national and "third flag" lines in each trade (new applications for member-ship are frequently rejected), and to avoid dominance by the major carrier, one vote is apportioned to each member line. A conference will normally control a trade flow in one direction only, and shipping companies will often be members of several of the 360 plus conferences in existence today. Conferences must therefore be regarded as price-fixing groups, but due to their peculiar circumstances they are generally exempt from mon-opoly laws that may apply in individual countries. In the USA, for example, special legislation was incorporated into the 1916 Shipping Act to exempt conferences from the country's rigid anti-trust laws.

As the conferences are all too eager to point out, it can take decades to build up a particular trade to the point where shippers have confidence in the future viability of vessel operation in the trade and are able to enter into firm commitments with overseas buyers in the knowledge that regular sailings exist at stable rates. Conference membership is therefore not freely available to those shipping lines who may intend operating in a particular trade on a temporary, or on an infrequent basis, and as the conferences further consider that the activities of these outsiders is undesir-able, they generally operate a "dual rate" system of charging freight. To those cargo owners who contract with the conference to ship by vessels belonging to member lines only, a freight dis-count of about 9.5% is granted, while cargo owners who prefer to choose their method of shipment and utilize conference ves-sels irregularly must pay the higher "non-contract" rate. The emergence of several national shipping lines is threatening the existence of the conference structure, and is encouraging the closed conference system whereby these new outsiders find mem-bership difficult to attain, while an extension of the dual rate principle has been designed to check non-conference activity.

This type of policy will continue until the point is reached where outside lines are seriously affecting cargo tonnages of conference lines, and the outsider will then be welcomed as a new member if only to stop rate cutting. Whether or not the outsider decides to join the conference will largely depend on his need for a regular cargo flow, and indeed the trend today is for outsiders to form themselves into groups and to offer services as regular as the conference but at cheaper rates. This more rigid attitude to non-conference lines is contrary to former practice, and very often government inspired nationalistic undertones will be present. The UNCTAD resolution to introduce bilateral cargo agreements, mention of which was made in Chapter 9, is a direct threat by the less developed nations to retaliate against the conference structure.

The Need for Consultation and Publicity

Conference affairs have traditionally been conducted behind closed doors, and information has not been freely available to shippers and to other interested parties. This secretiveness has been the cause of much criticism levelled at the conferences, and requests have often been made that freight tariffs should be available for inspection, and that annual cost/revenue accounts should be published. A more open attitude was in fact adopted in 1973 by the Far Eastern Freight Conference who were the first to produce publicly an annual report, but it is still difficult in particular to persuade conferences to account for freight rate increases. The relationship between conferences and shipping companies on the one hand, and shippers on the other, has therefore never been entirely harmonious, and until rate increases and other sometimes apparently unwarranted actions are justified by the conferences, this relationship is likely to remain. Mention should be made, however, of the various shippers' councils representing the interests of the cargo owners, and in particular of the British Shippers' council, an independent trade association formed in 1955. Similar bodies were soon to become established in the rest of Europe, and the councils were formally recognized in 1963 by the Committee of European National Shipowners

Association (CENSA). Shippers' councils throughout the world perform a valuable service for cargo owners by making their views known to the conferences, especially when freight rate alterations are envisaged, and these representations are today on the whole well received by the conferences. Some conferences though are less willing than others to listen to the councils, preferring instead to be guided by CENSA, even in cases where the recommendations of the council are obviously just, and have been adopted by other conferences. In other cases the amount of consultation that takes place between a shippers' council and a conference or shipping company is insufficient to allow a fair exchange of views, and the rate adjustment will take place before firm recommendations can be put forward by the council for review. In spite of these difficulties the British Shippers' Council has on several occasions been successful in amending a proposed freight increase by showing that the basis of calculation of the increase has been incorrect. Following currency devaluations, for example, conferences have sometimes been in the habit of raising freight rates by the full amount of the devaluation, even though some costs are incurred in the devalued currency, and the British Shippers' Council has succeeded in lowering the proposed increase to its correct level. Shippers' councils do not therefore regard all proposed freight increases as inevitable, and while condoning rises that have allowed shipping companies to revert to profitability, they are ever watchful for unjustified increases that have become hidden behind "inflated operating costs" or other vague terms. Prior to the UNCTAD meetings in Geneva where a code of conduct for liner conferences was drawn up, the British Shippers' Council had played a leading part in negotiating the first code of liner conference practice in 1971 which was accepted in western Europe, and it is this code that is generally used today as a basis for calculating bunker and currency surcharges.

A New Rating Structure

Conference freight tariffs are large and unwieldy, and in their present form are the cause of a very large number of shippers being charged incorrect rates. Apart from difficulties associated with identifying a product within the pages of individual tariffs, there is often no relationship between product descriptions in the tariffs of different conferences. The more involved the tariff, the more likely it is that the unwary shipper will be incorrectly charged, and until tariffs of different conferences are drawn up on a similar basis the shipper will continue to find that conferences have different interpretations of the same product. For example, a dump truck will be rated by one conference as a vehicle, while another will classify it as machinery which carries a higher rate. It should be possible to compare rates in different trades, and adoption of a common standard would allow such comparison to take place. Use of the Brussels Nomenclature system, which many countries utilize for classifying goods prior to levying customs duties, would avoid anomalies by allowing the shipping company freight clerk to correctly identify products, and quote the appropriate rate. If the shipper then made sure that this number appeared in the bill of lading, the freight account could be prepared in accordance with the quoted rate. Use of the internationally adopted Standard International Trade Classification (SITC) commodity code system, which is interrelated with the Brussels Nomenclature system, would prove to be equally beneficial, and ACL has indeed already drawn up its own tariff based on the SITC.

A complete rating review should also include an examination of the basis for assessing freight charges. Although conferences maintain that rates are based on demand, they are in fact usually based on what the traffic can bear, and although shippers often complain that because of the latter system they are subsidizing the movement of low-value products, the system is in fact a lesser evil than the "freight of all kinds" (FAK) method. Advocates of FAK, under which a fixed charge per container would be levied irrespective of contents, maintain that a discriminatory rating structure is unfair to shippers of high-value products, and that charges should be assessed on each container strictly in accordance with the costs involved. But an FAK rate would be so high that it would become uneconomic to ship many products previously taking a low rate, and developed countries would be further assisted at the expense of the less developed. Commodity prices would rise, and low-value low freight earning goods would be left to those lines using more conventional methods of assessing freight. While discussing fairness in charging freight, it should be understood that if it is decided to use the discriminatory tariff system, rate adjustments should be made on a percentage basis, and not as a standard charge irrespective of the level of the basic rate. In cases where a standard charge is levied, the shipper of low-value, low-rated items will once again have to carry most of the burden of the increase.

Anomalies also exist where rates controlled by an eastbound conference are radically different from those controlled by the westbound conference in the same trade. While some of the variation will be due to trade in particular products being more buoyant in one direction or due to these products commanding a higher selling price when moving in one direction (rates on American exports to Japan in the Pacific trade can be up to 90 per cent higher than on Japanese exports to the United States), the differences will often be due to the conferences' lack of knowledge concerning their traffic flows, and due to the unprofessional manner in which several conferences are run. Where operating costs in both directions are similar, rates should show some similarity, and rule of thumb methods of assessing freight should not be used. Attention has already been drawn to the practice of imposing "additionals" such as container service charges, and of the distortionary effect of these charges. If a conference is unable to maintain freight costs (which have traditionally included stevedoring charges), it should say so and announce its intention of raising freights, without resorting to additionals which can only hide the true level of freight costs.

Stability of Rates

A recurrent criticism of the conference system arises from the lack of competition associated with the grouping of shipping lines or consortia. But shipping must be based on a firm financial footing, in common with industry in general, and controlled collusion will benefit both the lines and the shippers if rate stability is maintained. It should not be forgotten that the non-conference lines are becoming stronger, and that if collusion became excessive a swing to these "outsiders" would soon be under way. It has already been explained how a weak conference can threaten stability, and a return to conditions that were evident in the North Atlantic trade only a few years ago when unofficial rebates were freely granted to shippers, should be avoided. Co-operation among the lines will also take place when a consortium is established, whether or not the parties to the consortium are conference members. The conference will usually be more far reaching in its membership than the consortium, but the consortium will play a very valuable role, even though confined to a small (but significant) number of lines, in adjusting individual vessel loadings to the amount of cargo on offer. Thus through revenue pooling schemes and slot sharing agreements the consortium members will be equally affected by fluctuating cargo volumes, and will be better able to manage during lean times through a "spreading" of the risks. Consortia activities are likely to become more significant as alternative methods of shipment such as the landbridge system are more fully developed, and as newcomers to a trade continue their policy of "skimming-off" highly rated cargo. One way of counteracting sporadic competition would be for the conference lines to introduce a system of quantity discounts, similar to those offered by the road haulage industry and the railways, whereby substantial shippers would be encouraged to support the conference lines. Economies of scale would then follow through from domestic movements to the realm of sea transport, erratic cargo swings between conference and non-conference lines would be checked, and relative stability would be enjoyed by both shippers and shipowners.

The conference system would appear to be a necessity then if only to maintain stability among its members. Without the conferences shipping lines would cut rates during periods when cargo was in short supply, often to uneconomic levels, hoping for an eventual rise in trade volumes. But it is during just these periods that stability is most needed in order to prevent lines withdrawing from a trade, and causing a situation of under-capacity later on which might take several months to correct. In these days of intense competition in overseas markets, transport systems must be efficient, and merchants must be able to rely not only on relative freedom from constantly fluctuating rates, but also on regular sailings. But as a last resort in cases where non-conference lines are offering predatory, and often subsidized rates, the conference may have to forego stability to prevent its own collapse. Open rates will be declared on a number of key commodities, the rates on these commodities being subject to rises and falls brought about by non-conference competition, and demand for and supply of vessel space.

A Change of Outlook

Today's conferences grew up in the late 19th and early 20th centuries, but as trading conditions have changed the conferences have not been able to adapt to accommodate current needs. The landbridge phenomenon for example has presented problems in the quotation of through rates by shipping companies, and it is still far from clear whether or not overland sectors of transit should fall under conference jurisdiction. In an effort to check Seatrain's landbridge service linking Europe and Japan via North America, the member lines of the Japan to Europe Freight Conference maintain that this particular landbridge is potentially harmful to the Conference, and should be under the control of the Conference. Rating levels are open to adjustment in cases where a conference is unable to control all sectors of a landbridge route, as the shipping company may find ways of subsidizing the overland sector at the expense of the sea freight.

In today's climate of free enterprise the newcomers to the world's trading routes are at pains to show that they too are able to operate competitively, but the fact that they are often only interested in the higher rated cargoes is to them immaterial. The non-conference Russian Far Eastern Shipping Company (FESCO) is taking highly rated cargo in the Pacific trade away from conference members by offering very competitive rates, which may force the United States to promote even more bilateral trade agreements with Japan and countries elsewhere. Nationalistic undertones run contrary to traditional conference policy, and it may be that the stronger maritime nations will gradually move away from the conference system. An example of non-conference domination in a trade is Orient Overseas Lines services linking Australia to Far Eastern ports. Orient Overseas has managed to secure 40 per cent of the northbound traffic, while the remainder has to be shared out among the other 25 lines (23 of which are conference members) in the trade. In situations like this shipping companies will seriously think about leaving the Conference, and may even join rival groups offering much cheaper rates.

Another threat to the conference system arises out of the increasing amount of government interference in conference affairs. Governments generally accepted the conferences and their methods of controlled collusion, but today it is becoming more and more apparent that governments are manipulating freight rates with a view to boosting their own national fleets, or to promoting exports by suppressing outward rates. As national fleets become stronger there will be little that the conferences will be able to do to re-assert their former power, and government interference in conference policy should be curbed now. The United States is particularly active in intervention, and their Federal Maritime Commission has powers to freeze freight rate adjustments. The FMC requires that conferences who are active within American waters must submit their tariffs for approval, and they have also on occasions tried to extend their control to conferences abroad. This type of activity, although appearing to be desirable, is in fact totally alien to a free flow of shipping services between countries, and changes the conference system from an organization with a commercial nature to one with a political bias.

In attempting to protect themselves from such outside influences as non-conference competition, government interference, and indeed discontent among their own members, today's outdated conferences have become parochial institutions with sometimes over-rigid rules. Self-policing schemes have been introduced that are totally lacking in flexibility, and shippers are having to pay such charges as rent and demurrage which would formerly have been open to negotiation with the shipping company in cases where it was difficult to apportion responsibility. If the conference system is to survive, a government-inspired international code of conduct regulating conference activities, and acceptable to all nations whether developed or less-developed, must be drawn up. The way will then be open for the much needed re-adjustment process between today's conflicting fleets to take place, and when the dust eventually settles a more efficient and competitive shipping industry should have emerged.

Bibliography

International Freighting Weekly, Maclean-Hunter Limited.

Export Management, The 'Syren & Shipping' Limited.

The Shipbroker, The Institute of Chartered Shipbrokers.

Freight Management, IPC Transport Press Limited.

Fairplay International Shipping Journal, Fairplay Publications Limited.

Seatrade, Seatrade Publications Limited.

Containerization International, The National Magazine Company Limited.

Commerce International, Investment Publications Commercial Limited (London Chamber of Commerce & Industry).

Business Week, McGraw Hill.

Lloyd's List, Lloyd's.

Lloyd's List Annual Review, Lloyd's.

The Journal of Commerce: International Edition.

British Shippers' Council Annual Reports, British Shippers' Council.

Containers—The Landbridge Pipeline, R.E. Lawless, Canadian National Railways (Ontario).

German Federal Railway Container Train Terminals, Dr E. von Krakewitz in *The Railway Gazette*.

The Role of Intercontainer, G. Flechon in *The Railway Gazette*.

The Economist, The Economist Newspaper Limited.

New Scientist, New Science Publications.

The Port of London Prepares for Containers, N.N.B. Ordman in *The Railway Gazette*.

European Chemical News, IPC Industrial Press Limited.

Cargo Handling and the Modern Port, R.B. Oram, Pergamon Press Limited.

A Brief History of the Port of Liverpool, Mersey Docks & Harbour Board.

The Times.

The Financial Times.

Investors Chronicle & Stock Exchange Gazette, Throgmorton Publications Limited.

Press releases and miscellaneous information issued by shipping companies, consortia, port authorities and handling equipment manufacturers.

Index

ACT 1, 174
ACT 2, 174, 176
ACT/ANL, 175–176, 183, 185, 186, 187
ACT Services Ltd., 166
African Container Express (ACE), 249, 250
African Container Line (AFCL), 250
Airships, 324–325
Aldington, Lord, 149
American Export Industries, 49
American Export Lines, 188, 194, 195
American Mail Line, 199
American Merchant Shipping Act (1970), 6
American President Lines, 189, 199, 207, 232
Anja, 250
Asialiner, 38
Associated Container Transportation Ltd.
    (ACT), 5, 9
Atlantica Line, 259, 275
Atlantic Container Line, 11, 55, 109, 115,
    192, 215, 281, 283, 286, 293, 316
Atlantic Gulf Service, 209
Australia and Europe, container service,
    174–184
Australian Endeavour, 177
Australian Wool Corp., 281

BACAT (barge-aboard-catamaran), 19, 21
Baltic Steamship Co., 224
Barge carrier (*see* LASH)
Beeching Report, 65–66
Belgium, container service, 278–282
Bell Lines, 4, 285
Bell Vanguard, 4
Benguela Railway Co., 252
Ben Line Containers Ltd., 166, 167
Bergen Line, 295
Bills of lading (*see* Documents)
Black Star Line, 251
Brian Boroime, 72
Bristow Committee, 147

British and Commonwealth Shipping, 63–64
British Rail, 91, 282
    shipping, 69, 71–75
British Shippers' Council, 148, 329
British Transport Act (1962), 65–66
British Transport Docks Board, 25, 27
Brussels Nomenclature system, 330
Bunker costs, 57–58
Burnett Steamship Co., 12

Canada
    container service, 214–223
    CP Ships, 52–54
Canadian Pacific, 52, 215, 216–217, 219–220
Capitalfin Vlasov, 50
Cardigan Bay, 165
Caribbean Overseas Lines (CAROL), 237–
    238
Carriage of Goods by Sea Act (1924), 95,
    98–99
    Amendment (1971), 96
Cast Europe (Containers) Ltd., 215, 217,
    220, 281
Casualization of dock labor, 143–146
Central Gulf Lines, 16, 233
Channel Tunnel, 27, 78–79, 81–86
Chassis system, 32–33
Clyde container handling equipment, 38, 39
Colchester, 71
Columbia Line, 275
Columbus Line, 186, 286
Comar Containerline, 52, 282
Combi Line, 16, 19, 208, 209, 283
Combined Transport documents, 103–112
    transmission of, 112–115
Committee of European National Shipowners
    Association (CENSA), 312–313,
    328–329
Common Market (*see* European Economic
    Community)

Compagne Maritime Belge, 242, 278, 281
Compagnie Générale Maritime, 268
Compagnie Nouvelle de Cadres (CNC), 78
Computers and automatic terminals, 316–
    317
Conference system
    change of outlook, 333–335
    consultation and publicity need, 328–329
    evolution, 326–328
    rating structure, new, 329–331
    and stability of rates, 331–333
Consortia and building problems, 4–7
Containerbases Ltd., 43
Container(s)
    equipment for handling, 31–33
    European movements, 132–135
        (*See also* Container service)
Container Marine Lines, 54–55
Container service
    Belgium, 278–282
    Canada, 214–223
    and dock labor, 143–157
    and domestic road haulage, 127–128
    East Africa, 244–246
    Europe/Australia, 174–184
    Europe/Far East, 164–174
    and export packer, 126–127
    France, 267–274
    and freight forwarder, 128–132
    Holland, 282–291
    India, 231–235
    Italy and Sicily, 258–263
    less developed countries, 161–163
    Mediterranean, 253–258
    New Zealand, 184–187
    and owners of conventional ships,
        117–121
    and pallet ships, 121–126
    Russia and Trans-Siberian Railway,
        223–231
    Scandinavia, 291–300
    South Africa, 238–244
    South America and Caribbean, 235–238
    Spain and Portugal, 263–266
    vs. traditional services, 116–117
    United States, 187–214
    West Africa, 246–252
    West Germany, 274–278
Container service charge, 60
Containerships
    beginnings, 3
    British Rail, 69, 71–75
    leasing, 6–7
Container Transport International (CTI),
    228–229
Control of through service by shipping
    company, 49–52
Cost
    Channel Tunnel, 81, 83
    through service, 57–64
Council of Economic Mutual Assistance
    (Comecon), 226–227

CP Ships, through service, 52–54
CP Voyageur, 218
Cunard Lines, 63

Daiwa Navigation Co., 319
Damage, causes of, 97–101
Dart Containerline, 9, 215, 278, 281
Datafreight Receipt, 109, 115, 316
DDG Hansa, 275
Deep sea terminals and feeder ports,
    158–161
Delta Steamship Lines, 16, 18, 208, 210,
    236
Demurrage costs, 58, 60
Deutsche Bundesbahn (DB) (*see* German
    Federal Railways)
Devlin Committee, 144–145
DFDS Line, 299
Doctor Lykes, 20
Documents
    combined transport, 103–112
    transmission, 112–115
Domburg, 71
Draft Convention on the International
    Combined Transport of Goods
    (TCM Convention), 110–111

East Africa, container service, 244–246
Elder Dempster Lines, 247, 249
Enterprise Container Lines (ECL), 242
Europe
    and Australia, container service,
        174–184
    container movements, 132–135
    and Far East, container service, 164–
        174
    roll-on roll-off movements, 135–143
European Economic Community
    and Comecon, 227
    container movements, 133–135
    roll-on roll-off movements, 136–137,
        140–141
European Unit Routes, 286
Export packers and containerization, 126–
    127

FAK (freight of all kinds) system, 201, 220,
    330
Far East and Europe, container service,
    164–174
Far Eastern Freight Conference, 166, 168,
    170–171, 172, 173, 308, 328
Far Eastern Shipping Co., 200, 204, 225,
    229, 230, 333
Feeder vessels, 51–52
Felixstowe
    port operation, 24–25
    container handling equipment, 34–36
Ferry wagon, 73–74
Fire hazard, 100
Fortaleza, 320
Forth container handling equipment, 39–40

France, container service, 267–274
Fred Olsen Line, 24, 34, 152, 295
Freight forwarder and containerization,
    128–132
Freightliners, 66–69, 70
French Railways (SNCF), 77–79
Furness Withy, 50, 63, 305

General Council of British Shipping,
    308, 310
General Steam Navigation Co., 120, 265
German Federal Railways, 79–81,
    272–273
Grodekovo, 223
Growth since containerization, 305–310
Guernsey Fisher, 72
Gulf Container Line, 209

Hague Rules, 95–96, 104
Halicon, 221
Hapag-Lloyd, 9, 62, 166, 275, 276, 283,
    286, 323
Harrison Line, 119, 283
Hengist, 72
Hijacking, 99
Hispania Maritime, 120
Holland, container service, 282–291
Holland America Line, 283
Horsa, 72

India, container service, 231–235
Inland terminals, 42–44
Insurance
    and combined transport documents,
        103–112
    and damage causes, 97–101
    and document transmission, 112–115
    established procedures, 94
    and risk spreading, 102–103
    and shipowners' liability, 95–97
Intercontainer, 75–77, 228
Interfrigo, 75, 79
International Agreement on Railway
        Transports (1961), 104
International Council of Containership
        Operators, 194
International Liner Services, 240
Irano-Hind Shipping Co., 235
Italy and Sicily, container service,
    258–263
Ivan Chernykh, 224

Japan/Nakhodka Line, 223, 224, 225
Jersey Fisher, 72
Johnson Line, 12
Johnson Scan Star, 293
Joint Liaison Committee on Documentation,
    12
Jones, Jack, 149
Jones-Aldington Committee, 149–151

Kamakura Maru, M/V, 164
Kangaroo service, 78
Kangourou, 181
Kavalerovo, 223
K Line, 171
Koninklijke Nederlande Stoomboot
        Maatschappij (KNSM), 283
Koninklijke Nedlloyd, 283
Kooringa, 186
Korrigan, 169

Labor
    dock, and containerization, 143–157
    "scheme" and "non-scheme" ports,
        24–25
Landbridge, 86–90, 178, 221, 222
LASH (lighter aboard ship)
    and BACAT, 21
    barge carrier, 12, 16–18
    vs. Seabee, 19
Latvian Steamship Co., 228
Leadenhall Insurance Co. Ltd., 105
Leasing of containerships, 6–7
Less developed countries, container
        service, 161–163
Liability (see Insurance)
Liverpool Bay, 114
Lloydiana, 259
Lloyd Trestino, 241, 243, 259
Lykes Lines, 209, 211, 214

MacAndrews-Swedish Lloyd, 263
Maersk Line, 171, 293–294
Malaysian International Shipping Corp.,
    172
Manchester Challenge, 213
Manchester Liners, 49, 54, 182, 212, 215,
    216, 217, 219–220
Manchester Vigour, 181
Maritime Coastal Container Line, 195
Maritime Container Lines, 192–193
Marples, Ernest, 30
Matson Navigation, 11, 199, 205
Maxton, SS, 3
McKinsey Report, 51, 146
McLean, Malcolm, 3, 187–188
McLean Industries Inc., 3
Med Club, 170, 256, 259
Mediterranea, 259
Mediterranean, container service, 253–
    258
Mersey, container handling equipment,
    40–42
Messageries, Maritimes, 169–170, 293
Mitsui OSK, 166, 243
Modular Automated Container Handling
        System (MACH), 32, 316
Moore McCormack Line, 188, 236
Moslash, 16
Mutsu, 323

National Dock Labour Board and "scheme" ports, 24–25, 143–144
National Freight Corp., 68, 69
Nationalism, 311–316
National Ports Council, 26, 28, 29–31
Neptune Orient Lines Ltd., 172
Netumar Line, 236
New England Express Line, 193, 286
New Zealand, container service, 184–187
Nigerian National Shipping Line, 249, 251
Nipponia, 259
Nippon Yusen Kaisha (NYK), 164, 166, 243
Novatrans, 78
Nuclear-powered vessels, 321, 323–324

Ocean Transport & Trading Ltd., 50, 63
OCL/ACT, 174
Orient Overseas Container Line, 171
Orient Overseas Line, 200, 334
Otto Hahn, 323
Overseas Containers Ltd. (OCL), 4, 9, 50, 63, 166, 167, 174, 183, 186, 187, 303, 305
Oy Finanglia Line, 299

P & O Lines, 49, 50, 63, 105, 186, 187, 305
Pacific, 12
Pacific America Container Express (PACE), 185, 186
Pacific Far East Line, 16, 119, 199, 205, 209
Pallet ships, 121–126
Polish Ocean Lines, 227
Ponape Maru, 319
Portainer, 31–32
Ports
    established structure, 22–25
    feeder, and deep sea terminals, 158–161
    grants, loans and subsidies for, 27–29
    investment needs, 25–27
    "scheme" and "non-scheme", 24–25
Portuguese Railways, 265
Profitability, move into, 303–305
Prudential-Grace Lines, 16, 18–19, 209, 257

Railways
    and Beeching Report, 65–66
    British Rail shipping, 69, 71–75
    and Channel Tunnel, 81–86
    freightliners, 66–69, 70
    French, 77–79
    future development, 90–93
    German Federal, 79–81
    Intercontainer, 75–77
    landbridge system, 86–90
Rate cutting, 54–57
Rate stability, 331–333
Rating structure, 329–331
Red Nacional de Ferrocarriles Espanoles, 263–264
Remuera, 184, 186, 187
Revenue pool, 190–192
Rhodri Mawr, 72

Road haulage, domestic, and containerization, 127–128
Rochdale Report, 29–30, 301–303
Roll-on roll-off vessels, 9, 11
    European movements, 135–143
Rudkobing VI, 19
Russia and Trans-Siberian Railway, container service, 223–231

Safmarine, 240, 241, 243
St. Eloi, 73
Savannah, 323
Scan Austral, 177, 291, 293
Scandinavia
    container service, 291–300
    pallet ships, 125
Scan Dutch, 169, 170, 174, 283, 293
"Scheme" vs. "non-scheme" ports, 24–25
Scindia Steam Navigation, 233
Seabee (sea barge carrier), 17, 20
    vs. LASH, 19
Sea Containers Inc., 7
Sea Freightliner 1, 71
Sea Freightliner 2, 71
Sea-Land Finance, 322
Sea-Land Service Inc., 3, 4, 9, 34, 52, 57, 194, 197, 204, 207, 210, 281, 286, 318, 321
Seatrain, 9
Shipbuilding industry and financing of containerships, 5–6
Shipowners
    of conventional ships, and container service, 117–121
    liability, 95–97
Shipping companies
    control of through service by, 49–52
    earnings in overseas trade, 304
Shipping Corporation of India (SCI), 233
Shipping Mortgage Finance Scheme, 5
Simplification of Trade Procedures Board (SITPRO), 112–113
Skyship, 325
Smith, Ian, 252
Sojusvneshtrans, 223–224, 225
South Africa, container service, 238–244
South America and Caribbean, container service, 235–238
Southampton, container handling equipment, 37, 39
Spain and Portugal, container service, 263–266
SPC Containers, 266
Springbok Shipping Co., 240
Standard International Trade Classification (SITC), 330
Standardization of vessels, 13–15
Stowage and cargo damage, 98–99
Subsidies, grants, and loans, 27–29
Suecia, 12

Taft-Hartley Act, 156
TCM Convention, 110–111
Terminals
    automatic, and computers, 316–317
    container handling equipment, 31–33
    deep sea, and feeder ports, 158–161
    inland, 42–44
Through service, 45–48
    control by shipping company, 49–52
    CP Ships, 52–54
    rate cutting, 54–57
    rising costs, 57–64
Tilbury, container handling equipment,
    34–36
Tonnage, 309, 314
Tor Line, 283, 294, 295–296
Townsend-Thoresen Ferries, 272
Trade, seaborne, 59
Transamerican Trailer Transport, 320
Transcontainer 1, 72
Trans-Europ-Container-Express (TECE), 76
Trans-Europ-Express-Marchandises (TEEM),
    76
Transport Act (1968), 92
Transports Internationale Routiers (TIR)
    system, 136–137
Trans-Siberian Railway, and Russia, con-
    tainer service, 223–231
Transtainer, 32
TRIP group, 164–169, 174, 275, 286, 318
Truckline Ferries, 272
Tung, C. Y., 171

United Kingdom
    dock labor, 143–156
    domestic road haulage and containeri-
        zation, 127–128
    Merchant Shipping Bill (1973), 315
    port developments, 33–34
    port structure, 22–25
    railway future developments, 90, 93
    shipbuilding problems, 4–7

United Kingdom Chamber of Shipping, 85,
    307, 312
United Kingdom/West Africa Lines Joint
    Service (UKWAL), 249
United Nations Conference on Trade and
    Development (UNCTAD), 162–163,
    311–313, 328, 329
United States
    dock labor, 156–157
    East Coast container service, 187–199
    Great Lakes container service, 211–214
    Gulf Coast container service, 208–211
    through service difficulties, 47–48,
        50–51
    West Coast container service, 199–208
United States Lines, 9, 57, 119, 195, 286,
    316

Vessels
    barge carrying, 15–21
    convertible container, 11–13
    feeder, 51–52
    ferry wagon, 73–74
    financing, 5
    fully containerized, 9
    new types, 317–325
    partial container, 9–11
    standardization, 13–15
Vishva Aditya, m/v, 233
Voorlooper, m/v, 242

Wallenius Line, 291
Waterman Steamship Corp., 16, 233
Weser Exporter, 250
West Africa, container service, 246–252
West Germany, container service, 274–
    278

Zeeland Steamship Co., 72
Zim Container Service, 172, 200, 256,
    286